Praise for *The Best of the Board Café,* Second Edition

"Solutions and inspiration—that's what readers will find in this updated edition of *The Best of the Board Café.* Busy board members need to optimize their time and efforts, and Jan Masaoka offers many suggestions on just how to accomplish this."

PAUL KAWATA, Executive Director, National Minority AIDS Council, Washington, DC

"These essays are concise and always helpful. Jan Masaoka cuts to the chase and helps board members stay motivated and focused."

PAUL SHOEMAKER, Director, Social Venture Partners, Seattle

"Every nonprofit executive and board member deserves to have a great mentor, but, if you don't, *The Best of the Board Café* is the next best thing. Jan Masaoka offers a clear, no-nonsense approach to thorny management issues. She helps readers ask the right questions and develop solution-driven plans."

PAMELA DAVIS, President and CEO, Alliance of Nonprofits for Insurance, Risk Retention Group, and Nonprofits' Insurance Alliance of California

"The information in this book is brilliant! No board member should be voted onto a board before reading this book. No executive director should start a first day of work before reading the book. This book is like having Jan Masaoka in the room giving you all you need to lead and manage your organization."

KRIS SINCLAIR, Executive Director, Association of California Symphony Orchestras, Sacramento

"Whether the reader is new to the world of board membership, or has served on multiple boards, he or she will find helpful tips, solid truths, and new ways of looking at nonprofit issues. This is an invaluable tool."

CARRIE AVERY, President, The Durfee Foundation, Santa Monica

"You can't be involved with a nonprofit organization if you don't have this book on your shelf. Period! You'll refer to this book often, checking out what it has to offer on various issues facing your organization—it's that relevant."

BARRY Z. POSNER, Dean and Professor of Leadership, Santa Clara University, Co-Author of *The Leadership Challenge* and *A Leader's Legacy*

"*The Best of the Board Café* offers current, practical advice on a broad array of issues facing nonprofit boards of directors. Best of all, it presents each topic — from recruiting board members and evaluating the executive director to invigorating board meetings— as a brief digestible morsel that can nourish board discussions. For the board veteran or the neophyte executive director, *Best of the Board Café* is an invaluable resource."

LESLIE T. HATAMIYA, Executive Director, California Bar Foundation

"The issues of nonprofit governance have never been as complex as they are today. This new edition of *The Best of the Board Café* challenges governance volunteers to be serious about their roles and to be respectful of the challenges in social impact work. Keep this book on your desk, not your bookshelf."

TESSIE GUILLERMO, President and CEO, ZeroDivide

Praise for the first edition of
The Best of the Board Café

"I've always found the *Board Café* to be a great resource tool. Now *The Best of the Board Café* pulls together timely and practical advice that boards and directors will refer to again and again."

> PATTI TOTOTZINTLE, Associate Director, Casa de Esperanza, Saint Paul, MN

"*The Best of the Board Café* is essential reading for board members and executive directors alike. It's filled with useful advice that can be applied to improve the board-staff relationship."

> PAUL C. LIGHT, New York University, the Brookings Institution

"*The Best of the Board Café* is destined to be a valued companion to nonprofit board members across the country. It offers up sound, practical guidance on issues relevant to all boards and, in short, is one of the best board handbooks I've seen. This one won't gather dust!"

> ANN LARSEN, Executive Director, MAP (Management Assistance Program, Inc.), Tampa, FL

"If you are a community-building practitioner, then you must read this book. It offers very useful and practical advice for developing strong community organizations. Don't leave home without it."

> FRANK J. OMOWALE SATTERWHITE, Ph.D., President, National Community Development Institute, Oakland, CA

"What a great compilation of digestible board tidbits that get at the heart of nonprofit leadership. Reading this book is the next best thing to talking through your board troubles with a trusted friend."

> MARLA J. BOBWICK, Vice President, BoardSource, Washington, DC

"I have consistently found the most practical, deft, and specific advice at the *Board Café*. To have all this useful wisdom in one book is a tremendous asset to all in the real work of improving governance."

> PEGGY MORRISON OUTON, Executive Director, Bayer Center for Nonprofit Management, Robert Morris University

"Wisdom, experience, and a good measure of common sense. *The Best of the Board Café* is informative, engaging, and filled with practical advice. An invaluable addition to the bookshelf of any nonprofit board member or executive director!"

> LESLIE P. HUME, Chair, Board of Trustees, San Francisco Foundation

"Practical and valuable information in a concise, easy-to-digest format. Busy board members will find succinct articles that address relevant topics that have immediate application."

> DENISE HARLOW, Director of Nonprofit Services, Council of Community Services of New York State, Inc.

"A powerful compendium of everything you need to know about making nonprofit boards work. This book is a 'must-read.'"

JUDITH ALNES, Executive Director
MAP for Nonprofits, Saint Paul, MN

"A powerhouse book . . . for today's fast-paced world, a comprehensive conceptual framework that is easy to use; individual articles that are brief, practical, easy to read, with useful tools, checklists, and more. Every board member should have a copy."

NANCY FUHRMAN, Vice President, Consulting, Executive Service Corps of Chicago

"This book is a distillation of the straight-talking, no-nonsense wisdom for which Jan Masaoka is so well-known and respected. Nonprofit leaders and board members will find here practical advice on all the important issues in nonprofit governance. It is clearly written, well-organized, and bound to be a favorite reference and training guide."

ELIZABETH T. BORIS, Director, Center on Nonprofits and Philanthropy, The Urban Institute

The best of the

board
café

The best of the
board
café

Hands-on solutions for nonprofit boards

Second Edition

Jan Masaoka

CompassPoint
NONPROFIT SERVICES

FIELDSTONE
ALLIANCE

SAINT PAUL
MINNESOTA

Fieldstone Alliance is committed to strengthening the performance of the nonprofit sector. Through the synergy of its consulting, training, publishing, and research and demonstration projects, Fieldstone Alliance provides solutions to issues facing nonprofits, funders, and the communities they serve. Fieldstone Alliance was formerly Wilder Publishing and Wilder Consulting departments of the Amherst H. Wilder Foundation. For information about other Fieldstone Alliance publications, see the last page of this book. If you would like more information about Fieldstone Alliance and our services, please contact Fieldstone Alliance at

800-274-6024
www.FieldstoneAlliance.org

Manufactured in the USA
First printing, July 2009

Typesetting by Kinne Design

Library of Congress Cataloging-in-Publication Data

Masaoka, Jan.
  The best of the Board café : hands-on solutions for nonprofit boards / Jan Masaoka. — 2nd ed.
     p. cm.
  Includes bibliographical references and index.
  ISBN 978-0-940069-79-4
  1. Nonprofit organizations—Management. 2. Boards of directors.
I. Board café. II. Title.
  HD62.6.B483 2009
  658.4'22--dc22
                              2009012939

The Best of the Board Café is one of a series of works published by Fieldstone Alliance (formerly Wilder Publishing Center and Wilder National Consulting Services) in partnership with CompassPoint Nonprofit Services of San Francisco, California. Together, we hope to strengthen the impact of nonprofit organizations and the people who work and volunteer for them as they strive to make our communities more vital and our democracy more just.

Other titles in this series include

The Accidental Techie by Sue Bennett et al.

Financial Leadership for Nonprofit Executives by Jeanne Bell Peters and Elizabeth Schaffer

Managing Executive Transitions by Tim Wolfred

Dedication

DEMOCRACY, IT HAS BEEN SAID, is the worst form of government, except for all the other ones. The same might be said of nonprofit boards: so often criticized, so seldom sincerely praised.

But volunteer board members—perhaps the two million of us in the United States and many millions more around the world—do work that would be unthinkable if boards were not already doing it. Board members, in small units of five, fifteen, or twenty-five individuals, effectively oversee billions of tax dollars and private donations. Board members debate community needs and struggle over the realization of values and dreams. Volunteer board members start new ventures, act as safety nets for organizations at risk, and close down stale institutions. Management expert and author Peter Drucker once commented that every important idea for social change has come from the nonprofit sector, meaning nonprofit organizations and movements have been brought to life, nurtured, and grown by volunteer community leaders, who are also known as board members.

This book is dedicated to nonprofit board members … who so often outshine their counterparts in other sectors and to whom we owe so much for the progress made toward social justice, for the opportunities to experience beauty, and for cohering our communities.

Jan Masaoka

2009 second edition

Contents

---

* Article is either new or revised from the
first edition of this book.

Acknowledgments

A VILLAGE HAS COME TOGETHER to write this book. Much of the content comes from the *Board Café* newsletter, a ten-year-old newsletter from CompassPoint Nonprofit Services that in 2008 evolved into *Blue Avocado*, a comprehensive, practical, and provocative magazine for nonprofits. In its first year, the *Board Café* was copublished with the Volunteer Consulting Group and subsequently for four years with the National Center for Nonprofit Boards (now BoardSource). The "kitchen staff" of the *Board Café* is its editorial committee, which has included Betsy Rosenblatt at BoardSource, Nora Silver of the Volunteerism Project, Brooke Mahoney and David LaGreca of the Volunteer Consulting Group, Pamela Davis of the Nonprofit Insurance Alliance Group, and Mike Allison, Tim Wolfred, and Pardis Parsa from Compass-Point. This committee suggests topics and scrutinizes each issue for content and style. Attorney Michael Schley volunteers his expertise on issues and articles that have legal implications.

I am grateful, too, to James Hormel and Timothy Wu, who generously underwrote the preparation of this manuscript. Tim and I worked together for six years at Compass-Point and together have agonized over, rejoiced over, learned from, and been inspired by the boards of our nonprofit organization clients.

I am also thankful to Betsy Rosenblatt who contributed many articles to this book and who served for years as a thoughtful writer and attentive editor. Judy O'Connor, Marla Bobowick, and Janis Johnston of BoardSource are also valued friends of the *Board Café*, as is Rick Moyers, now at the Meyer Foundation in Washington, DC

CompassPoint has been, of course, instrumental in the success of the *Board Café* and now *Blue Avocado*. CompassPoint staff have served as writers, fact-checkers, editors, technical support, promoters, and, perhaps most important, as critics. In particular I am grateful to current and former staff Nelson Layag, Jeanne Bell, Pardis Parsa, Cristina Chan, Roald Alexander, and Karen Aitchison.

Blue Avocado's staff has been equally important to the quality of the content of this book. In particular, Senior Editor Lynora Williams is a constant and wise editor, and copy editor Karen Aitchison keeps us technically correct and readable. *Blue Avocado*'s warm graphics and friendly web design are due to Patrick Santana, who along with his colleagues, Paulette Traverso and Darryll Dunn at Traverso Santana, has been instrumental in every success.

Some of the articles in the *Board Café* are revisions from an earlier book, *Action Handbook for Boards*, which I cowrote with Jude Kaye of CompassPoint and which was published by the National Minority AIDS Council (NMAC) under the leadership of Executive Director Paul Kawata and Jackyie Williams. The book was excellently and heroically edited by Ellen Clear; others who were instrumental include Harold Phillips and members of NMAC's Washington staff, as well as Mim Carlson, Andy Cochran, Brenda Crawford, Gary Levinson, Omowale Satterwhite, and Tim Wu.

A critically important contributor to *Action Handbook for Boards,* as well as to this book, is Mike Allison, CompassPoint's director of consulting and research. For ten years Mike and I have worked together in management under CompassPoint's board and, as consultants, jointly with the boards of client organizations. Through many long and thoughtful (and sometimes mutually maddening) discussions, Mike has been a principal architect of the concepts behind this book.

The many executive directors and board members with whom all of us have worked as colleagues or clients are also partners in the development of this book. Among the many boards that I have been honored to work with and learn from are those of the Asian and Pacific Islander Wellness Center, the San Francisco Foundation, the Black Coalition on AIDS, Unity/Journalists of Color, ACLU of San Francisco, the Y and H Soda Foundation, the National Black Women's Health Project, Project Hired, the Armenian Women's Archive Association, Asian American/Pacific Islanders in Philanthropy, the Academy of Television Arts and Sciences, Golden Gate Kindergarten Association, Kimochi, and the Hispanic Scholarship Fund.

Perhaps most of all, I want to thank current and former members of CompassPoint's board of directors, who have led CompassPoint well, and whose examples as board members have been instructive as well as inspiring. I give special affectionate thanks to Katherine Webb Calhoon, Sally Carlson, Liz Harvey, Rod Hsiao, Mary Lester, Jules Mayer, Jeff Mori, Clare Phillips, Kathleen Schuler, Elizabeth Share, and Joe Valentine.

About the Author

JAN MASAOKA is a leading writer and thinker on nonprofit organizations with particular emphasis on boards of directors, business planning, and the role of nonprofits in society. She is the director and editor-in-chief of *Blue Avocado*, an online magazine for nonprofit staff and volunteers, and continues to write the popular *Board Café* column, which appears in each of its issues.

Jan has written for *Stanford Social Innovation Review,* the *Grassroots Fundraising Journal, Leader to Leader,* the *Foundation Center, BoardSource,* and other publications. Her research work includes studies on nonprofit executive tenure, nonprofit workforce issues, women executive directors of color, and all-volunteer organizations. The same practical, visionary, and irreverent spirit that infuses the *Board Café* also makes her a popular conference keynoter and workshop presenter.

Jan recently left her job of fourteen years as executive director of CompassPoint Nonprofit Services, a consulting and training firm for nonprofits based in San Francisco and Silicon Valley. In that role she was named Nonprofit Executive of the Year by *NonProfit Times* in 2003. She was a member of the Governance and Fiduciary Working Group, convened by Independent Sector to advise the U.S. Senate Finance Committee in 2006. She has served on the boards of a wide range of nonprofit organizations, including New America Media, Asian and Pacific Islander Wellness Center, the San Francisco Foundation Community Initiative Funds, and the Rooftop PTA. She serves on the advisory committees to the California Diversity in Philanthropy Initiative, Stanford Social Innovation Review, BoardSource, and Asian Americans for Community Involvement, and she served two terms on the Telecommunications Commission of the City and County of San Francisco. She lives in San Francisco and can be reached at jan@blueavocado.org.

About the *Board Café* and *Blue Avocado*

THE BOARD CAFÉ began more than ten years ago as a two-page, faxed newsletter for nonprofit board members. Founded by CompassPoint Nonprofit Services, the *Board Café* was designed to speak directly to board members, providing them with practical information beyond what might have been given them by their executives. With its motto "Short enough to read over a cup of coffee," the *Board Café* quickly found an audience. In the first few years CompassPoint's fax machine ran all night every night for a week to get out the issues. Restricting the newsletter to two faxed pages enforced the rules of brevity, practicality, and snap.

In 2008, the *Board Café* expanded to become *Blue Avocado*, a magazine for nonprofits that takes advantage of the Web 2.0 environment. With early support from key supporters and a remarkable leadership council, *Blue Avocado* has built a team of editors, writers, graphic professionals, and technology wizards. The *Board Café* is now a regular column in *Blue Avocado*, appearing in each of its twenty-four issues per year. As this second edition of *Best of the Board Café* goes to press, *Blue Avocado* has 50,000 subscribers and includes news articles, OpEds, columns on nonprofit human resources and finance, and articles that reflect and support the inspiring, dedicated, wacky, and curious sides of the people who work and volunteer in community nonprofits. Subscriptions are free by sending an e-mail to editor@blueavocado.org with "Subscribe" in the subject line, or at www.blueavocado.org.

About CompassPoint Nonprofit Services

CompassPoint Nonprofit Services is one of the nation's leading management consulting and training firms for nonprofits. CompassPoint conducts more than seven hundred workshops and six conferences each year on topics such as nonprofit strategic planning, finance, boards of directors, technology applications, volunteerism, organization development, and executive director transition. CompassPoint's Consulting Group contracts with more than three hundred nonprofits annually, conducts and publishes research studies, and   works with collaborative ventures linking nonprofits, government, and private philanthropy. The organization maintains offices in San Francisco and San José.

San Francisco
731 Market Street, Suite 200
San Francisco, CA 94103
415-541-9000
415-541-7708 fax

Silicon Valley
Sobrato Center for Nonprofits
600 Valley Way, Suite A
Milpitas, CA 95035
408-719-1400
408-719-1444 fax

info@compasspoint.org
www.compasspoint.org

Preface to the Second Edition

SINCE THE FIRST EDITION of this book, there have been both positive and negative developments related to nonprofit organizations and nonprofit boards:

- The U.S. Senate Finance Committee proposed legislation in 2006 about nonprofit boards that spurred a frightened reaction from the nonprofit sector.

  The good: It drew attention to the role of boards. And the proposed regulations—which would have had strong negative impacts on nonprofits—were eventually dropped.

  The bad: The mainstream nonprofit national organizations responded in part by calling for "self-regulation" ideas that were more appropriate for institutional nonprofits (such as hospitals and universities) than for the vast majority of nonprofits, which are community organizations.

- Federal Form 990—required annual form for nonprofits—was revised (starting with 2009 filings), including a greater focus on nonprofit board practices.

  The good: The new questions—especially the suggestion that board members see the 990 before it is filed—will help boards think more about the message their 990 sends to the world. And Form 990-N, which is required for organizations previously too small to file the 990, will act as "proof of life" and provide a more accurate count of active nonprofits.

  The bad: more and more complicated paperwork. Despite consensus that Sarbanes-Oxley has done little to improve for-profit corporate governance, the government continues to bring similar process requirements to the nonprofit sector.

- A wave of new nonprofits has continued to grow, often Internet-based, often self-identified as social entrepreneurs.

  The good: People continue to see nonprofits as the vehicles for changing the world and are creating new ways to do that work.

  The bad: Some nonprofits are overlooking their roles as community representatives, not just community service providers, and as movement builders, not just service factories.

- The United States elected a president for the first time from the nonprofit sector: Barack Obama is a former community organizer, and his wife, Michelle Obama, is a former nonprofit executive director.

  The good: A president who has an appreciation for community, for movement building, for social justice, and for the nonprofit sector.

  The bad: As we go to press, too early to tell. Given the challenges in the world, many people—not just those who supported his candidacy—are hopeful.

On a smaller scale, the response to *The Best of the Board Café* has been phenomenal. The book went into multiple printings, and CompassPoint and Fieldstone Alliance gave me the opportunity to work on this second edition. And it's been nothing but exhilarating to see the *Board Café* grow and change with its new home, *Blue Avocado*. We are continuing to provide the ultra-practical, real-world tools for nonprofit board members, and these can be seen more clearly now as part of our efforts to champion and to support community nonprofits more broadly.

Community nonprofits are not just little factories putting out services. Nor are we the stereotype often heard about: too small to have an impact, too amateur to be well managed, and too softhearted to see hard realities clearly.

But community nonprofits take heat from almost everyone. Government tells us we're too small or mismanaged; consultants urge us to make a hundred management improvements; donors tell us there are too many nonprofits; corporations tell us to be more businesslike (like Bear Stearns or Enron?); and foundations tell us that our logic models aren't good enough. These stereotypes are so common that some of us in community nonprofits have unconsciously adopted them ourselves. It's easy to become discouraged when faced with this onslaught of negativity. But community nonprofits and people—the overwhelming majority of the nonprofit sector—are the ones doing most of the work, coming up with the most innovative ideas and making the most meaningful investments in community life.

Management expert and author Peter Drucker once said, "In the last hundred years, every important idea for social change has come from the nonprofit sector." Community nonprofits arise to meet self-identified community needs and are the vehicles through which we take care of our communities and act for social change. Much more than individual corporations providing units of services, we are vital components of movements ranging from healthcare access to environmental health, immigration rights, ending racial discrimination, and raising our individual and collective spirits.

I recently met with some women from a public housing project who were trying to raise a few thousand dollars to start a drill team for middle school girls. The money was for instruments and uniforms. After talking with them, I realized that some people might assume that the YMCA or the Boys and Girls Club would do a better job of starting such a drill team. After all, they have experts in youth development and professional purchasing departments. While these are great organizations, I hope you would all agree with me that there is a unique and greater value in having mothers in a housing project start and lead such a team. They will not only provide "units of service," but in the process will create and nurture a community of parents and youngsters, a community that will realize many more impacts than just "unduplicated clients served."

In addition to our greater impact, community nonprofits are actually more effective and more efficient than nearly all government agencies and corporations. We break new ground (unlike foundations) and take personal risks (unlike funders). As community nonprofits, we do more than provide services. We are part of, and we lead movements for, social change. And we hold ourselves accountable to our constituencies.

All of our organizations are like the drill team for girls: We not only develop and provide important services, but in doing so we create community and bring about long-term, varied, and unexpected benefits. In our own work, we all share the heart, spirit, and meaning of the drill team mothers. Let's claim not only our explicit outcomes, but all the impacts we have.

Thank you for being a part of the *Board Café*—and now the *Blue Avocado*—community. I look forward to hearing from you.

Special thanks for this second edition to:

- The *Board Café*'s Editorial Advisory Committee: Mike Allison, Pamela Davis, Tim Wolfred, Mike Schley, and Nora Silver.
- The co-founders and sponsors of *Blue Avocado*: Pamela Davis of the Nonprofit Insurance Alliance Group and Jeanne Bell of CompassPoint Nonprofit Services.
- The early funders and advertisers of *Blue Avocado*: the Nonprofit Insurance Alliance of California, the Alliance of Nonprofits for Insurance Risk Retention Group, the Wallace Alexander Gerbode Foundation, the Evelyn and Walter Haas, Jr. Fund, and Chapman and Associates.
- *Board Café* and *Blue Avocado* readers, who don't just request—but *demand*—high-quality, purely practical, inspiring material in every article and every issue.

Jan Masaoka

CHAPTER ONE

Introduction

The *Best of the Board Café* consists primarily of articles that first appeared in the *Board Café*, a newsletter for members of nonprofit boards. Beginning in 2008, the *Board Café* expanded into *Blue Avocado*, an online magazine for nonprofit board members, staff, and volunteers, and the *Board Café* continues as a column in *Blue Avocado*. Over its ten years of publication, the *Board Café* has covered a broad spectrum of issues, and this book brings the best articles together in one place. Chapter 1 describes *The Best of the Board Café* and includes

About the *Board Café*

The *Board Café* column in *Blue Avocado* magazine addresses the real-life demands of board members—including the need for materials that speak to different kinds of organizations. The practices and structures of a large, staffed, multisite organization will be different from those of a small organization that runs on volunteers or has a small staff. Even individual organizations differ, depending on whether there is a strong executive at the helm, a weak executive, or the position is vacant. A dance company will need different skills from its board members than does an organization advocating for toxic-waste cleanup.

Board Café articles reflect the CompassPoint Board Model for Governance and Support. This conceptual model, developed by CompassPoint Nonprofit Services* over the years, is based on research about both nonprofit and for-profit boards, on theoretical work about governance, and on an original analysis of the reasons why boards so seldom live up to the expectations set for them.** It has been tested and refined in consulting work with hundreds of nonprofit organizations. Chapter 2 focuses on explaining and understanding the CompassPoint board model, although it is "behind the scenes" throughout the book. In addition to this model, the *Board Café* draws on the practical experiences of thousands of board members.

How is this book different from the *Board Café* column in *Blue Avocado*?

The editors of the *Board Café* receive dozens of letters and comments in response to articles published in the newsletter. These letters almost always contain thoughtful criticisms and additions. For example, after the article "A 360-Degree Look" was published (see page 112), several readers wrote to say that the article seemed to equate the evaluation of the organization with the evaluation of the executive director. The version of this article in *The Best of the Board Café* has been rewritten to take these important comments into account. Similarly, the article "Young Voices in the Boardroom" (see page 155) sparked many favorable responses, including several that have been incorporated into this version.

In other words, *The Best of the Board Café* also includes the best thinking of the 50,000 subscribers to *Blue Avocado*.

What you'll find in this book

Written for both the new board member and the veteran, this book is a just-in-time guide to the issues at hand. Because your time is scarce, each article is short— "short enough to read over a cup of coffee." Each article takes on a specific question, and each article understands that you—a nonprofit board member—need plug-and-play solutions, right now. This compilation of articles provides practical, hands-on advice for board members, executive directors, and other staff. Examples throughout the book are based on real-life organizations, although all the organization names—taken from the names of trees—are fictitious.

---

* CompassPoint Nonprofit Services is a consulting and training firm in northern California—and a nonprofit itself.

** Jan Masaoka and Mike Allison, "Why Boards Don't Govern," in *Taking Trusteeship Seriously: Essays on the History, Dynamics and Practice of Trusteeship* (Indianapolis: University of Indiana Press, 1995), 165.

Chapter 1 includes a list of terms and separate pieces of advice for executive directors and board members. It also discusses popular myths about nonprofit organizations and includes a story illustrating the board's role as a safety net.

Chapter 2 describes the CompassPoint Model for Governance and Support. It also discusses some of the basics of nonprofit boards, including bylaws and board-staff relationships, and it has special sections on advisory boards, all-volunteer organizations, taking public policy stands, and Sarbanes-Oxley.

Chapter 3 focuses on the unique and paradoxical relationship between the board and the executive director. It includes articles on executive director pay and performance evaluation, on the transition from one executive director to another, and even on firing the executive director.

Boards of directors frequently come face-to-face with big decisions, including what strategies and plans should guide the organization and, in some cases, whether to close down or merge the organization. Chapter 4 looks at these big decisions and the criteria and processes that boards can use to make and implement them. Also included are a Dashboard Tool and a "360 Look" at the organization.

Nonprofit boards have a duty not only to govern their organizations but also to manage their own affairs. Chapter 5 examines issues such as board self-assessment, conflict of interest, and integrating new board members. It also tackles the difficult issues of nonproductive and disruptive board members.

Chapter 6 addresses the question, Who is on the board and how did they get there? It contains ideas for recruiting new board members and questions to ask prospective board members. The chapter also suggests principles for achieving diversity on non-profit boards.

Chapter 7 discusses the structure of nonprofit boards, including how large a board should be and whether a board should have committees. It gives job descriptions for board officers and various board committees. Helping to create effective committees (and to disband others) is an important goal of this chapter.

Being on a board and going to board meetings are almost synonymous. Chapter 8 contains many ideas for holding good board meetings. A crucial concept introduced in this chapter is the Critical Path for the board: a way to bring strategy into every meeting agenda.

Chapter 9 takes up the topic of fundraising and business strategy. It distinguishes between the board's governance role and support role in raising money for the nonprofit. It discusses how to develop strategies for financial sustainability, as well as suggests ways individual board members can raise funds and support earned-income strategies.

Chapter 10 addresses the twin to fundraising: finance and financial accountability. It explains what it means for the board to have oversight of the nonprofit's budget. The chapter also contains advice on cash and investment management, federal Form 990, and A Board Member's Guide to Nonprofit Insurance.

Finally, Concluding Words provides some thoughts about the important role nonprofits play in society at large.

The resource section at the end of this book contains suggestions for further reading and for organizational assistance. You will also find information on how to subscribe to the *Blue Avocado* at the back of the book.

Like a café menu, this book offers many choices for boards and organizations. It discusses why different choices are appropriate for different situations. The various articles will be useful to you at different times. Like any café patron, you won't want to or even be able to digest everything on the menu today, but you'll want to return and select different items later.

How to use this book

This book is intended to promote discussion among board members, executive directors, and staff. The articles have been formatted as handouts so that they can be easily shared. You might share the articles in these ways:

- Photocopy an article or a few pages and pass them out or fax them to fellow board members, the staff of your organization, and friends.

- Photocopy articles and distribute them with board packets. For example, if a discussion is coming up on finances, you might include the article "A Board-Staff Contract for Financial Accountability" (see page 220).

- Reprint pertinent articles in your organization newsletter or other literature. The sidebar Reprint Policy on the following page gives more information about using articles from this book.

The Best of the Board Café is intended to be the *beginning* of a discussion, not the last word. As your board circulates and discusses these articles, you'll inevitably come up with additional ideas, criticisms, and suggestions. You are invited to share these experiences and ideas in future issues of *Blue Avocado* so that they can contribute to the important work of social service and social change. (See page xiv for information on how to contact the *Blue Avocado*.)

Reprint policy

The Best of the Board Café is written for the hundreds of thousands of volunteer board members who govern and support nonprofit organizations in the United States and Canada. Please observe the following rules for reproducing or reprinting articles from this book.

A. Making copies of articles to share with fellow board members, staff, or friends who serve on boards: go ahead! You are encouraged to make handouts. Please do not remove or cover the copyright notice on the handout.

B. Reprinting five or fewer pages in another publication: this is fine as long as you comply with the following two simple rules:

Along with the reprinted article, print the following:

• **Copyright 2009 CompassPoint Nonprofit Services. Excerpted from *The Best of the Board Café* with permission. Free subscriptions to *Blue Avocado* magazine for nonprofits (in which *Board Café* is a column) and an order form to purchase the book are available at www.blueavocado.org. *The Best of the Board Café* is published by and available at www.FieldstoneAlliance.org.**

• Send two copies of the publication where pages have been reprinted to *Blue Avocado,* 731 Market Street, Suite 200, San Francisco, CA 94103. If you are reprinting materials in an e-mail newsletter or on the web, please forward the e-mail or send the link to editor@blueavocado.org.

C. Reprinting six or more pages at once in another publication: request permission by contacting *Blue Avocado* at the above address, by e-mail at editor@blueavocado.org, or by phone at 415-722-4703.

The intent of the policy is not only to encourage the friendly use of this book but also to keep *Board Café* writers and *Blue Avocado* editors informed of how it is being used.

Terminology and titles

Board: This book uses the term *board* for the board of directors of a nonprofit corporation—the legal, governing board.

Board member: Members of nonprofit boards of directors may be referred to as *trustees, governors,* or *directors.* The term *board member* is used to cover all these titles.

Executive director: This is the top paid staff position in the organization. Although some nonprofits use *CEO* (chief executive officer), *president,* or *director,* the term *executive director* remains the most widely used and is the term used throughout this book.

Board chair: This is the head of the board of directors. Again, other terms are in use, including *board president, CVO* (chief voluntary officer), and *chairperson,* but here the term *board chair* will most often be used.

Client: There isn't one word that accurately describes the direct beneficiaries of nonprofit activity. Health clinics serve *patients*; caseworkers serve *clients*; theatres welcome *patrons*; environmental justice groups have *members*; independent schools teach *students*; magazines have *subscribers*; nonprofit radio stations have *listeners.* The term *client* seems to come closest to a generic term and is the term most often used in this book.

Nonprofit: Although the Internal Revenue Service (IRS) defines many kinds of nonprofit corporations, this book uses the term *nonprofit* to refer to 501(c)(3) corporations, which are eligible for tax-deductible donations.* Other terms in use are *not-for-profit* and *charity.* Recently there have been attempts to gain coinage for *public benefit organization, human change organization,* and other terms in the same way. These are worthy efforts; but, at least for now, the term *nonprofit* is still more recognizable.

Community-based organization (CBO) and community nonprofit: To differentiate from other types of nonprofits, the term *CBO* is used frequently by government agencies and others to identify nonprofits that are NOT. Some examples are churches or other religious entities; labor unions; condominium associations; charitable foundations; professional associations; or large, institutional nonprofits such as private universities and hospitals. The term *CBO,* however, has come to connote a nonprofit human service provider with county and state contracts for services delivery. More broadly,

---

* The *Board Café* is written for an audience predominantly in the United States, although readers in dozens of countries find it useful as well.

we use the term *community nonprofit* to mean a community organization, led by members of the community and serving that community, however broadly defined.

About Nonprofit Boards and Executives

Boards of directors can be tremendous sources of strength, solace, support, and inspiration for staff, volunteers, clients, and the larger community. They help keep organizations on track by providing vision, by raising money and political support, and by representing constituents in the halls of power. They can be looked to for advice on what to include in the new brochure or where to buy inexpensive furniture. Boards are safety nets for organizations in crisis. Perhaps most important, boards can be a vital link between our communities and the agencies that have grown out of them. To be as successful as we can be, we need boards to function well.

But too often, the board experience is unsatisfying and frustrating to both board members and staff. Board members are often uncertain about how to be effective. Sometimes they get burned out by too much work and too much responsibility; at other times (or even at the same time) board members feel irrelevant and ignored. People on staff sometimes complain that board members are micromanaging, meddling, and stepping on the toes of the professional providers who know better ways to do things. At other times staff feel that the board isn't paying enough attention, is ineffective, or isn't "doing its share," particularly in terms of fundraising.

In turn, executive directors—the people in the top staff job—are often irritated by board members, or even simply by the existence of the board. Many executive directors feel the pain of governance reflected in expert Richard Chait's comment that "board members are part-time amateurs supervising the work of full-time professionals." Executive directors are often exhausted from the hours and responsibility of their jobs, and it can seem as if the board neither appreciates them nor helps out. It's particularly aggravating when board members aren't doing what they are supposed to be doing, yet they feel that they can oversee and give guidance to their executive director. Finally, executive directors are understandably reluctant to tell the board what to do; after all, the board is the boss.

The unique and multifaceted relationship between the board and its executive is perhaps the most important relationship leading to organizational success or failure. Like the two partners in a skating competition, each side can either bring out the best in the other or prevent the other from skating well.

The following two brief sections separately address two very different parties: *executive directors* and *board members*. Each side brings different resources and different concerns to the table, making it appropriate to offer different suggestions on how to approach the work of the nonprofit board.

A special word to board members

As rewarding as board service can be, many board members often find it maddening as well. Others on the board may have differing views about how matters should be addressed, and you may feel at times that they simply aren't doing their part.

As a board member, working with the staff can have its ups and downs as well; at one moment staff may ask you to do hours of menial labor, yet at the next they take offense at a suggestion and accuse you of micromanaging. Sometimes staff members demand that the board "set a direction," while at other times it seems as if they only want you to rubberstamp decisions they have already made. Meetings often are clogged with administrative details, yet you joined the board intending to engage in meaningful discussions about the needs of the community.

This book is for you, your fellow board members, and the executive director of your organization. It is meant to establish a framework in which your work can be more effective and in which you can make a meaningful contribution to the agency's work. By using this book, over time, both the board and staff will know more and will have more concepts in common.

> **Although the key reason people join boards is to give something back and bring about social change, much more is to be gained.**

Although the key reason people join boards is to give something back and bring about social change, much more is to be gained. For example, by volunteering to serve on the board of an arts education organization, a person can learn a great deal about young people, politics, art theory, and educational philosophy. Boards are significant ways to meet new people, some of whom will become close friends, business associates, and customers. Board service is a way to learn new skills—and apply those skills—in important ways.

Imagine being on the board of a business in which you have invested $100,000 of your own money. You would probably attend every meeting and read the advance materials carefully. You would learn more about the field to be sure that your company is staying abreast of developments and trends. You would ask tough questions to be sure that your investment is being used to your best advantage. Of course, you probably have not put $100,000 of your own money into the nonprofit organization on whose board you participate. However, you do represent government, foundation, and individual entities who have contributed funds to that organization. All of us look to you, the board of directors, to ensure that the community's investment pays off by improving the lives of the individuals served and the communities in which we live.

A special word to executive directors

The executive director's role in managing and assisting the board is perhaps the most paradoxical of all relationships in the nonprofit sector. On the one hand, the board is the "boss and the leadership," and leads and directs the organization's vision. On the other hand, the executive director informs, advises, and often provides leadership to the board.

Executive directors often wonder why they have to go through the motions of board involvement when staff really knows best. Most executive directors wish at least once for a board that simply does what it's told—in addition to heaping praise on the staff and raising lots of money on its own.

Executive directors often wonder why they have to go through the motions of board involvement when staff really know best.

Rather than ignore the paradox or the frustrations, this book seeks to turn the paradox into an advantage. In some ways the role of board members is to support the staff, and in other ways the board's role is to govern, with staff submitting to the board's authority. All along the way, this book provides conceptual and practical tools for the various roles executive directors have to play when working with their boards.

Other members of your staff may be less experienced or knowledgeable about how boards work. Giving this book to your staff may help them understand board members' actions or be more receptive when you ask them to perform tasks for the board. As the executive director, you can be a facilitator of meaningful exchange between staff and board, rather than a gatekeeper who maintains control of all information flowing in either direction.

And don't forget: board members, too, need praise and recognition for their good work, both individually and as a group. It would be easier for them to go home after work rather than come to a board meeting where there is likely to be at least one boring stretch and at least one aggravating stretch. Simply because they want to help, board members give up Saturdays for retreats, fold flyers for benefits, call their friends and ask for contributions, and argue with each other over the right steps for the organization.

It's hard to get around to working with the board when there always seem to be more immediate concerns in the office. But strong boards are critically important in the long-term struggles for healthcare, civil rights, education, a clean environment, economic prosperity, and the arts in our communities. As the executive director, the leadership *you* provide to the board may not be recognized or appreciated, although ensuring that the board is effective is one of your most important responsibilities. This book seeks to help you and your boards in the efforts ahead.

Use this book to build common understanding

One way you can use this book to help bring board members to a common understanding is to photocopy separate sections and distribute them with board packets. For example, if a discussion on finances is coming up, you might send out information from Chapter 10, Boards and Finance.

Alligators in the Boardroom
Myths and Urban Legends about Nonprofits

It is worth noting that some common assumptions about nonprofits are actually urban legends. Like the legendary alligators in New York sewers, these stories have been passed along through so many people they've gained a measure of credibility just by their longevity. Some of these myths may need to be dispelled among your fellow board members.

Nonprofits can't make a profit. In fact, the Internal Revenue Service (IRS) guidelines do *not* say that nonprofits can't have profits, but they *do* clearly state that any profits can't be simply distributed to board members (as corporate profits are to shareholders). The IRS requires surpluses ("profits") to be reinvested in the organization's work. Such cash reserves—built through surpluses—are needed by nonprofits to even out their cash flows, to provide reserves for emergencies, and to allow them to pay for equipment, research, staff development, building renovations, and other necessary investments.

Nonprofits can't charge for their services. In fact, many nonprofits exist solely or mostly on fees charged, such as nonprofit preschools that charge tuition or community choirs that sell tickets to their concerts.

Nonprofits are poorly managed compared to businesses. Compared to which business? Compared to Lehman Brothers, Enron, Merrill Lynch, General Motors, World-Com? In fact, nonprofits often achieve growth rates well above for-profit companies of comparable size, and they do so while undercapitalized and highly regulated and while maintaining the highest of ethical standards. But comparisons between nonprofits and for-profits often aren't very useful; they have different bottom lines, different measures of effectiveness, different resources, and different financial flows.

Nonprofits can't lobby. Nonprofits cannot engage in any *electoral* activity—they can't support or oppose candidates. However, they *can* support or oppose ballot measures (such as *for* public school bonds or *against* new immigration laws). In addition, nonprofits can encourage legislators to support or oppose various pieces of legislation—as long as such lobbying activities are an "insubstantial" part of their activities. In fact, legislator education and lobbying may be centrally important for long-term impact. (For more information, see the web site of Center for Lobbying in the Public Interest: http://www.clpi.org/.)

A nonprofit budget has to be balanced. Instead, in some years a nonprofit will want to budget for surpluses, in order to create a cash reserve or to save up for new equipment. In other years the same nonprofit might plan for a deficit, for example, to do onetime programs with windfall money or to invest in a new fundraising director or a publicity strategy. Over time, the financial goal of a for-profit is to maximize profits; in contrast, the financial goal of a nonprofit is to *sustain sufficient working capital for program continuance and strategic choices.*

I don't benefit from nonprofits. Nonprofits help other people. In fact, each and every one of us benefits from nonprofits every day. We may have a daughter in Brownies or an aging father in a nonprofit nursing home. We may watch public television, take in a play, or take a walk in a restored natural habitat. We drive safer cars because nonprofits have developed and advocated for consumer safety legislation. We benefit from medical research at nonprofit research institutes and from the cleaner air and water that have resulted from nonprofit advocacy. Nonprofits aren't about *us* helping *them*; nonprofits are the vehicle through which communities organize to help *ourselves.*

Nonprofits don't contribute to the economy. Surprisingly, nonprofits generate 8 percent of the gross domestic product (GDP) in the United States and employ one in every fourteen American workers. Nonprofits mobilize the efforts of an army: 61.2 million adults volunteering 12.9 *billion* hours each year toward community and public benefit—the equivalent of 7.6 million full-time staff.*

---

* Amy Blackwood, Kennard T. Wing, and Thomas H. Pollak, *Nonprofit Almanac 2008: Public Charities Giving, and Volunteering* (Washington, DC: National Center for Charitable Statistics, The Urban Institute, 2008).

Also Try

Why Do Nonprofits Have Boards? p. 18

Nonprofits and democracy

Board members typically think of volunteer work on a board as helping that particular organization and the cause or services it represents. But it's important to be reminded of the role of nonprofits in fostering democracy. After all, starting a business takes a fair bit of money, and getting elected to political office takes the support of many people, but a nonprofit can start with an idea and the commitment of just a few people. Because of the inherently democratic nature of nonprofit origins, nonprofits as a whole help keep new ideas arising and growing. They are an intrinsic counteraction to tyranny.

For this reason, many emerging democracies actively encourage the development of nonprofit organizations. In fact, this has become a cornerstone strategy for democratic leaders in Eastern Europe, the Middle East, Asia, and elsewhere.

A Board Leads an Organization Out of the Abyss

Perhaps the least-appreciated aspect of nonprofit boards is their role as a safety net. Even boards that don't seem to be doing much, or that may even have contributed to deep problems, rise up and do heroic work to fix things. Here we tell a board chair's story about such a breakthrough—how an organization walked to the precipice of bankruptcy and then walked away.

Tom Siino, longtime board member of Big Brothers Big Sisters of the East Bay, tells the inspiring story:

"Three years ago our financial troubles started when we lost our executive director. Then we made a couple of false steps in hiring a replacement. At one point we were down in the ashes with one staff person and a lot of debt. Our budget had gone from $700,000 to $75,000. Now we're back to seven staff and a budget of $400,000, all our liabilities cleaned up, cash in the bank, a great new executive director, and more and more kids in the program every day.

"When we were close to broke, we made the decision not to hire a new ED because we didn't want any obstacles to a possible merger that we were exploring, and to save the cash. We all agreed that keeping the program staff was the most important thing, and board members took on management tasks. Sometimes we were meeting once a week! We lost a number of board members—they didn't want to come to meetings where it was always bad news being discussed and we were faced with dealing with immediate needs instead of strategic planning. We voted to have everyone's board terms end on June 30 and required each person to proactively choose to rejoin the board. A couple of times we had to loan money to the organization to make payroll.

"After several months we realized a merger wasn't going to happen. We reversed strategy: We turned our attention to hiring a new leader and creating an organization that could attract such a leader and make him or her able to succeed. At this point instead of keeping the program staff, we let all the program staff go and kept only the fundraiser. We contracted with another nonprofit to manage our volunteer-based programs as an interim measure. We put a government grant on hold.

"All this time we were holding our bowling tournament, our big annual dinner, monitoring cash on a daily basis. Our landlord allowed us to cancel our lease and even gave us free space in the building—it was like a big closet, had no windows, and no air at first—but it was free.

From *Best of the Board Café* (a column in the online magazine *Blue Avocado*), Copyright © 2003 and 2009, CompassPoint Nonprofit Services, published by Fieldstone Alliance, www.FieldstoneAlliance.org. Subscribe free to *Blue Avocado* at www.blueavocado.org.

We talked about closing down and set some guidelines, such as "If we haven't raised X dollars by X date," we would consider bankruptcy. It was hard to raise money but we tried to keep focus on our optimistic view of the future. We monitored toward those guidelines, and they were motivating.

"What kept me going? I was a Big Brother for a Little Brother from when he was seven years old 'til he was eighteen; today he is thirty-one, and we still keep in touch. I was a Big Brother for another boy for two years until he moved away. I've seen so much of the program firsthand—such as seeing the 'Bigs' and 'Littles' together. I know what this program does. We can't let this program go away. I'm sold for life.

"We on the board wouldn't—couldn't—go through this process again. But seeing it successful—we all have a big sense of pride in how everybody stepped up to the plate—not just people on the board but volunteers and community people and businesses. We now have five new great board members ready to take on leadership and an executive director that is truly leading the organization to new heights and reconnecting with our community leaders and volunteers. My wife understood how important this program is to me and she never complained about all the evenings and weekends I spent doing board work—now I have more time to spend with her and our own kids again!"

Our thanks to Tom for sharing this heartbreaking and heartwarming story. If this had been a business, it probably would have closed. But the board stepped up and saved the organization's services for hundreds of young people hungry for a stable, nurturing relationship with an adult. All of us owe Tom—and the millions of board members nationwide—our thanks.

CHAPTER TWO

Responsibilities of the Board
The CompassPoint Board Model for Governance and Support

This book focuses on practical tools, but they are more than just commonsense ideas. These tools are based on a conceptual framework for nonprofit boards of directors called the CompassPoint Board Model for Governance and Support. This chapter describes the CompassPoint Model in detail. It also discusses the legal basics of nonprofits and the board's relationship with staff and volunteers. This chapter includes the following articles:

Why Do Nonprofits Have Boards?

All corporations, whether nonprofit or for-profit, require boards of directors, and these boards have formal responsibilities for directing those corporations. As a result, it's appropriate to begin a discussion about nonprofit boards with a discussion of the nonprofit corporation.

A group of people sitting around a kitchen table decides to take a more organized approach to realizing a vision for community change or service. They decide to launch a new nonprofit organization as the means for doing so. To give the organization a legal framework, such a group would typically choose to incorporate, that is, to form a corporation. A corporation has the ability to act as a fictitious person: instead of the real individuals involved, it can sign leases, hire staff, and engage in business activity.

A next step is to obtain nonprofit, tax-exempt status for the corporation (at both the federal and state levels). Nonprofit corporations, identified as 501(c)(3) organizations (named after the section in the Internal Revenue Code that describes them), enjoy several important tax advantages.

Nonprofit 501(c)(3) corporations

• Do not pay corporate income tax on income made by the corporation.

• Can accept donations that are then tax deductible to the donor.

• Are eligible for foundation and government grants that are only for nonprofits.

• Are eligible for the nonprofit bulk mail postage rate.

• Are eligible for state and county tax benefits in some areas.

Society has granted these tax advantages to nonprofits* for several reasons. Nonprofits provide services to society that may not be provided through the commercial or government sectors, such as support for low-income families caring for an elder with Alzheimer's. Community-based nonprofits can often perform important community roles that are less successful when done by government agencies, such as reaching young people with information on sexually transmitted diseases. Finally, nonprofits may speak out for groups or champion issues that would be ignored by either the commercial or government sectors. For example, civil rights groups, AIDS organizations, and environmental justice advocates play important roles by bringing new issues and perspectives to the attention of the public.

In a *for-profit* corporation, the board represents the stock owners—the shareholders—of the company. On behalf of the owners and shareholders, the board hires and oversees the head of the company, reviews financial performance, and makes sure that the company is headed in a direction that will result in profit for the shareholders.

In a *nonprofit* corporation, there are no such owners. Instead of representing shareholders, the board of directors represents, in a general way, the interests of the public. For example, the board represents the interests of government in ensuring that the organization's funds are used for its nonprofit purpose, rather than to make the board members or staff members wealthier. The board represents the interests of clients, patrons, and beneficiaries, ensuring that services are of good quality, appropriate, and accessible. Finally, the board represents the interests of the organization's donors, ensuring that funds are spent appropriately and for maximum impact.

The formal responsibilities of boards of directors are

- To ensure that the organization stays in compliance with laws and regulations relating to nonprofit corporations.
- To determine the organization's mission, strategies, and program priorities.
- To ensure that the organization uses its resources toward fulfillment of its tax-

exempt purpose as stated in its application for exemption.

- If appropriate, to hire an executive director or chief executive officer to manage the corporation.
- To fulfill these responsibilities, board members must be in control of important decisions and have adequate knowledge of the organization's operations. This important work often takes the form of detailed discussions about administrative and financial matters. A constant challenge for board members is to remain aware of the link between these administrative responsibilities and their accountability to clients and the community.

Community-based organizations need boards not only for legal reasons but also because boards contribute immensely to an organization's ability to succeed. By the very act of serving on the board, board members embody both the commitment of the community to the nonprofit and the commitment of the nonprofit to community leadership. Acting for the community, the board of directors also has a special role as the conscience of the organization—ensuring ethical and effective work that makes a difference in the world.

---

* BoardSource estimates that the total of these taxes foregone is approximately $30 billion per year.

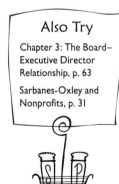

Also Try

Chapter 3: The Board–Executive Director Relationship, p. 63

Sarbanes-Oxley and Nonprofits, p. 31

The CompassPoint Board Model
for Governance and Support

There are two fundamental types of nonprofit board responsibility: governance and support, each of which has distinctive characteristics, shown in the chart on page 21. On one hand, the board, acting as the formal representative of the public, governs the organization's affairs. At the same time, board members help support the organization by volunteering, raising money, and advising.

Much of the confusion about board responsibilities is confusion between what the board should do as a group and what individual board members should do. For example, although the board as a whole is responsible for evaluating the executive director, the board president as an individual doesn't have the authority that a supervisor has with a subordinate. The board president is not a supervisor, but instead acts as a convener and leader for the board, which as a group provides feedback and direction to the executive director.

As a result, board members frequently have to switch roles. The CompassPoint Board Model reflects the "role switching" that board members do. For example, an individual may meet with the organization's finance staff to lend expertise in formats for cash-flow statements. In this role, the person can make suggestions, but the finance staff report to the executive director and can choose not to take that advice. Subsequently, the same person can go to the board meeting where the budget is being considered. In this setting, the individual is acting as a part of the board in its governance role. The board as a body does not report to the executive director and can, for example, direct staff to revise the budget in a certain way.

On the outside looking in— or, on the inside looking out?

When acting in its governing role, the board represents the interests of the community. It asks: Is this organization using public and private resources to benefit the community and the public? In a sense, the board stands *in* the community, looking through the door into the organization. It represents the community and speaks to the organization in the community's voice.

But at the same time, the board also represents the organization's interests to the community. Board members individually act as ambassadors from the organization to the community. Board members promote the organization's work in the community, build support for the organization's

The CompassPoint Board Model: Governance and Support

The board acts to **GOVERN** the organization	The board acts to **SUPPORT** the organization

Objectives

• To represent the *community's* interests within the *organization*	• To represent the *organization's* interests in the *community*

Process for action

• The board acts as a body	• Board members act as individuals or through committees

Responsibilities

• Direction: Determine mission and purpose	• Fundraising: Contribute to the organization's fundraising success as appropriate to the individual (such as making a financial contribution, volunteering at a fundraising event, making business contacts for the organization, soliciting cash and noncash contributions); assist staff in raising funds
• Legal: Ensure compliance with federal, state, and local regulations and fulfillment of contractual obligations	
• Financial: Safeguard assets from misuse, waste, and embezzlement	
• CEO: Select the chief executive officer (usually called the executive director); monitor and evaluate performance	• Public relations and community contacts: Act as ambassadors to the community on behalf of the organization and its clients
• Fundraising: Approve a fundraising strategy and monitor its effectiveness	• Volunteerism: Recruit volunteers
• Planning: Determine strategies and overall priorities	• Advisory: Advise staff in areas of expertise; act as a sounding board for the executive director and other executive staff
• Programs: Determine the organization's program priorities, monitor implementation, and conduct program evaluations to measure impact	• Reputation: Lend name and personal credibility to the organization to use in brochures, grant proposals, and other formats
• Efficiency and impact: Ensure a realistic budget that maximizes use of resources	

From *Best of the Board Café* (a column in the online magazine *Blue Avocado*), Copyright © 2003 and 2009, CompassPoint Nonprofit Services, published by Fieldstone Alliance, www.FieldstoneAlliance.org. Subscribe free to *Blue Avocado* at www.blueavocado.org.

initiatives, and represent the board at city council meetings. In this sense, the board stands in the organization facing *out* and speaks to the community in the organization's voice.

This is the CompassPoint Board Model at work: As a group, the board represents the public in keeping the organization accountable; and as individuals, board members represent the organization to the public.

Who's in charge now?

In organizations with paid staff, there are times when the board acts in its governing role, as "the boss and in charge," but there are other times when individual board members act to support the staff. Boards and staff often get confused over these differences. For example, when it comes to fundraising, some people think that fundraising is an intrinsic board responsibility while others think fundraising is only a requirement for boards that have chosen to accept the responsibility. This conundrum—often the source of tension between staff and board—can be cleared up with the CompassPoint Board Model, first discussed here related to strategic planning and then to fundraising.

When an organization undertakes a strategic planning process, it's ultimately the board's responsibility to adopt a plan.

When an organization undertakes a strategic planning process, it's ultimately the board's responsibility to adopt a plan. In this setting the staff prepares reports and proposals for the board

to consider. The board is clearly functioning in its governance role—in charge of the organization's direction and future. On the other hand, in the *implementation* of the plan—program delivery—board members frequently volunteer as individuals. Whether as museum docents or as workers at a neighborhood fair, board members often volunteer under the direction of staff. They may be trained as grief counselors by a staff person or work on painting a house as directed by staff.

In fundraising, the board, in its governing role, is responsible for seeing that there is a realistic plan for bringing in the funds the organization will need and for monitoring progress on the plan. This funding plan might include fundraised (contributed) dollars, but it could also include fees, interest income from investments, foundation grants, money from the sale of books, and so forth. What's important is that ensuring the existence of the plan is a governance responsibility, one in which the board acts as the "boss" and provides oversight to the staff-developed plan.

But in the support role, board members as individuals also help carry out that plan. In this role, they often act with direction from staff. For example, staff might generate a list of people who need to be called for an upcoming event, and distribute those names among board members. In this situation, the staff organizes the work and delegates tasks to board members acting as individual volunteers.

In short, there's an up-and-down switch as well as an inside-out switch. The board as a group oversees the staff's development of a fundraising plan, but the staff frequently oversee the implementation of fundraising activities by board members.

Who's responsible for the board doing its job?

A frequent source of frustration for executive directors is a board that is inactive and passive. These executive directors cry out, "My board doesn't do anything!" But the frustration comes from more than the lack of board activity. It also comes from a sense of helplessness, a sense that there is nothing the executive can or *should* do to get the board going. In many instances, both board members and executives believe that it would be inappropriate for the executive to play a leadership role with the board. Many strong executives draw back from appearing to provide too much direction to their "bosses."

This approach comes from the conventional wisdom that "the board sets policy, and staff implements it." This statement fails to distinguish between the governing and supporting roles of the board and, in practice, often devolves into arguments over what is policy and what is not.

In fact, telling an inactive board—or even an inactive board telling itself—that it *should* be active is seldom an effective strategy. Even if one or two active board members insist that all board members *must* be active, little is likely to change. In

short, an approach that makes the board solely responsible for its own functioning is an approach that succeeds with strong boards but simply doesn't work with weak boards.

The approach advocated by the Compass Point Board Model may at first seem surprising, but in fact is common practice by many seasoned executive directors: *The executive director must be largely responsible for the board fulfilling its governance role.* The truth is that the executive director is in the best position to ensure the effective functioning of the board. He or she is the primary staff support to the board, attends meetings, and is usually more in touch with board members than anyone else. Moreover, the executive director is responsible for the organization's performance and, because board governance and support are both needed for high performance, must develop an active board for the sake of organizational performance.

Perhaps more important, this approach *works.*

The executive director cannot ensure the board's effectiveness by ordering board members to perform various tasks or to adopt certain attitudes. The executive can work more closely with individual board members, take an active role in the recruitment and orientation of board members, and develop processes that the executive and the board can use to work together for better governance.

Just about any approach works when there is both a strong executive and a strong board. But the CompassPoint Board Model also works when (a) there is a weak executive and a strong board; or (b) there is a strong executive and a weak board. The model provides a basis for strong boards to deal with weak executives, as well as a basis for strong executives to help change weak boards.

Management expert Peter Drucker has long said that the effective functioning of the corporate board is the responsibility of the chief staff person. This responsibility can be written into the executive director's job description, and it should be one of the responsibilities for which the board holds the executive director accountable.

As paradoxical as it may seem at first, it makes complete sense for the board to evaluate how well the executive director has elicited board effectiveness. And the wise executive director willingly accepts the responsibility, knowing that with a strong board there will be a working partnership and knowing that in the absence of a strong board, he or she must develop one.

The CompassPoint Board Model is not a deeply scientific theory like the theory of atomic energy. It is, however, a framework that helps clarify discussions on boards and about boards. It rests on research and theoretical work on the economic and social roles for nonprofits, on research and thinking about governance in the for-profit corporate sector, and on the extensive research, literature, discussion, and experiential knowledge about the nonprofit board.

This model is not directly referenced in most of these articles, although it lies beneath them—like the continuous root of the bamboo which is not visible above ground, but sends up many shoots in many locations that appear at first to be unconnected.

Many veteran board members and executive directors will find that the CompassPoint Board Model articulates principles that they have practiced for years. Less experienced board members and executive directors will find that it can act as a decoder—decoding the puzzling ways that boards act at times. For the *Board Café*, it serves as the cooking principles upon which many different kinds of dishes are based.

Also Try

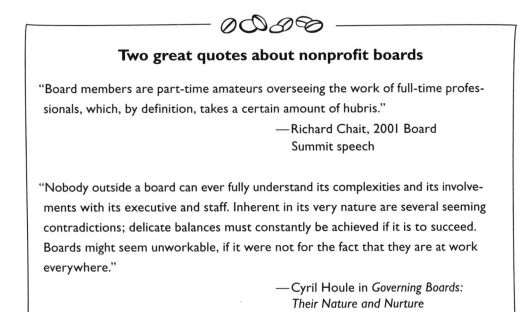

Two great quotes about nonprofit boards

"Board members are part-time amateurs overseeing the work of full-time professionals, which, by definition, takes a certain amount of hubris."

—Richard Chait, 2001 Board
Summit speech

"Nobody outside a board can ever fully understand its complexities and its involvements with its executive and staff. Inherent in its very nature are several seeming contradictions; delicate balances must constantly be achieved if it is to succeed. Boards might seem unworkable, if it were not for the fact that they are at work everywhere."

—Cyril Houle in *Governing Boards:
Their Nature and Nurture*

A Board Member Contract*

One way to be sure that everyone on the board is clear on his or her responsibilities is to adopt a board member contract. The board's discussion about what to put in its contract or agreement is valuable in itself. This sample may help get that discussion started.

The board chair should sign two copies of this agreement for each board member. Each new board member should sign both, return one copy to the board chair, and keep the other for reference.

---

*One of the five most reprinted *Board Café* articles.

Also Try

Orientation and Integration of New Board Members, p. 134

Conflict of Interest, p. 131

A Board-Staff Contract for Financial Accountability, p. 220

Sample Board Member Contract

I, _____, understand that as a member of the Board of Directors of _____, I have a legal and ethical responsibility to ensure that the organization does the best work possible in pursuit of its goals. I believe in the purpose and the mission of the organization, and I will act responsibly and prudently as its steward.

As part of my responsibilities as a board member

1. I will interpret the organization's work and values to the community, represent the organization, and act as a spokesperson. In turn, I will interpret our constituencies' needs and values to the organization, speakout for their interests, and on their behalf, hold the organization accountable.

2. I will attend at least 75 percent of board meetings, committee meetings, and special events.

3. Each year, but no later than Thanksgiving of each year, I will make a personal financial contribution at a level that is meaningful to me.

4. I will actively participate in one or more fundraising activities.

5. I will act in the best interests of the organization and excuse myself from discussions and votes where I have a conflict of interest.

6. I will stay informed about what's going on in the organization. I will ask questions and request information. I will participate in and take responsibility for making decisions on issues, policies, and other matters.

7. I will work in good faith with staff and other board members as partners toward achievement of our goals.

8. If I don't fulfill these commitments to the organization, I will expect the board president to call me and discuss my responsibilities with me.

In turn, the organization will be responsible to me in the following ways:

1. I will be sent, without request, quarterly financial reports and an update of organizational activities that allow me to meet the "prudent person" standards of the law.*

2. Opportunities will be offered to me to discuss with the executive director and the board president the organization's programs, goals, activities, and status; additionally, I can request such opportunities.

3. The organization will help me perform my duties by keeping me informed about issues in the industry and field in which we are working and by offering me opportunities for professional development as a board member.

4. Board members and staff will respond in a straightforward fashion to questions that I feel are necessary to carry out my fiscal, legal, and moral responsibilities to this organization. Board members and staff will work in good faith with me toward achievement of our goals.

5. If the organization does not fulfill its commitments to me, I can call on the board president and executive director to discuss the organization's responsibilities to me.

Signed:

_____ Date _____
Member, Board of Directors

_____ Date _____
Chair, Board of Directors

---

* The "prudent person rule," applied in many legal settings in slightly differing language, states that an individual must act with the same judgment and care as, in like circumstances, a prudent person would act.

Key Documents
Bylaws, Incorporation Papers, IRS Ruling Letters, and Others

Most of the time, board members don't pay much attention to the legal documents forming and governing their organizations. However, when there's a legal challenge to the organization, when there's deep conflict on the board, or when an aggressive or unscrupulous board member tries to take over, everyone's attention is drawn to the key legal documents. And too often, those documents were drawn up years ago and haven't been looked at since.

Here is a brief recap of the nonprofit organization's key documents.

1. IRS Form 1023: application for incorporation

This form is used for both nonprofit and for-profit corporations at the time of formation. Form 1023 requires that the organization state its purpose.

2. IRS determination letter

In response to the Application for Public Charity 501(c)(3) Status, the IRS issues a Determination Letter stating that it has determined that the organization has a nonprofit purpose and has been granted nonprofit status. (Prior to September 2008, the IRS issued Temporary Determination Letters, which could then become permanent after a five-year period.) If you have lost the Determination Letter, you can request a duplicate from the IRS.

3. State determination letter

Most legal aspects of nonprofit organizations are determined at the state level. Each state has a State Charity Official, although these individuals have different titles and work in different departments depending on the state. For example, in New Mexico, the Registry of Charitable Organizations is in the Consumer Protection Division in the Attorney General's Office. (A complete list of relevant regulators can be found through the National Association of State Charity Officials at http://www.nasconet.org/.)

4. Articles of incorporation

The articles of incorporation (in some states called a "certificate of incorporation" or "charter") is a publicly filed document that describes the organization's most basic legal structure and states the organization's name, the state in which it is located, and the purposes of the corporation.

5. Bylaws

Various aspects of bylaws are governed by the states. For example, in Ohio and New York, nonprofit boards must have a minimum of three members, but in California the minimum is one. It's important to obtain the applicable state laws and make sure that the bylaws are in compliance. In addition, some cities have further regulations for nonprofits. Ask the city attorney's office for guidance. For example, some states and cities have different rules for nonprofit organizations for which the board automatically includes an elected official or government employee as a result of that individual's election or employment.

Here is a checklist to be sure the most important provisions are included in your bylaws:

- Indemnification. A statement that limits the personal liability of board members.

- Whether the organization has members (such as members of a neighborhood or professional association) and, if so, what their rights are. For example, in a true membership organization, members have the right to elect officers. Even if you don't have members with legally enforceable membership rights such as voting rights, you can still have people called "members," but the distinction should be clarified in the bylaws.

- Minimum and maximum number of board members. Example: minimum of five and a maximum of fifteen board members. Some states specify a minimum, and some specify a formula for a minimum and maximum, so check your state's law.

- The number required for a quorum.* Many states specify the minimum required for a quorum; for example, in California a quorum may be as low as one-fifth of the board.

- Terms and term limits. Example: two years, with term limits of three consecutive terms (making a total of six years); after a year off, a board member may be permitted to return. Similarly, terms can be staggered so that, for instance, one-third of the board is up for reelection each year.

- Titles of officers, how the officers are appointed, and their terms. Example: appointed by majority vote at a regular meeting of the board; an officer term is for one year with a maximum of two consecutive officer terms.

- Procedure for removing a board member or officer. Example: by majority vote at a regularly scheduled meeting where the item was placed on the written agenda distributed at least two weeks ahead.

- Conflict of interest policy. Alternatively, many bylaws simply state that there will be a conflict of interest policy but will keep its exact wording out of the bylaws.

From *Best of the Board Café* (a column in the online magazine *Blue Avocado*), Copyright © 2003 and 2009, CompassPoint Nonprofit Services, published by Fieldstone Alliance, www.FieldstoneAlliance.org. Subscribe free to *Blue Avocado* at www.blueavocado.org.

- Minimum number of board meetings per year. Example: four, with one in each quarter.

- How a special or emergency board meeting may be called.

- How a committee may be created or dissolved.

- What committees exist, how members are appointed, and powers, if any.

- Conference calls and electronic meetings. Example: votes by e-mail or web forum are prohibited. Meetings may be held by conference call if all members can simultaneously hear one another.

As Internet usage grows, some boards are adding sections to the bylaws that describe how to hold a board meeting on the Internet, or whether and how decisions can be made by e-mail.

Each board member should be given a copy of the articles of incorporation, the IRS and state determination letters, and the bylaws. Some organizations also post their bylaws on a password-protected section of their web site.

Every few years, it's important to review the bylaws. Occasionally, individuals are invited to join boards without much scrutiny and are later found to be disruptive and destructive. Too often the board looks for the bylaws to see how to remove such a person, only to discover that the bylaws were written twenty years ago (and seldom looked at since) and have no such provision. Appropriate changes to the bylaws should be recorded in the board minutes, added to copies of the bylaws, and, in some cases, reviewed by an attorney experienced in nonprofit law.

---

* A quorum is the minimum number of board members who must be present for official decisions to be made. For example, if an organization currently has fifteen members, and the bylaws state that one-third of the members constitutes a quorum, then official decisions can only be made at board meetings where five or more members are present. Note: states may determine the minimum percentage for a quorum.

Also Try

From *Best of the Board Café* (a column in the online magazine *Blue Avocado*), Copyright © 2003 and 2009, CompassPoint Nonprofit Services, published by Fieldstone Alliance, www.FieldstoneAlliance.org. Subscribe free to *Blue Avocado* at www.blueavocado.org.

Sarbanes-Oxley and Nonprofits

Somehow, all the publicity about Sarbanes-Oxley made it seem as if this legislation applied to nonprofits, too. But contrary to what is frequently thought (and said in nonprofit boardrooms), Sarbanes-Oxley is not applicable to nonprofits, albeit with just a couple of exceptions. In other words, there are a couple of small points to note (templates later in this article), a lot to relax about, and a lesson to be learned in nonprofit leadership.

You may remember that this multi-component legislation (nicknamed SOX) was passed by the U.S. Congress in 2002 in response to a large number of for-profit scandals involving Enron, Tyco, WorldCom, Arthur Anderson, and others. Extreme fraud, conflicts of interest on boards, unethical executive compensation practices, and improper auditing led to the failure of these megacompanies and deep, negative impacts on consumers, shareholders, employees, and many other individuals and institutions.

In response, Sarbanes-Oxley set in place a number of required processes for publicly held corporations (corporations that issue stock to the public), of which the best known may be the requirement that the CEO personally vouch for the accuracy of financial statements and that the external audit firm be different from the firm providing financial consulting.

There are only two aspects of Sarbanes-Oxley that are applicable to nonprofits:

- Strengthened whistleblower protection, and
- Retention of documents related to lawsuits

Form 990-N also asks whether you have policies related to these two areas, making it more important to get them adopted. To make it easy, nationally recognized attorney Tom Silk of Silk Nonprofit Law has created model policies in each of these areas and made them available at no charge to the nonprofit community through CompassPoint Nonprofit Services. *Blue Avocado* is pleased as well to be able to present these for use by nonprofits. See the end of this article for links to these templates.

Perhaps the most intriguing aspect of Sarbanes-Oxley is that many of the provisions it mandated for for-profit businesses were already common, nearly universal practices in nonprofits, including the

- Requirement that the audit committee be comprised of board members
- Requirement that audit committee members not be on staff, and

- Prohibition of loans from the organization to board members

Although Sarbanes-Oxley was not aimed at nonprofits and its key provisions are already widely practiced in nonprofits, some voices in the nonprofit sector saw the law's passage as a wake-up call for nonprofits to adopt a variety of governance and financial practices. For example, Independent Sector, the national coalition that proposes standards for nonprofit governance, now suggests that nonprofit boards include at least one "financial expert" and provide "financial literacy training" to all board members. While such practices may be good ideas for some organizations, turning them into requirements would be, for most organizations, defensive, unnecessary moves. (Two white papers that explore possible implications are "The Sarbanes-Oxley Act and Implications for Nonprofit Organizations" from BoardSource and "Ten Emerging Principles of Governance of Nonprofit Corporations and Guides to a Safe Harbor" by Tom Silk.)

The bottom line for nonprofits and Sarbanes-Oxley?

A. Adopt and implement a whistleblower policy

B. Adopt and implement a document retention policy

C. Consider formalizing such non-required practices such as:

- Have your audit committee comprised of board members who are not also on staff, and if you are audited but don't have an audit committee, consider forming such a committee or task force
- Prohibit loans from the organization to board members (some states' corporate laws prohibit this)
- Work with a financial consulting firm that is different from your auditing firm
- Have the full board approve compensation for the executive director and the top staff financial officer
- Adopt an Ethics or Conflict of Interest Policy

Special thanks to attorney Michael Schley and CPA Steve Zimmerman for assistance on this article as well as to the brilliant and generous Tom Silk.

Model Whistleblower Policy for Nonprofits

Board resolution: The board of directors approves the inclusion of the following statement in the Employee Handbook and directs the chief executive officer to ensure that it is given to and acknowledged by all employees. In addition, the chief executive officer will ensure that whistleblower protection notification is posted in the workplace(s) as required by state law.

Notes: The Model Whistleblower Policy extends beyond the law by encouraging reporting of law violations as well as prohibiting retaliation. Whistleblower Posters can be downloaded from each state.

If any employee reasonably believes that some policy, practice, or activity of <u>NAME OF ORGA-NIZATION</u> is in violation of law, a written complaint may be filed by that employee with the chief executive officer.

It is the intent of _____ to adhere to all laws and regulations that apply to the organization, and the underlying purpose of this Policy is to support the organization's goal of legal compliance. The support of all employees is necessary to achieve compliance with various laws and regulations. An employee is protected from retaliation only if the employee brings the alleged unlawful activity, policy, or practice to the attention of _____ and provides _____ with a reasonable opportunity to investigate and correct the alleged unlawful activity. The protection described below is only available to employees who comply with this requirement.

_____ will not retaliate against an employee who, in good faith, has made a protest or raised a complaint against some practice of _____, or of another individual or entity with whom _____ had a business relationship, on the basis of a reasonable belief that the practice is in violation of law or of a clear mandate of public policy.

_____ will not retaliate against an employee who discloses or threatens to disclose to a supervisor or a public body any activity, policy, or practice of _____ that the employee reasonably believes is in violation of a law, or a rule, or regulation mandated pursuant to law or is in violation of a clear mandate or public policy concerning health, safety, welfare, or protection of the environment.

My signature below indicates my receipt and understanding of this Policy. I also verify that I have been provided with an opportunity to ask questions about the Policy.

_____ Date _____

Employee Signature

Retention of Documents

Notes: This document management policy is designed to conform with the charitable laws of states that give the Attorney General unusually long statutes of limitations (ten years) within which to bring an action for breach of charitable trust. In addition, organizations with medical patients, psychology clients, and other types of clients may have retention guidelines that are specified by federal or state contracting agencies, by licensing authorities, or by relevant professional societies.

Document Retention Policy

Document	Retention Period	Location/Storage
Accounts payable ledgers and schedules	10 years	
Accounts receivable ledgers and schedules	10 years	
Audit reports of accountants	Permanently	
Bank statements	10 years	
Capital stock and bond records: ledgers, transfer payments, stubs showing issues, record of interest coupon, options, etc.	Permanently	
Cash books	10 years	
Checks (canceled, with exception below)	10 years	
Checks (canceled, for important payments; i.e., taxes, purchase of property, special contracts, etc. [checks should be filed with the papers pertaining to the underlying transaction])	Permanently	
Contracts and leases (expired)	10 years	
Contracts and leases still in effect	Permanently	
Correspondence (general)	4 years	
Correspondence (legal and important matters)	Permanently	
Depreciation schedules	10 years	
Duplicate deposit slips	10 years	
Employee personnel records (after termination)	7 years	
Employment applications	3 years	
Expense analyses and expense distribution schedules (includes allowance and reimbursement of employees, officers, etc., for travel and other expenses)	10 years	
Financial statements (end of year)	Permanently	
General ledgers and end-of-year statements	Permanently	

Document Retention Policy (continued)

Document	Retention Period	Location/Storage
Insurance policies (expired)	Permanently	
Insurance records, current accident reports, claims, policies, etc.	Permanently	
Internal reports, miscellaneous	3 years	
Inventories of products, materials, supplies	10 years	
Invoices to customers	10 years	
Invoices from vendors	10 years	
Journals	10 years	
Minute books of Board of Directors, including Bylaws and Articles of Incorporation	Permanently	
Payroll records and summaries, including payments to pensioners	10 years	
Purchase orders	3 years	
Sales records	10 years	
Scrap and salvage records	10 years	
Subsidiary ledgers	10 years	
Tax returns and worksheets, revenue agents' reports, and other documents relating to determination of tax liability	Permanently	
Time sheets and cards	10 years	
Voucher register and schedules	10 years	

Warning: All permitted document destruction shall be halted if _____ is being investigated by a governmental law enforcement agency, and routine destruction shall not be resumed without the written approval of legal counsel or the Chief Executive Officer.

Thanks to attorney Tom Silk and to CompassPoint Nonprofit Services for the development and provision of these model documents.

Also Try

Conflicts of Interest, p. 131

Key Documents, p. 28

A Board Member's Guide to Nonprofit Insurance, p. 239

Table of Contents for a Board Binder

A new board member needs a guide to the job and the organization, and longtime board members need an easy way to keep reference materials. One convenient way is to provide each new board member with a Board Binder kept in a three-ring binder and to distribute updated sections to all members each year. Some boards make use of electronic binders, such as Yahoo! Groups.

Along with the Board Binder, consider holding an orientation session for new board members if several have joined the board at the same time. Such a session can bring new members up to speed on current issues and can establish personal relationships between new members and veterans. Based on suggestions from dozens of *Board Café* readers, a proposed table of contents for the Board Binder follows:

1. A welcoming letter signed by the board president and the executive director, including an offer to take the new board member on a tour of the facility, to introduce the new board member to staff, and to meet to further familiarize the new board member with the agency

2. An order form for a free subscription to the *Blue Avocado*, which includes the *Board Café* column

3. Corporate and historical documents
   - Description of programs and constituencies, or an "At-a-Glance" factsheet
   - Annual report
   - Bylaws and amendments
   - Incorporation documents (IRS Form 1023, IRS Determination Letter, State Determination Letter)
   - Most recent Form 990 filed with the IRS
   - Recent articles in the press about the organization
   - A history of the organization, if available
   - Brochures and other descriptive materials
   - Current strategic and annual plans, including mission and vision statements

4. Rosters
   - Roster of board members, including occupations, contact information, and the dates on which their terms and term limits expire
   - Committee list: names of committees and membership on each
   - Résumés of the executive director and other key staff

- Names, titles, telephone extensions, and e-mail addresses of staff with whom board members are most likely to interact
- Organizational chart

5. Calendar of meetings for coming year, with locations

6. Responsibilities
   - Statement of agreement or job description for board members
   - Conflict of interest policy
   - Conflict of interest statement (two copies presigned by the board president, with one copy to be signed by the new board member and returned)

7. Financial information
   - Current budget
   - Current financial statements
   - Audit report from previous year
   - Copy of the declaration page and proof of payment for directors and officers insurance, if purchased

- List of funders and individual contributors

8. Working tools
   - Membership application form (for membership organizations)
   - Contribution response envelope
   - Some letterhead stationery and envelopes (in a plastic sheet holder or in a pocket of the binder)
   - Bumper sticker, pins, T-shirt, or other materials

Some organizations use the Internet to store the materials that are more traditionally in a Board Binder. Board members have passwords that allow them to access the bylaws or budget, for example, as well as materials for the next meeting such as agenda or meeting location. It's a good way to save paper and keep track of materials, but it takes more Internet skills than staff and all board members may have.

Also Try

A Board Member Contract, p. 26

Conflict of Interest, p. 131

Orientation and Integration of New Board Members, p. 134

Key Documents, p. 28

Alligators in the Boardroom, p. 11

How to show staff you appreciate them

As just one way to let hardworking staff know the board appreciates their efforts, take it upon yourself to take the staff out after work one Friday afternoon. Meet the staff at a restaurant or pub near their office, buy some snacks and beverages, and be sure to toast them for their everyday commitment and caring and for serving the community sidebyside with the board. (If you live several states away from the office, ask the executive director to take everyone out and send you the bill.)

From *Best of the Board Café* (a column in the online magazine *Blue Avocado*), Copyright © 2003 and 2009, CompassPoint Nonprofit Services, published by Fieldstone Alliance, www.FieldstoneAlliance.org. Subscribe free to *Blue Avocado* at www.blueavocado.org.

The Board and the Staff

Not all nonprofit organizations need or have paid staff. But in those that do, one of the most important dynamics is the relationship between board and staff. When there is tension, animosity, and mistrust between board and staff, an organization can become paralyzed or even destroy itself. But when both sides are strong and have a respectful relationship, the partnership can drive remarkable achievements.

Following are two components to the board-staff partnership:

1. The lines of authority and processes that keep board and staff roles distinct, respectful, and mutually supportive.

2. The special relationship between the board and the executive director.

Guidelines exist for the partnership between board and staff in specific areas such as in fundraising and financial accountability. However, the following three general principles underlie the board-staff relationship:

1. The board's two-way responsibilities are to govern the organization as a group and to support the organization as individuals.

2. The staff's responsibilities are to deliver the programs of the agency, to engage volunteers and the community in that work, and to manage the business of the agency.

3. No matter how clear the relationship is, both sides need to be capable. Sometimes individuals on the board or staff need to leave and different individuals need to be recruited before the relationship can be productive.

These principles represent only a starting point for a complex relationship that will develop out of the skills and personalities of the people involved. Consider the complexity of a relationship between just two people; then consider the far greater complexity of a relationship between two groups totaling thirty people. Negotiating this complex relationship takes focused attention from both sides, yet many boards and staff successfully negotiate this partnership every day.

Should staff contact with the board be restricted?

Should board members have contact with staff independent of the executive director? For many executive directors, this issue raises blood pressure faster than almost any other.

While everyone would agree that nonprofit executive directors must work closely with board members, opinion is divided about whether and how other staff should interact with board members. Executive directors often feel that independent board-staff contact undermines their authority and creates the potential for staff to give misleading and undermining information to the board. Board members want to respect the authority of their executive director, but they also know that they can often serve best by meeting separately with staff on program or fundraising issues, and they value the independent viewpoint they can develop when not all their information is filtered through the executive director. And when staff-board contact is prohibited, the board is often the last to know about serious problems such as financial troubles, lawsuits, and and reputational issues.

Some boards regularly ask program managers to give presentations to the board on developments in the field and on how the organization is responding. For example, the board of an arts organization might ask for a presentation by the development director on the concept of audience development, or the board of a jobs program might ask the director to speak to the board about welfare-to-work initiatives and about how the agency is working with those programs. Some boards assign a board member to each program manager, although other boards feel that doing so can create "special interests" on the board.

Restricting contact between board and staff usually results in suspicion on the part of the board and resentment from the staff. The following guidelines can help clarify board-staff contact:

- There are no restrictions on contact, but the executive director must be informed about meetings. (Example: a voicemail message from the controller saying, "Hey, I just wanted you to know I'm meeting with the board treasurer next week to go over cash-flow projections. Let me know if you have any concerns or things you want me to bring up.")

- Many of the ways that board members support the organization—such as soliciting donations, advising finance staff—involve meetings between staff and board members. Both sides should be sure to keep these meetings within bounds; for example, in a meeting between a board member and the development director to discuss board member donations, it would be inappropriate for them to discuss whether the board or the executive director is acting responsibly in finance.

- Board members can request information and reports (such as another copy of the budget or last month's client statistics report), but they must stop short of directing staff work by asking for reports that are not already prepared. New reports can be requested of the executive director.

Also Try

The Board's Role in Human Resource Administration, p. 43

Annual Report from a Board Committee, p. 187

A Board-Staff Contract for Financial Accountability, p. 220

Chapter 3: The Board–Executive Director Relationship, p. 63

• Personnel grievances must go through the channels specified in the personnel policies. Board members should direct staff complaints to those channels.

Finally, many organizations feel that there should be a defined channel by which staff can raise concerns to the board about the way the executive director is running the organization. Other organizations feel that any authorized way that staff can complain directly to the board is a mistake that leads to factions on the board and the undermining of executive authority over staff.

There *does* need to be a way for serious concerns about mismanagement or malfeasance to come to the board from staff. One way to do this is to direct serious complaints and concerns only to the board president, not to any other board member. As representatives of the public, the board needs to know if staff have serious criticisms to raise, but it's only fair to the executive director and to the board president for these to be handled in a defined way. The board president can choose to raise the concerns to the executive director or to bring them to the board for investigation.

Bio book for board and staff

Board members and staff often don't know enough about one another to make use of each other's skills and backgrounds, or even enough to have an enjoyable conversation. To help board and staff become better acquainted, create a board and staff directory. Such a directory includes short biographies of each board and key staff member, including their professional and volunteer titles and affiliations, as well as length of service, community or professional involvements, and other interests and hobbies. Include a recent photo with each bio to help board members and staff identify each other. Everyone will learn things that will help open up communication, encourage strategic thinking, or spark a new friendship.

From a reader

One item we don't have in our board handbook is a board member bio sheet. The board originated as a group of people who were already acquainted, but over the years, especially in the past six months, we have brought on several new members, so now it's an excellent idea.

—T. D., Symmes, Ohio

Meaningful Acts of Board-Staff Appreciation

"We [board members] do this huge amount of work, and we're volunteers, but the staff never seems to have any response but criticism for us not doing more!"

"I'm the executive director, and the board just seems to focus on what we haven't accomplished, instead of giving me credit for all the things I have accomplished!"

How many times have we heard (or thought) something similar? Despite admonishments to "give positive feedback," it often seems that efforts between board and staff to communicate appreciation feel trivial at best and hypocritical or enraging at worst. What are some ways to express authentic appreciation that are meaningful to the recipient and send the right message about values? Following are seven quick ideas:

1. The day after a board meeting, whatever your role, phone the two people who helped make it a good meeting—the board president, the executive director, the treasurer, or anyone who helped move a discussion forward. A quick phone message can be remarkably encouraging.

2. To acknowledge a board member, write, print, and frame a proclamation unique to the board member; or, celebrate the board chair's running the board meetings especially well, a member negotiating the new lease, or the treasurer helping to choose new accounting software.

3. For the staff as a group, have an annual board discussion on the subject of attracting and retaining the right staff and how crucial it is to an organization's success. Start (for instance) with a report from the executive director and Finance Committee on current salaries and what comparable salaries might be. Bring a plan to the board, perhaps taking a two-pronged approach. Suggest some near-term raises for the positions that are the most underpaid and undertake a three-year process to increase salaries in an affordable way. Make sure this is communicated to staff so that the seriousness with which the board takes the matter and the reality of budget constraints is understood.

4. Ask the executive director to suggest individual staff the board can recognize. The board can then pass a board resolution detailing accomplishments and have a board member present it and read it aloud at a staff meeting.

5. As a new board president or at the start of the year, attend a staff meeting. As a volunteer leader, explain

how you and the board see your most important tasks over the coming year and invite questions and comments.

6. For a coalition or an association where board members work at other organizations and also spend considerable time in board service, consider grants to their organizations to show the value of the board service. Help pay, for example, for substitutes or overtime work performed.

7. When possible, have the organization pay for travel expenses for board members, to demonstrate that board membership is not based on ability to pay.

On the other hand, keep in mind some things not to do:

- Staff should not say, "Board members, thank you for helping us." Unintentionally this implies that the staff is the core of the organization and board members are ancillary participants who are the helpers to staff. Instead, say, "I'm proud to work for an organization with a board that _____ as effectively as ours does," or "I'm grateful to work at an organization where board members contribute so much."

- Board members shouldn't say, "Thank you, staff, for doing all the administrative things we hate doing" (heard, for example, in a mostly volunteer organization). Instead, say, "I really value the way your work makes it possible for us volunteers to do so much more."

Celebrate accomplishments and getting through tough periods. Present small gifts and certificates, for example, to all the members of the board-staff strategic planning committee, to the executive director search committee, or to the group that "successfully got us through the accreditation process."

These quick ideas are, of course, only part of a larger picture for how both appreciation and criticism are shared. Consider taking up just one or two of these ideas and see how people can bloom in their roles when given meaningful thanks and praise.

Also Try

The Board and
the Staff, p. 38

The Board's Role
in Human Resource
Administration, p. 43

What Are the Board's
Responsibilities for
Volunteers? p. 47

The Board's Role in Human Resource Administration

The human resources in a nonprofit organization are staff and volunteers. Frequently, the best practices for managing staff are also the best practices for managing volunteers, and it often works best for these two types of resources to be managed in tandem. This article, however, speaks primarily to paid human resources, or staff.

I once served on the board of a group whose executive director adamantly insisted that managing staff was her responsibility, not the board's. We stayed hands-off until we started to hear rumors of favoritism. After we prevailed in a battle with her about getting a listing of staff pay, we were shocked to discover that her assistant was paid $20,000 more than the program director and nearly as much as the development director. A lesson—actually several lessons—learned.

The role of the board of directors in personnel or human resource administration is frequently a sticky issue for nonprofits. Should the board approve all salaries or just the executive director's? If a staff member has a grievance, should it come to the board? How can the board's finance committee members, for example, be helpful in hiring accounting staff, but not usurp the hiring role of the executive staff? How can a board member appropriately give feedback to the executive director on the behavior of a staff person?

Boards tend to be at one extreme or another: Some insist on approving every raise for every staff member, while others never see a salary report. This article proposes specific guidelines for board oversight that don't take away from the chief executive's authority or responsibility. The board can approve various policies such as salary ranges, while not interfering with the staff's ability to manage. However the board structures its oversight, it needs a formal process to exercise that oversight. These guidelines provide such a process and follow the principle that the board as a whole governs the organization, while individual board members can be helpful advisors to staff.

Guidelines for the board's role in human resource administration

1. *Committee(s):* The board establishes a board-staff committee that works with matters related to paid staff. Only board members have votes on the committee. This committee makes recommendations to the board for approval (rather than deciding matters on its own). Following are the areas for this committee's scope of examination.

2. *Personnel policies and employee manual:* The executive director is responsible for ensuring that personnel policies and procedures are disseminated and implemented and that the policies are reviewed as appropriate by the board. Individual members of the human resources committee may be able to bring their human resources expertise to make suggestions. Every two years or so, the human resources committee (or a task force) reviews the policies with staff and, if appropriate, drafts changes or a complete revision.

3. *Salary scales:* The executive staff drafts a rate schedule (salary ranges for each position or category) of salaries, which is reviewed by the human resources committee or task force. This ensures that the board has considered the strategic matters related to salaries: whether the schedule is in line with the organization's values, whether there is appropriate internal equity or differences among positions and departments, whether specific positions are appropriately placed on the scale, whether compensation is in line with that at similar organizations, and whether the compensation supports (rather than hinders) the organization's ability to recruit qualified staff. The committee or task force sends the salary schedule to the whole board for approval. In this way, the executive staff is still responsible for salaries, but the board approves the range of salaries.

4. *Salary scale compliance:* Once a year, the human resources committee or task force reviews the specific salaries of the staff (by name and position) against the salary schedule to ensure that no individuals are being paid outside the range for that person's position. The committee's job is to protect against favoritism and ensure compliance with the salary schedule, *not* to review whether any specific individual deserves a particular salary.

5. *Benefits:* The benefits schedule—health insurance, long-term disability insurance, 401(k), and so forth—is reviewed annually as part of the budget process, with costs projected for the coming year. The human resources committee should review the benefits package at least every two years and suggest changes (additions or subtractions), and their financial implications, to the executive director, the board's finance committee, or both.

6. *Hiring:* In some cases, at the request of the executive director, one or two board members may help with hiring. A common example is the board treasurer helping to interview and select the chief financial officer (CFO) or accountant. It should be made clear to everyone involved that the final decision is made by the staff person to whom the new hire would report. In these situations individual board members are acting as advisors to staff.

7. *Diversity:* If an organization has established goals or principles regarding a staff that is diverse in race, ethnicity, gender, age, disability, or other characteristics such as client status, there will be an HR role to play in implementing the policies and goals. A board-staff diversity committee, or the board or board-staff HR committee, can assist with making sure that recruitment efforts reach out effectively (for example, through the ethnic press), be on the alert for indicators of weak management of a diverse workforce (such as a string of resignations from Latina nurses), and assist with monitoring progress toward goals.

8. *Layoffs:* A management decision to lay off staff usually reflects a financial situation that should already have been shared with the board. In this context, the steps that management is taking to deal with that financial situation— whether layoffs, paycuts, new income strategies, or others—should be discussed with the board and the board should bless or put a hold on management actions. Although in most staffed organizations the decision of whom to lay off and when and how are management decisions, it's critical for the board and management to be in sync about how the organization is responding to financial problems.

9. *Grievances:* Grievances on the part of employees must first go through the written procedures outlined in the employee policies manual. If an individual has exhausted the grievance process and that process has been documented, individual employees may be permitted (if it is so written in the policies) to raise a grievance to either the board chair or the board's human resources committee, which then acts as the final arbiter. This may be especially appropriate where the complaining employee reports to the executive director and has an unresolved complaint about the executive director.

10. *Serious charges about the organization's management:* Sometimes a staff member has a serious charge against management, such as the illegal or improper use of funds, sexual harassment, discriminatory behavior, or improper accounting methods that cannot be taken up in the grievance process. To provide an outlet for such matters (other than a complaint to the state attorney general), some organizations allow staff members to raise such concerns with the board chair. When other board members hear such complaints, they have a responsibility to direct the staff person to the board chair. By making the board chair the sole recipient of such charges, the board can prevent a disgruntled staff member from trying to develop allies on the board against the executive staff, and can provide a way to bring an organizational matter to the attention of the board as a whole.

Delegating personnel work

The board can choose how to delegate personnel-related work. The most common choices are

- A standing (permanent) human resources committee,
- A human resources task force (that is, a temporary committee),
- A board-staff standing committee, or
- A board-staff task force.

Committee members might include the staff human resources director (if there is one), executive director, or nonboard volunteers such as a human resources attorney. (Note that if nonboard individuals are members of the committee, they should be nonvoting advisory members of the committee or the committee's recommendations should come back to the board for approval.) In some cases, the human resources committee is also responsible for developing plans and strategies for appropriate recruitment and utilization of volunteers, while in other organizations the human resources committee looks only at paid personnel.

Each organization will want to choose its own guidelines on these sensitive and important issues. Striking the right balance between board and executive director authority may initially be challenging, but it's far from impossible. In the end, sorting this out will strengthen your organization while making life easier for board members and staff.

Also Try

The Board and the Staff, p. 38

Should the Board Hold Executive Sessions? p. 205

Sarbanes-Oxley and Nonprofits (includes Whistleblower Policy), p. 31

Try recruiting volunteers over the web

Where is there a free online site to post "help wanted" ads for volunteers? Try out VolunteerMatch, at http://www.volunteermatch.org/. People seeking volunteer jobs—whether one day once, many days over time, or as a board member—will spot your ad and send an e-mail to you. Or if you're looking for another place to volunteer, you can scan the ads on the web site, too!

What Are the Board's Responsibilities for Volunteers?

by Susan J. Ellis

Does your organization involve volunteers in service delivery? (It already involves at least some volunteers—on the board!) If so, when did the board last focus attention on this subject?

Don't allow volunteer involvement to be the invisible personnel issue. If something is neglected, it may thrive by accident. But proactive support of volunteer involvement dramatically increases its potential achievement level. So what can a board of directors do?

1. Regularly devote time to the subject of volunteers at board meetings. This sends a strong message to everyone that volunteers are important. Develop thoughtful policies about and goals for volunteer participation. Budget adequately to support the work volunteers do. Become as involved in "raising people" as in raising money.

2. Develop an organizational vision for volunteer involvement and set standards in line with that vision. If you think of frontline volunteers as friendly but low-skilled helpers, that's exactly whom you'll attract. On the other hand, if you make it clear that community participation is an important element of your organization's work, that volunteers are a part of your resource mix, and that you expect to involve the best, highest-skilled people as volunteers—then you'll get that type of volunteer.

3. Ask for and analyze data about volunteer involvement. Make sure you get reports on the types and scope of volunteer activities. Recognize that this is necessary to have a complete picture of the organization and of the resources available to it. Ask questions about what volunteers do and make it clear that the board expects the best!

4. Participate in volunteer recruitment. The more people spreading the word about volunteer opportunities, the better. Just as board members should be alert to fundraising potential, they should be on the lookout for ways to recruit volunteers. For example, each board member can

   a) Recommend or refer prospective volunteers, with the understanding that they must go through the regular application process just like any other prospective volunteer.

b) Distribute recruitment materials at your workplace or during visits to community sites.

c) Identify company newsletters, special events or meetings, display booths, e-mail list managers (such as Listserv), or other ways to communicate with your colleagues. Be a visible advocate—explain why you chose to volunteer on the board of this particular organization.

5. Take part in volunteer recognition events. Attendance by the board shows other volunteers that they are valued at the top. Recognition events provide a great opportunity to mingle and talk with supporters of your organization, whose opinions may prove illuminating. Once at the event, contribute to its success with active participation, not observation from a segregated table. And, remember, you have also earned the thank-yous given to the organization's volunteers!

6. Make volunteers as visible as possible. Make sure your annual report includes volunteer accomplishments. Incorporate information about volunteer opportunities into your organization's web site for both recruitment of new volunteers and recognition of current ones. Make sure volunteers are included in any public forum or media outreach and as agency representatives when appropriate.

7. Create a board committee on volunteerism. Some boards form a volunteer program advisory committee to offer ongoing advice, expertise, community contacts, and other resources to the volunteer program staff. In the absence of paid coordinating staff, you may want a board volunteer development committee to plan the outreach strategies necessary to recruit the best volunteers. If yours is a membership association, volunteer-related issues may need to be considered by several committees, including the nominating committee and the membership development committee. Educate yourself about the growing volunteer management field.

Too many organizations are thought*less* when it comes to volunteers. Help your board to become thought*ful* on the subject. It will make a real difference.

Susan J. Ellis is the president of Energize, Inc., a Philadelphia-based consulting firm focusing on volunteerism, and a copublisher of the excellent newsletter e-Volunteerism.com. This article appeared in the June, 1999, issue of the Board Café *and was adapted with permission from* From the Top Down: The Executive Role in Volunteer Program Success *by Susan J. Ellis (Energize, 1996). You can order the book and reach Susan at www.energizeinc.com.*

Also Try

All-Volunteer Organizations, p. 50

Different ways to talk about volunteers

"Men don't volunteer as much as women do," or so says conventional wisdom. But Susan Ellis of Energize, Inc., counters: "Men volunteer a lot; they're just not called volunteers. They're called coaches and firemen!"

With new waves of stimulus-package volunteers and retirement-age volunteers coming down the road, it's even more urgent that we change the way we talk—and think—about volunteers.

Old language (often said in apologetic tone): "We have only a few staff, so we have to rely on volunteers." *New language:* "Because we have so many volunteers, we don't need more than a few staff."

Old: "Our volunteers help us [staff] so much!" gushes a nonprofit staff person. *New:* "Volunteers help the *patients* so much!"

Old: "We have a couple of volunteers who help with the newsletter," said the director of a nonprofit legal services organization, adding, "Oh yeah! And some pro bono attorneys." *New:* "Our organization is lucky to have pro bono attorneys, pro bono writers, and pro bono graphics and layout staff."

Old: "We have 25 staff and 175 volunteers," said a museum director starting a speech. *New:* "We have 200 staff, of whom 175 are volunteers and 25 are paid."

To quote Susan Ellis again: "Paul Revere made his living as a silversmith. But he's remembered for what he did as a volunteer."

If you're a volunteer (messenger, revolutionary, American hero like Paul), print out this article and give it to the volunteers and staff you work with. Let's change not only the world, but the way we talk about it.

All-Volunteer Organizations*

Volunteerism is an enormous economic force, yet it is never mentioned in business school or in economics departments.

—*Walter Hoadley, former chief economist for the Bank of America*

All-volunteer organizations (AVOs) are a major economic force, albeit one that is seldom given credit for its work. Through all-volunteer organizations, people clean up beaches, care for the dying, coach basketball teams, advocate for gun control, rescue abused animals, raise their voices in song, publish literary journals, raise scholarship funds, preserve local history, serve as volunteer fire departments, organize protests, exchange heirloom seeds, host visitors from foreign countries, help people conquer alcoholism, change public perception about the disabled, help adoptees and birth parents find each other, and, in thousands of ways, make our communities, however defined, work better.

That these and countless other services are provided by volunteers and not by paid staff (of a nonprofit, business, or government agency) would come as a surprise to many. In fact, individuals *in* all-volunteer organizations often don't even think of themselves as the important economic and social force that they and their organizations represent. An all-volunteer organization is a nonprofit organization where volunteers manage the organization and do most or all of the work. Some all-volunteer organizations *do* pay individuals: soccer leagues pay referees for Saturday games, historical preservation societies pay gardeners, and PTAs often pay after-school art teachers. The difference is that while all-volunteer organizations sometimes pay people to work, they don't pay people to *manage*. The job of management is done by the volunteer leaders, usually the board.

In all-volunteer organizations, the term *board* means the group of people that runs the organization. Some groups elect officers, while in others whoever wants to can join the "core group," or the "steering committee." Because many all-volunteer organizations haven't taken the legal steps to form a nonprofit corporation, there may not be a legal board of directors. Nonetheless, the term *board* is a convenient way of identifying this leadership group.

In a nonprofit with paid staff, an important function of the board is its governance function: to hold staff accountable to the community purpose. In its governance role, the board ensures that the organization is complying with tax and legal requirements, and is using funds efficiently toward the organization's priorities. In their supporting role, board members often assist staff in the work of the organization, whether that's helping to raise money, assisting with accounting, or volunteering in a women's shelter, a thrift shop, or a community center.

In an all-volunteer organization, there are no paid managers. As a result, it's often hard to distinguish between what the board does and what the organization does. For example, the same person—let's call her Cristina—may wear two "hats" when volunteering for the local garlic festival or the Martin Luther King Jr. march. When she's wearing her board member hat, Cristina and the other board members must obtain local permits and decide how much to spend on publicity. When she's wearing her volunteer staff hat, Cristina and the other volunteers may direct cars to parking areas and design the newspaper ad. It's confusing because it's the same Cristina, and because, whichever hat she's wearing, she's still a volunteer.

One of the biggest questions in AVOs is whether to strive to become a staff-managed organization, where ultimately most of the work is done by paid staff. For some all-volunteer organizations, there is a clear goal to "grow up" to be a large, staffed organization. (Sierra Club, Red Cross, NAACP, American Diabetes Association, Mothers Against Drunk Driving, and countless other powerful organizations started as all-volunteer organizations—and many do most of their work through all-volunteer local chapters.) The board of such an all-volunteer organization needs to develop a plan that phases in paid staff and a change in roles for the board. Many AVOs that aspire to become staffed organizations stumble when they first hire someone to manage the organization. After years of acting in both management and governance roles, it's often difficult for boards to find a way both to be supportive of management staff and to provide adequate oversight or governance. Some AVOs hire an interim director or a program coordinator before hiring a director as a way for the organization and the board to make the change in stages.

The board of such an all-volunteer organization needs to develop a plan that phases in paid staff and a change in roles for the board.

For other organizations, staying all-volunteer is an intrinsic part of their mission and heart. In church groups, volunteer rescue squads, hospital auxiliaries, Kiwanis, or the PTA, the all-volunteer character of the organization is a lot of what makes working in it satisfying and rewarding. All-volunteer organizations need not feel that they "should" aspire to being a staffed organization. Rather than thinking, "We're all just volunteers," AVOs should be proud to say, "Being all-volunteer is just right for us: we don't really need or want staff."

Two responsibilities in particular are uniquely critical in all-volunteer organizations. One is the job of recruiting new leaders and turning over responsibilities to them. In large corporations developing a "succession plan" is an important job of the executive director. In an all-volunteer organization, the departure of key leaders may be an even more critical crossroads for the organization.

For some organizations that have trouble retaining volunteers, there may be something in the way the board works (or the way some individuals behave) that discourages people from thinking they can become part of the leadership. Sometimes longtime leaders and volunteers view the organization as "their baby" and are sharply critical and undermining of anyone whose approach is different. They may constantly find fault with new volunteers or refuse to allow new people to have real responsibility. If the board members truly believe in the organization's work, they will want to ensure that they encourage new volunteer leaders (even if the new leaders seem to be doing it all wrong) and let the organization grow into its own future. (This may mean allowing current activities to die out and new activities to take their place.)

Some people who are wonderful "workers" are reluctant to see themselves as prospective board members. They may feel that board members are experts or must be specially trained. In fact, the boards of all-volunteer organizations are among the best places in the world to find training and become an expert in managing people and organizations. It helps if current board members seek out valued volunteers and encourage them to stretch their skills by joining the board. This is just one way that each person's self-interest and the organization's interests can grow together.

When the board presidency or other leadership position changes hands, many AVOs find that the organization's papers and obligations get lost in the move. At the very least, one sturdy box should be "the organizational safe." It can contain the official documents and be easily passed along from one president to the next. Some organizations have one box for each position of responsibility; these are ceremonially presented at a meeting or installation dinner to the incoming generation of leaders.

The second crucial job for the board is also intangible: the role the board plays in establishing a tone for the organization. Through example, leaders build a spirit where others contribute gladly, not reluctantly or guiltily. By paying scrupulous attention to financial matters, leaders establish an atmosphere of accountability and integrity. By ensuring that government and other paperwork is filed properly, the board demonstrates a commitment to doing things right.

Some of today's all-volunteer organizations will be tomorrow's multimillion-dollar, influential, and powerful organizations that change laws, change public opinion, and shape society. Others will continue to be the invisible but strong glue that keeps people connected to one another—connections that form the framework for strong communities. In a thousand ways, board members in all-volunteer organizations are the grassroots leaders and "keepers of the spirit" upon which so much of community cohesiveness and social change depend.

---

* Excerpted from *All Hands on Board: The Board of Directors in an All-Volunteer Organization (AVO)* by Jan Masaoka; published in 1999 by the National Center for Nonprofit Boards, and available for free download at http://www.blueavocado.org.

How to Take a Public Policy Stand

When the Colorado Association for Recycling was approached to endorse the No Child Left Inside legislation, they didn't know what they would decide, but they did know how to decide (see what they decided at end of this article). They already had a procedure in place for deciding which public policy stands to take. But many nonprofits aren't as prepared.

Would it support your cause or help your constituencies if your organization took an official stand on a public policy issue? Is it legal to do so? And how would you go about it? Your board may be thinking of taking a stand on an international issue, on Food and Drug Administration regulations, on public school policies for students with disabilities, on a proposed hospital closure, on pending legislation, or on whether dogs should be allowed in a local park.

The worst time to decide on how to take a policy position is when an issue suddenly erupts. Having a policy or procedure in place *before* a controversy develops eliminates the need for the board to make two difficult decisions at the same time: *how* to take a stand, and *whether* to take a particular stand.

We'll look first at a sample procedure for how organizations take stands and then offer a questionnaire that one organization uses when asked to sign onto letters. Finally, we'll provide some links to additional information.

First, is it legal for a nonprofit to take a stand on a policy matter? Answer: Yes! What is prohibited for nonprofit, 501(c)(3) organizations is supporting or opposing candidates for election. But it is completely legal for a nonprofit to take a stand on U.S. foreign policy, on local zoning codes, on Social Security, on air quality standards, on tax issues, and on proposed regulation of nonprofits. In fact, some of our country's most important social gains have been won through nonprofit policy work, such as Mothers Against Drunk Driving on blood alcohol limits, the American Civil Liberties Union on discriminatory hiring practices, and Communities for a Better Environment on air quality standards. (A caveat: In an election season, if the policy issue is strongly identified with a particular candidate, it might appear that you are actually advocating for the candidate.)

Don't forget, too, that holding a discussion on a policy stand is one of the best ways for the board to learn about an issue and what the organization already does (or doesn't do) on the matter.

Sample Policy on Taking Public Policy Stands

Introductory statement: We believe that taking stands on appropriate policy matters, and promoting those positions, are important ways in which we serve our constituents and our cause. We must not only serve our communities, but we must also advocate for our communities. We will use our voice strategically and thoughtfully. The following outlines the principles by which we will consider taking policy stands and the process we will follow when making such a decision.

1. Only the board of directors, by a majority vote, can decide on an official policy stand by the XYZ Organization.

2. Suggestions for taking a policy stand can come from anyone. These suggestions should be sent in writing to the chair of the board of directors and to the executive director.

3. The chair and the executive director can bring the suggestion to the board meeting for discussion, or can refer the issue to a public policy committee or task force.

4. The criteria used by the board and committee or task force are based on factors listed below. We will consider taking an organizational stand if all factors are true.

   • The issue directly or indirectly affects our constituents or our organization.

   • The issue draws on our expertise and knowledge as an organization. (For example, if we are an environmental health organization, does this matter draw on what we know about how environment affects health?)

   • Along with the policy stand, we develop a realistic plan for how to communicate our stand to the appropriate people and what we will do to implement the stand. (For example, in some cases an organization will want to take a leadership role on an issue and assess its ability to play that role. In other cases a board will decide that taking a stand will be heartening to clients and to staff, but undertaking a large campaign is not realistic for the organization.)

5. Letters to officials, letters to editors, and open letters to the public on this stand will be signed by the chair of the board of directors and the executive director.

6. Public policy stands will be posted on our web site.

7. Public policy stands expire after one year from adoption unless the board acts to extend the period. (This keeps an organization from having positions on stale issues or ones where a new stand might be required.)

8. If we foresee that public policy stands will use significant time or financial resources, or if this is an election season, we will consult with an attorney to be sure that we are in compliance with regulations.

The fine print: Nonprofits are not prohibited from lobbying, but they *are* prohibited from using "substantial" amounts of resources on lobbying, including calling on the public to take a stand. If you believe that your organization is using significant staff time, volunteer time, or money in lobbying, you can apply—it's not difficult—for a 501(h) election, which provides a clear and mathematical test for what level of activity exceeds the proscribed limits. For more information, see the Alliance for Justice's set of factsheets available at http://afj.org/.

If you are frequently asked to sign onto letters and petitions

Some organizations receive many requests to sign onto letters and petitions—sometimes as often as weekly. What's the best way to manage so many requests? One organization, the Northwest Women's Law Center, sends people with such requests a questionnaire. It's a smart way to weed out the blast e-mails and to tee up an issue for the board. Include a brief statement about your organization, when and how you take policy stands, and ask for an explanation of the endorsement being requested.

Example Request for Endorsement

The Northwest Women's Law Center, as an advocacy organization dedicated to advancing women's legal rights, engages in litigation, legislative and administrative advocacy, and education about issues that concern women and their families. The Law Center is part of a community of organizations working for social justice and progressive change in Seattle, Washington State, the Pacific Northwest, and the nation. The Law Center is frequently asked to endorse or support initiatives and campaigns on a variety of issues.

The Northwest Women's Law Center endorses only initiatives, actions, or campaigns that relate to its mission of advancing legal rights for women. To facilitate our decision-making about endorsements, the Board of Directors asks that you answer the following questions:

1) Why are you seeking the endorsement of the Northwest Women's Law Center? What will our endorsement add to your effort?

2) What will be the effect of the proposed action, campaign, or initiative on women? Please be specific, including describing the population(s) of women who will be affected.

3) What resources (money, staff time, volunteer time), if any, are you requesting that the Northwest Women's Law Center provide to your effort?

4) Please give us information about your organization: How long has it existed? Is it a 501(c)(3) organization? Who are your members? What other organizations have endorsed this effort?

NOTE: As a nonprofit, 501(c)(3) organization, the Law Center is prohibited from endorsing any candidate in any election. Please return this form to _____.

And as for the Colorado Association for Recycling? Executive Director Marjorie Griek reports: "Our organization decided to support the No Child Left Inside coalition. We were asked to support a national bill that would provide grants to ensure that teachers have the necessary knowledge and skills to teach environmental education, and provide grants to enhance state and national capacity for environmental education. States that create environmental literacy plans, detailing how all graduates will be environmentally literate, will be eligible for this funding.

"Our board thought it important to support this as part of the education covered would be about recycling and waste diversion issues. We signed on to the group, and sent information to our members about it, and will send letters of support as needed."

Special thanks for assistance in this article go to attorney Michael Schley of Santa Barbara, to Lisa Stone of the Northwest Women's Law Center, and to Marjorie Griek of the Colorado Association for Recycling.

A Board Member's Guide to Nonprofits and Copyrights

There are two things to worry about regarding copyrights: protecting original material that your organization has created and making sure that your organization isn't improperly using material that someone else owns.

Blue Avocado asked copyright attorney Kate Spelman to help us with these issues, and she generously gave all of us her expertise and time.

Q: Should we be copyrighting things we publish in print, on our web site, in our music CD, and elsewhere? Is it enough to put © on things?

Kate: It's a good idea to put the © symbol (a "c" in a circle) on original materials, along with the year and the copyright owner. But a copyright can't be enforced unless the work has been registered. See www.copyright.gov for the official site of the U.S. Copyright Office.

Q: Is it hard to register a work?

A: Not really. Works can be registered at the United States Copyright Office for $45 each, and the benefits include having facts asserted in the application taken as true by a court, and the ability to ask for attorneys fees and statutory damages. The filing of a copyright application is intended to be done by citizens, not lawyers. It consists of answering nine questions—three of which are your address!

Q: What's the most common copyright question that arises for nonprofits?

A: A frequent problem is who owns a work. Is it the nonprofit? The staff person who wrote it on the job? A volunteer? This usually doesn't become an issue until there is financial success. But photographers, writers, authors, musicians, artists, and others may create work where the question will arise. Sometimes, for example, a volunteer will write something for an organization that turns into a book that the author wants to sell.

Q: What should our organization be doing about this?

A: It's best to establish who will own the copyright at the very beginning—of the volunteer's work or of the employee's project.

Q: What steps should the board take to make sure that our organization respects the copyrights of others?

A: Make sure the staff knows that it's important to the board both to respect the rights of others and to protect the organization's work. If your organization publishes frequently, adopt a policy that requires an agreement on copyright to be signed by employees, contractors, and volunteers in advance of work done and that requires a report to the board before any agreement is signed that gives those rights to others. When you look at work produced by your organization—whether written, musical, photographed, drawn, programmed, or translated—check to see that the copyright mark is present, and if the work is a major one, ask if it has been registered. When you see something reprinted in your organization's newsletter, ask to be sure that permission was appropriately granted.

Q: Is there a good place on the Internet where I can download sample copyright forms and other documents?

A: Unfortunately, no. But have a look at http://copyright.gov/ for a good place to start.

Q: How would you sum this all up?

A: A proactive version of the "Golden Rule" applies to copyright: get permission and be clear in advance of who owns what; and give credit generously, as you would have others do unto you.

Kate Spelman is an attorney at Cobalt LLP in Berkeley, California, with a national and international practice in copyright law. She has worked for Fortune 500 companies as well as many nonprofits. She is a board member of the American Intellectual Property Law Education Foundation and loves used bookstores and fly-fishing. She can be reached at kate@cobaltlaw.com.

Also Try

A Board-Staff Contract for Financial Accountability, p. 220

Allow limited copying and distribution: the Creative Commons approach

A common dilemma for nonprofits—especially those that publish online—is the desire to have materials used and disseminated as widely as possible combined with the need to protect original content. Creative Commons is an internationally recognized nonprofit that has developed an approach and accompanying free tools for granting various "some rights reserved" licenses. For example, a work can be licensed to users provided that it is used for noncommercial purposes, is attributed to the author, and is not modified. Creative Commons licenses have been welcomed by much of the intellectual property legal community. More information and licenses to download are at http://creativecommons.org/.

What Is an Advisory Board and Should We Have One?

Many Board Café *readers have written to say their organizations are considering creating advisory boards or advisory committees of one kind or another. At the same time, others write to ask how to abolish troublesome or obsolete advisory committees. Here are some guidelines for advisory committees, as well as a sample letter inviting an individual to join such a board.*

The board of directors of a nonprofit organization is its legal, governing body. In contrast, an advisory board does not have any formal legal responsibilities. Rather, an advisory board is convened by the organization to give advice and support.

There are three common reasons why organizations choose to convene advisory boards, illustrated in the following examples:

• The board of directors of Eucalyptus AIDS Services* is composed of wealthy, well-connected members who see their role as centering on fundraising. But most of the board members are not well connected to the low-income client population, nor are they experts in the AIDS field. As a result, Eucalyptus AIDS Services convened an advisory board composed of low-income clients, social workers, and medical personnel. The advisory board meets four times a year to give input, to react to ideas from staff, and to make suggestions. Several staff and board members attend each meeting. For example, the last advisory board meeting focused on developing a policy around case management for dual-diagnosed clients.

• The Banyan Asian Artists Co-op doesn't have its own 501(c)(3) status but works under the fiscal sponsorship of another organization. As a result of not having incorporated separately, Banyan cannot legally have a board of directors. Its advisory committee acts in many of the same roles that a board of directors does but doesn't have the same legal responsibilities. If Banyan decides to incorporate separately, the advisory committee members will form its board of directors.

• Along with recreational, senior, and housing loan programs, one of the programs of the Manzanita Community Center is a program called "Living with Breast Cancer." Manzanita's board of directors must be concerned with all the center's programs, and the staff of

From *Best of the Board Café* (a column in the online magazine *Blue Avocado*), Copyright © 2003 and 2009, CompassPoint Nonprofit Services, published by Fieldstone Alliance, www.FieldstoneAlliance.org. Subscribe free to *Blue Avocado* at www.blueavocado.org.

Living with Breast Cancer wants a group from the community that can focus more exclusively on their activities. As a result, they convened an advisory committee that meets monthly to advise on the program—but not the finances or personnel—of the Living with Breast Cancer program.

Some guidelines for having advisory boards

1. Develop a written description of the responsibilities, activities, and limits on authority of the advisory board. An advisory board needs its own informal job description that spells out its activities, the extent and limit of its authority, how members are appointed, length of terms, term limits, and frequency of meetings.

2. Establish a formal relationship between the advisory board and the governing board. For example, at the Manzanita Community Center above, a board member can be the liaison to the Living with Breast Cancer Advisory Committee, attending meetings and communicating between the two groups.

3. Distinguish between the role of the governing board of directors and the advisory board. For example, a board of directors hires the executive direc-

tor of the organization; an advisory board may draw up a suggested list of qualifications for the person or people hiring the executive director. A board of directors can direct staff to take certain actions; an advisory board can suggest actions to staff and can be angry if its suggestions aren't taken, but an advisory board can't compel staff to act.

4. Don't establish an advisory board if you cannot commit the time to preparing for effective advisory board meetings and to making the experience meaningful and rewarding for members. Some organizations have erred by creating advisory boards where members felt ignored, or as if they were being asked for donations in the disguise of being asked to advise.

5. Consider asking a community leader to chair the advisory board and act as a spokesperson for the agency in the community.

---

* This is a fictitious name for an organization and, like other such fictitious groups in this book, is named after a tree.

Also Try

What Are the Board's Responsibilities for Volunteers? p. 47

Sample Invitation to Join an Advisory Committee

Use this letter as a model to ask individuals to join an advisory committee.

Dear _____,

We would like to invite you to join the Advisory Council of Parents Act for Children's Cancer Treatment (PACCT). This council consists of thoughtful community leaders who meet three times per year to advise the PACCT board of directors. We have tremendous admiration for the work you have done with children in the SW neighborhood of our city, and we would be very grateful to have your thinking as we go forward.

The responsibilities of Advisory Council members are to:

• Attend at least two meetings per year, each held on a weekday from 8:00 a.m. to 9:45 a.m.
• Contribute your expertise and thinking to the current and future work of PACCT
• Be available for four to five telephone calls each year from staff seeking advice
• Allow PACCT to publish your name as a member of the Advisory Council

In return, PACCT promises you:

• A delicious breakfast three times a year and meetings that start and end on time
• A complimentary PACCT membership during your term on the Advisory Council
• An appreciation of your time and a commitment not to abuse your time or your generosity

Advisory Council terms are for two years. Enclosed is a roster of current Advisory Council members and a schedule of meetings for the coming year.

One of us will be calling you within the next few days to answer your questions and to give you a personal invitation to join the council. Thank you, and we look forward to talking with you.

Tom Lamothe, Chair, PACCT Board of Directors
Jennifer Judy, Executive Director

The Board–Executive Director Relationship

Imagine a figure skating competition for pairs. The best couple is the one where each of the skaters is wonderfully skilled and graceful, and together they create breathtaking beauty as they skate. The opposite case is the pair where neither of the partners is very skilled. And perhaps the most painful to watch is the couple where one partner is a strong, talented skater, while the other just can't keep up.

The board–executive director partnership can be compared to these skating pairs. The best partnerships are ones that combine a strong board with a strong executive director. With that combination, organizations can have major, lasting impact on their communities. And when problems arise in the partnership, strong partners can find ways to work them out.

On the other hand, if one side is weak, the other side *cannot* fully compensate. An executive director, no matter how talented, can never make the case in the community the way that board members can. Nor can a strong, committed board create a positive office climate or maintain control of the expense budget.

Just as important, emphasizing greater *clarity on roles* will not solve the problem by itself. It may be necessary for the executive director to leave, or for the board's composition to change, in order for matters to improve significantly.

The CompassPoint Board Model gives some guidance on how to handle this crucial relationship. First, in its governance role, the board, acting as a body, is responsible for hiring, supervising, supporting, and maybe firing the executive director. In this regard, the board is the executive director's "boss."

However, unlike individual bosses, the board is a *group*. The board president is *not* the executive director's supervisor. Instead, the board chair plays a more complex role: The board chair must be a *leader*. Because the board performs its governing and oversight work as a group, the board chair must guide and lead the group—a much more difficult matter than simply making decisions. In doing so, the most important partner is the person who is responsible for the execution of plans: the executive director.

Second, as board members do their work to support the organization, the board chair must be a model of an individual supporter: taking the organization's cause to the community, providing encouragement and support to staff, and participating in fund-raising and public events.

The executive director is so central to an organization's near-term success that boards of directors sometimes even have trouble discussing the relationship. To help boards better understand the relationship, this chapter contains several articles addressing the most common matters that arise in this board–executive director partnership.

Succession Planning for Nonprofits of All Sizes

by Tim Wolfred and Jan Masaoka

The term *succession planning* brings to mind a large corporation with a long-time CEO first choosing, then grooming, a successor. But this practice is sharply declining even in large corporations and is even less relevant to most community-based organizations. At the same time, more and more nonprofits are realizing that executive director transition is a crucial moment in an organization's life: a moment of great vulnerability as well as great opportunity for transformative change. Succession should be a topic broached even when no one is anticipating a change in leaders. And of course, illness and other events can lead to sudden and unanticipated departures.

Planning for executive director transition is called succession planning—thinking in advance about how to set the stage for a strong transition. The *Board Café's* sponsor, CompassPoint Nonprofit Services, has developed a comprehensive set of services for nonprofits anticipating or going through such a transition; in fact, CompassPoint's fastest growing consulting area is in Executive Transition and succession planning.

Succession should be a topic broached now . . . whether or not you are anticipating a change in executives. Here are some questions and issues to be addressed now, and some that draw attention to longer-term planning. Taking steps now will increase your readiness for this inevitable occurrence and increase the likelihood of a positive transition.

- If the executive is suddenly unable to serve, is it clear to everyone who will be the acting executive until the board can meet and decide? Who will speak to the press? Consider creating an emergency or contingency succession plan just in case.

- Does the board of directors have the right mix of members for hiring the new executive? Sometimes a board that is best at supporting a strong executive is different from one that is well equipped to hire a new executive. For example, a board of all corporation vice presidents may raise a lot of money but may not understand the qualities that make for a successful nonprofit executive or know how to look for and screen candidates. One criterion for board recruitment should be: "Will this person be a good addition to a hiring process?" Executive directors should ask themselves: "Do I want this person on the board that hires my replacement?"

• Is the executive director's job doable—that is, could the job be done by a regular human being? Too often a successful executive director has, over time, taken on so many responsibilities that it would be nearly impossible to find another such superhero. In a similar light: "Are management team members able to do their jobs?" Sometimes a broadly skilled executive will "carry" one or more management team members who can't handle their responsibilities on their own. If an organization can, for instance, transfer some finance responsibilities from the executive director to the newly created position of chief financial officer, the executive director's job will become more doable and as a result, the board can hire from the pool of talented professionals rather than from the very small pool of superheroes.

Too often a successful executive director has, over time, taken on so many responsibilities that it would be nearly impossible to find another such superhero.

• Is the salary of the current executive director much lower than what you should pay a new executive? Sometimes a successful, longtime executive is being paid much too little—which ends up pushing other salaries down and makes it unlikely that qualified candidates would accept such a salary. On the other hand, sometimes an executive is making much more than is appropriate. Succession planning should include a longer-term effort to bring all staff salaries—including the executive's—in line with the market.

• Can you get through a fundraising or income dip? The chief money raiser or rainmaker in most nonprofits is the executive director. It will take time for his or her successor to develop the relationships with donors and paying clients that are essential to the incumbent's revenue-producing success. Succession planning should include raising funds for the transition: one twenty-five-year executive we know is in the midst of a "legacy campaign" to give donors a chance to honor his community achievements with gifts to an agency endowment fund. Fundraising and business relationships can also be institutionalized by bringing board members and other staff into relationships now held only by the executive director.

• Are there any obvious candidates for the job? In some cases an executive director may have been grooming someone internally for the job. In other cases it may be assumed that the associate director or program director wants and will get the job. There may be a board member who feels that he or she would be the best choice. The decision to hire is the board's and any such unspoken assumptions should be brought to the board. If, for example, it does seem appropriate to groom a particular individual, the board should be part of that process. At the same time, it would also be a shame if a valued staff or board member were to depart on the mistaken assumption that the job has been promised to someone else.

- When was the last time that succession was on the board meeting agenda?

The executive director may worry that bringing up succession planning is a signal that she is planning to leave. At the same time, board members may worry that bringing up the topic will incorrectly send a message to the executive that they *want* her to leave. One easy way to broach the topic without either of these fears coming to pass is to begin the discussion with a distribution of this article.

Also Try

Hiring the Executive Director, p 68

Job Description for an Executive Director, p. 70

Searching for a New Executive Director, p. 73

How Much to Pay the Executive Director? p. 76

Firing the Executive Director, p. 95

Hiring the Executive Director

How long do executive directors stay? A national study* by Compass-Point Nonprofit Services indicated that the average tenure is four to six years. Perhaps more critically, the study also showed that 65 percent of executive directors are holding this top job for the first time. Together, these findings suggest that most nonprofit board members are likely to participate in hiring an executive director during their tenures on the board.

Whether an executive director is leaving after many years of glorious achievement or after having been fired by an angry or disappointed board, his or her departure always represents a stressful time for board members. As with the boards of for-profit corporations, the selection of a new executive director is likely to be the most important decision a nonprofit board will make in many years.

But this stressful period of executive transition is also an exceptionally powerful moment for change in an organization's life: It is an opportunity for the kind of transformative change that is usually far more difficult and more protracted to achieve if the same executive director stays throughout. Nonprofits make great leaps into new areas of service, dramatic changes in scope, or shifts in whom they serve when led by a new executive director who both reflects and initiates transformative change.

Rather than seeing executive transition as a trying period to muddle through, boards can view it as an opportunity to take big steps toward the realization of a vision.

So what are the keys to successful hiring?

First, boards should recognize the importance of the hiring decision and make sure they have enough time to do it right. Hiring an experienced interim executive director may be one way to "hold down the fort," make a few changes, and give the board time to plan and think about what kind of person they really want and need. The Presbyterian Church offers an intriguing model: congregations seeking new pastors engage in year-long planning and assessment processes for which they hire an interim pastor. These interim pastors have undergone special training and have access to support to enable them to do their jobs well.

Today in the wider nonprofit sector there are individuals who see themselves as "professional interims"; in fact, the director of the Executive Transitions Program at CompassPoint, Tim Wolfred, has held sixteen interim executive director assignments.

Second, the board must consider what changes in leadership are appropriate for this point in the organization's development. Even the best executive director will not have had all talents and skills, and a changing environment may demand new aptitudes not needed before. Board members might decide this is the right chance to hire an executive director with a more personal connection to the agency's mission, rather than the administrative manager they've had before. Or, because of growth in the organization, they might decide to bring in someone with experience in larger organizations. Or this may be the time to choose an executive director who more closely reflects or is connected to the client population or to choose one with specialized experience, such as in earned income or in political action.

Third, the board should consult others about what kind of person to hire, and involve others in seeking the right candidates. Staff, funders, the leadership of similar agencies, clients, and other constituents may have valuable insights into the right kind of leader for the agency, and they can often help recruit and identify strong candidates. Some agencies have had good experiences with search consultants and board consultants who help

them work through these decisions as well as help them find good applicants.

Finally, the board should be prepared for changes in its own makeup. Executive transition typically interrupts the natural turnover on a board. When an executive director leaves, some board members usually decide to stay on a little longer than they might have in order to see the transition through. Some board members may leave because of their close connection to the departing executive, while others may leave because they don't like the new hire. Many board members have found themselves in all three of the above situations at one point or another. In any case, the new executive director can view this change in board composition as an opportunity to build a board that is better suited to the new situation. However, these changes can also leave just two or three people on the board with all the knowledge and clout, which can create special challenges for the new executive or for incoming board members.

---

* Jeanne Peters et al., *Daring to Lead: Nonprofit Executive Directors and Their Work Experience* (San Francisco: CompassPoint Nonprofit Services, 2001). This study is available to download for free or in hard copy by paid order at www.compasspoint.org.

Job Description for an Executive Director

At a recent gathering of nonprofit executive directors it was amazing to discover how many didn't have job descriptions—and almost no one had a job description that had been recently updated. Too often boards only look at the executive director's job description when they're unhappy with their executive or when they're hiring a new one. It's hard to write a job description from scratch, and the sample on page 71 may be helpful as a starting point.

In addition, many national and local organizations are willing to share their executive director job descriptions with others. It's worth a call or two to friends on other boards to see if they have good ones to share.

Whatever job description you use, test it to see both that it provides everyday guidance for the executive director and that it can serve as an evaluation tool at the end of the year. Be sure to revisit and revise the job description as the job and the organization change.

Also Try

Evaluating the Executive Director's Performance, p. 82

How Much to Pay the Executive Director, p. 76

Firing the Executive Director, p. 95

Should the Executive Director Have a Vote on the Board? p. 93

Sample Job Description—Executive Director

The executive director is the chief executive officer of _____. The executive director reports to the board of directors and accepts responsibility for the organization's consistent achievement of its mission and financial objectives.

In program development and administration, the executive director will

1. Assure that the organization has a long-range strategy that achieves its mission, and toward which it makes consistent and timely progress.

2. Assure that the board of directors is an effective, diverse body that governs the affairs of the organization and assure that individual board members can contribute in meaningful ways to the organization's achievement of its mission and financial objectives.

3. Provide leadership in developing program, organizational, and financial plans with the board of directors and staff, and carry out plans and policies authorized by the board. Act quickly to respond to rapidly changing conditions.

4. Promote active and broad participation by volunteers in all areas of the organization's work.

5. Maintain official records and documents and ensure compliance with federal, state, and local regulations.

6. Maintain a working knowledge of significant developments and trends in the field.

In communications, the executive director will

1. See that the board is kept fully informed on the condition of the organization and all important factors influencing it.

2. Publicize the activities of the organization, its programs, and its goals.

3. Establish sound working relationships and cooperative arrangements with community groups and organizations.

4. Represent the programs and point of view of the organization to government agencies, organizations, and the general public.

In relations with staff, the executive director will

1. Be responsible for the recruitment, employment, and release of all personnel, both paid staff and volunteers.

2. Ensure that job descriptions are developed, that regular performance evaluations are held, and that sound human resource practices are in place.

Sample Job Description—Executive Director (continued)

3. See that an effective management team is in place and that it serves as a leadership development body as well as a coordinating body.

4. Encourage staff and volunteer development and education, and assist program staff in relating their specialized work to the total program of the organization.

5. Maintain a climate that attracts, keeps, and motivates a diverse staff of top-quality people.

In budget and finance, the executive director will

1. Be responsible for developing and maintaining sound financial practices.

2. Work with the staff, the finance committee, and the board in preparing a budget; see that the organization operates within budget guidelines.

3. Ensure that adequate funds are available to permit the organization to carry out its work.

4. Jointly, with the president and secretary of the board of directors, conduct official correspondence of the organization, and jointly, with designated officers, execute legal documents.

Qualifications

1. Bachelor's degree or graduate degree in a field related to the organization's purpose; or equivalent experience and expertise.

2. A minimum of five years of experience in administration—directing a business firm or nonprofit agency and involving supervision of a diverse staff and management of significant funds.

3. Experience working with volunteers and a commitment to volunteer leadership and involvement.

4. Demonstrated success in fundraising and public relations.

5. Exceptional management ability and a sincere commitment to the goals and values of the organization.

Searching for a New Executive Director

Hiring and firing an executive director are two of the most important and difficult tasks a board must be prepared to perform. This article addresses the search process, often a neglected component of the hiring process.

Many of the principles used in hiring staff are also sound principles for boards to use in seeking and hiring new executive directors.

1. Place high priority on developing a sizable pool of strong applicants. Too often boards focus on selecting the right person from the pool, rather than on having a great pool from which to select. Give yourself enough time and consider allocating funds for this work.

   • Remember that most executive directors are on the job for the first time, so don't limit your search to people who have already served in this position.

   • Advertise widely, in the neighborhood and ethnic presses as well as in citywide newspapers and national newsletters.

   • Make telephone calls. Repeat: make telephone calls. Headhunters succeed *not* by placing lots of advertisements but by telephoning contacts, asking them for suggestions, and following up all suggestions by phone. Good people to call: executive directors of collaborative and competing organizations (such as other affordable housing organizations), foundations and corporations that give grants to your organization, former board members, longtime volunteers (such as docents at your natural history center), religious leaders in the community, clients (such as adult children whose elderly parents are in your program), and patrons (such as season ticket holders).

   • Register with local employment assistance organizations, such as a nonprofit that helps women with career choices.

   • Send job announcements to dozens of similar and other community organizations and ask them to circulate and post the job announcement.

- Look outside your immediate field for candidates. For example, an HIV-prevention organization might find good candidates with backgrounds in heart disease prevention or in child abuse prevention. A film preservation archive may find candidates with backgrounds in film, libraries, art preservation, museums, or literary journals.

2. Remember that at different times an organization will need executive directors with different abilities. At one time an organization may need an executive director with a strong program background; at another, a director with a strong financial background.

3. Establish an executive director transition committee that gathers input from board members, staff, and others in the field about the qualifications and requirements for the position. The committee can write a job announcement and a job description, and screen applicants for final interviews with the full board.

4. Consider contracting with an executive search consultant or firm. Search consultants may have contacts in less familiar fields and the time to call people who may have suggestions. But be careful: Some organizations have had negative experiences with search

consultants who end up doing little or who inappropriately screen out potential candidates.

5. Confirm degrees, licenses, and other qualifications. Write to the university or state board to confirm, for example, a master's degree or a nursing degree. For some positions it is appropriate to conduct a criminal background check.

6. Contact references in addition to the ones provided by the candidate. If a candidate has previous executive director experience, for example, contact several board members from that organization as well as some funders of that organization.

7. Take the opportunity to consider whether you want to change the employment terms for the executive director position. Perhaps a wider salary range should be considered or a one-year employment contract instead of an open-ended hire. Authorize two individuals to conduct negotiations on salary, benefits, and other matters once you have identified your top candidate.

8. Take your time. Selection of the executive director is perhaps the most crucial decision the board will make for the next five years. Let committees meet with the top candidate and spend some informal time with the

Also Try

Job Description for an Executive Director, p. 70

How Much to Pay the Executive Director, p. 76

Eleven Ways to Set a New Executive Director on a Path for Success, p. 79

Succession Planning for Nonprofits of All Sizes, p.65

top candidate before you make a decision to offer someone the job. It may be appropriate to ask an existing staff member to serve as acting executive director in the interim; some organizations have hired an individual from the outside to serve as temporary or interim executive director.

9. After you have hired the new executive director, introduce him or her to the staff and to the community. Some boards hold a series of informal dinners or receptions at which the new director can begin to forge important relationships.

How Much to Pay the Executive Director

Some nonprofit boards have a difficult time holding a discussion about how much to pay the executive director. One reason for this reluctance is the general secrecy about salaries, especially in a group where salaries are likely to differ widely. In fact, it is believed that the salaries of the board members are one of the strongest drivers in setting executive director compensation: If all the board members have salaries around $35,000, they are unlikely to pay their executive director, for example, as much as $65,000. The same-sized organization with board members who have salaries around $200,000 is unlikely to pay as little as $65,000.

Nonetheless, compensation is an important part of retaining key staff. Distributing this article to board members may help break the ice on the subject and provide a starting point for the discussion.

In a national study of nonprofit executive directors, most were reasonably satisfied with their compensation,* despite salaries often between $40,000 and $60,000 in some of the country's most expensive urban areas. On a scale of 1 to 5 (5 is "very satisfied"), respondents' average rating of satisfaction with pay was 3.47, although a substantial portion—27 percent—rated their compensation packages a 1 or 2. It is also noteworthy that 6 percent of executive directors receive no salary at all—they're volunteers.

The study also showed disturbing gender differences in salary. Despite the predominance of women in nonprofit executive positions around the country, male executives make significantly more than their female colleagues do. This is true at five of the six sizes of organizations studied. The gender gap is especially wide at agencies with budgets of more than $5 million: the mean salary nationally for women executives of nonprofits with budgets between $5 million and $10 million was $82,314; at this same budget size, the mean salary for men was $98,739.

This question of how much to pay usually arises in one of two quite different settings: when hiring a new executive director and when discussing a raise for a current executive director. When hiring a new executive, a board typically chooses a salary that strikes a balance between what the organization can afford and the going rate in the market for the talent and experience desired. But later, the same board can tend to ignore changes in the job market and focus only on percentage increases. Whether discussing salary for a new hire or a long-tenured director, objectives and factors to take into consideration include the following:

1. *To be competitive in the market for talent.* For what organization is your executive director most likely to leave? If the answer is a similar nonprofit, look at the salaries of comparable nonprofits in the area. (But keep in mind that salaries at very similar nonprofits can differ by factors of ten or more.) If the answer is government, look at the kinds of positions your executive director might take and at what salary and benefits are being offered.

2. *To be fair internally.* How much are other employees making? What salary is appropriate relative to other staff?

3. *To recognize the contribution the executive director will make in the coming year.* Rather than being a reward or a punishment for previous performance, salary for the coming year should be consistent with the performance that is anticipated. Of course, the best indicator of next year's performance is last year's performance.

4. *To send the appropriate signal.* Words are important but so is money. Praising executive directors while keeping their compensation flat ends up conveying a message that the board doesn't really value their work. In the same way, giving inadequate executives a raise while quietly considering their termination sends a mixed signal you may later hear about in a wrongful termination lawsuit.

5. *To avoid putting financial stress on the organization.* The board has a responsibility to keep the total costs of the organization (including the executive director's salary) in an affordable range. On the other hand, when hiring a new director, it may be appropriate to invest "venture capital" by offering a higher salary. In an experiment by the Neighborhood Investment Corporation, grants of $5,000 and $10,000 were made to local groups to raise the salary offered to a new executive. The corporation hypothesized that by offering more, a better-qualified person could be hired, and such a person could raise enough money to meet the new costs as well as to bring all salaries up. In some cases, boards did succeed in hiring at a new level of competence, and the model was proven correct. But in other cases, boards still were unable to attract talent with which they were satisfied.

Information on salaries may be found at

• Abbott, Langer, and Associates, Inc., which provides (for a fee) salary survey data from about 11,000 nonprofit organizations, typically larger, institutional organizations. See www.abbott-langer.com.

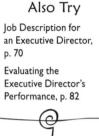

Also Try

Job Description for
an Executive Director,
p. 70

Evaluating the
Executive Director's
Performance, p. 82

- GuideStar, which draws salary data from 58,000 Form 990s filed annually by nonprofits with annual revenues of $25,000 or more. Salaries reported are $50,000 or higher. It's also possible to look up organizations in your community with which you are familiar to see the salaries of their key employees. Keep in mind that the data are typically a few years old and do not include hours worked and certain other types of benefits. See www.guidestar.org.

- Local sources: in some areas United Ways or community foundations conduct compensation studies on area nonprofits. Local studies on for-profits are often conducted by local business newspapers or the local chamber of commerce.

- *Chief Executive Compensation: A Guide for Nonprofit Boards* covers IRS regulations on excess pay, more ways to research comparable nonprofit salaries, and a list of national and regional compensation surveys. This twenty-page booklet is available from BoardSource, 800-883-6262.

---

* Jeanne Peters et al., *Daring to Lead: Nonprofit Executive Directors and Their Work Experience* (San Francisco: CompassPoint Nonprofit Services, 2001). This study is available to download for free or in hard copy by paid order at www.compasspoint.org.

Executive director, CEO, or president?

This book uses the term *executive director* to describe the top paid position in a nonprofit, 501(c)(3) organization. Although a variety of titles are used for this position—sometimes president, or director, or chief executive officer (CEO), for example—the term *executive director* remains the most widely used.

Eleven Ways to Set a New Executive Director on a Path for Success

by Tim Wolfred and Jan Masaoka

When a new executive is hired, the board has usually been working extra-hard for weeks or months. In addition to meetings about candidates, board members have often taken on additional tasks, such as managing a fundraising event or overseeing the audit. (The board, acting as a body, has been working hard on its governance responsibility of hiring, while board members, acting as individuals, have also stepped forward to support and help.)

Following are some ideas for the board and for board members:

1. Don't drop the ball quite yet! It's understandable that board members may want to relax once the new executive director is in place. In a tough situation—where new income streams need to be found, for example—board members may want to step back and hope the new executive will pull the organization forward. At the same time, a new executive may be reluctant to ask board members to do more, or may be new to the community or field and thus be unsure of the kind of board help to seek. Stay in there at continued intensity for a while longer, and make sure the executive gets off to a great start. Tip: Have a committee or an officer take on the job of monitoring and supporting the transition for the first six months.

2. Write and send out a press release— either by e-mail or in hard copy. Send it to local and neighborhood newspapers, local ethnic presses, newsletters for the field (such as disabilities or theatre), national office and affiliates (if you're a chapter organization such as Planned Parenthood), and local television and radio stations.

3. Don't forget that the most important recipients of the press release may not be the press: Be sure the press release is sent to funders, donors, significant volunteers, former staff and board members, city officials, and organizations with which yours is in contact. They'll appreciate the news, and it gives you a chance to tell them more about the new executive and spark their positive interest in working with her.

4. Have the board president or chair introduce the new executive to the staff. Doing so sends a message that

the board has hired this executive to manage the staff and who reports to the board.

5. At a board meeting, make a list of the influential people your new executive should meet and see which board members can set up coffees or lunches with them. A board member can invite the new executive to lunch along with other Chinatown leaders, for example, or have coffee with the school superintendent.

6. Make a personal donation to the organization *now* to demonstrate your confidence in the new executive and the organization's future. Bonus: She'll really appreciate it.

7. Set the new executive up for success by giving positive messages to the community about him, especially ones that point the way for working together. If you have some private reservations about the new executive, keep them to yourself. Example: "We are so thrilled we were able to hire him—he's just what our organization needs for the future. In particular, I think you'll appreciate his experience with innovative programs involving kids and sports."

8. If you're the board chair, take extra care working with the new executive on board meetings and board packets. She'll just be finding her way in a new environment, and you can help find a balance between what the board is familiar with and her style as it develops.

9. Take your new executive out to lunch, and listen. Don't forget that he's in the process of forming his big ideas, and you can help him by listening, asking questions, and encouraging him to be creative and bold. You can also help him think through which kinds of issues need to come to the board and which are appropriately up to him. While reminding him of what the board expects in terms of support and information from its executive, in turn, ask him how he'd like to be supported by the board. Any relationship in life has a better chance of thriving when the expectations of all parties are explicit.

10. Look for opportunities, especially at board meetings, to praise the new executive. "The directions you're talking about are just the ones we were looking for," or "The board packets were excellent—I especially appreciated the inclusion of the article about changes in funding for neighborhood arts."

11. Even the best baseball players work with batting coaches and fielding coaches. Suggest to your executive that a good use of organizational funds may be to pay for a coach—perhaps in fundraising, or public speaking, or general leadership development.

Don't let all good feelings distract you from the board's responsibility to establish and monitor benchmarks for performance. Clear performance goals for the first year will go a long way toward keeping the board and the executive focused on what's important. Some boards ask the new executive to use the first forty-five days to learn and then present a set of draft benchmarks to the board, while others establish the benchmarks together as part of the hiring process. Either way, be sure the board fulfills its collective responsibility as a board to oversee its chief executive. If things begin to go bad quickly, such benchmarks will allow early termination. If things go well, such benchmarks will have been a reason for success.

Also Try

Job Description for an Executive Director, p. 70

How Much to Pay the Executive Director?, p. 76

Should the Executive Director Have a Vote on the Board? p. 93

Evaluating the Executive Director's Performance, p. 82

Evaluating the Executive Director's Performance
Three Approaches

Because the executive director is so central to the success or failure of the organization, evaluation of the executive director by the board is an important component of the board's governance responsibilities. But too often evaluations (and job descriptions) are undertaken only when the board has become unhappy with the chief executive. An annual, written evaluation both documents the executive director's achievements and shortcomings and helps the executive understand areas for improvement or areas where the board is insufficiently informed.

A surprisingly common, deeply felt complaint of executive directors is that their boards must be prodded and prompted to conduct ongoing evaluations. Don't let this be the case with you! Decide on a regular time for evaluation—perhaps at the end of the fiscal year—and make sure the evaluation is scheduled for that time each year.

The many tools for evaluating executive performance can be grouped into three approaches, here described as

1. Board Survey Assessment
2. Report on Performance to Plan
3. Strengths and Weaknesses Review

In the following sections, each of these approaches is discussed briefly, with examples of questions and formats to be used.

1. Board survey assessment

In a board survey approach, board members complete a performance evaluation worksheet, which is then compiled and discussed by the board officers or evaluation committee. The most common tool is a list of items for which board members supply a rating.

> Please rate the performance of the executive director as "1–Needs Improvement," "2–Satisfactory," or "3–Excellent":
>
> 1. Meets or exceeds program goals in quantity and quality
> 2. Meets or exceeds revenue goals

Such an annual survey gives the executive director a clear picture of the criteria that will be used in his or her evaluation and provides a straightforward way in which board members can provide feedback to the director. A major weakness of a board survey is that the results are based on the perceptions of board members, rather than objective data. For example, in the sample rating above, board members may be mistaken in believing that revenue goals have been met.

A second shortcoming is that the numerical nature of the board survey tends to attribute the same level of importance to all tasks, and success with smaller tasks can overwhelm a big failure. For example, if an executive director does wonderful program, community, and administrative work but has incurred a huge deficit leading the agency close to bankruptcy, the problem will only show up as one or two negative "grades" and won't affect the "grade point."

If you use a board survey, be sure that the evaluation *starts* with the numbers but goes well beyond the numbers. The director's performance should be assessed as a whole, not just as an accumulation of tasks.

See the article "Executive Director's Performance Assessment: Sample Board Survey" on page 87 for a complete template for a board survey.

2. Report on performance to plan

Because the executive director accepts responsibility for the organization's overall performance, it makes sense to assess the executive's performance by looking at the organization's performance. Like most staff, the executive director is responsible for *results*, not simply for the completion of activities. For example, the executive director is responsible for raising $50,000 in foundation grants, rather than responsible for writing ten grant proposals. In its governance role representing the interests of the community, the board is rightfully concerned with what the *organization* has achieved.

Some organizations prepare annual or two-year plans that incorporate objectives for the organization to achieve.

In such plans, the board sets measurements ("metrics") that evaluate achievement rather than activity. These achievements are typically of three types: internal achievements, activity milestones, and community outcomes.

An organization's board and staff will need to work together to establish the objectives and goals for the year as part of the organization's annual or two-year plan. This plan not only serves as a guide for staff and board as months go along, but also becomes the plan against which the executive director's work is measured.

There are two key advantages to this approach. First, it builds on the idea that the executive director's job is to make the organization successful, not to accomplish a long list of tasks. Too often a weak executive can point to a great many activities, although those activities have not resulted in the intended impacts. Second, this

Sample Report on Performance to Plan

Plan	Performance	Notes
Internal achievements • Meet or exceed revenue and expense goals		
Activity milestones • Conduct thirty workshops in six counties on farmland preservation		
Community outcomes • Farm acreage lost to development decreased by 15 percent from previous year		

approach draws the organization's attention to measurable outcomes throughout the year.

For some organizations, however, looking only at organizational performance does not give enough guidance to the executive director. In these organizations, board members are likely to have worked directly with the executive over the year, perhaps through a board committee, a fundraising event, or in program delivery. Board members have closer, more personal relationships with the executive and are inclined to have an evaluation process that more closely resembles the kind of evaluation done by a supervisor in a work setting.

3. Strengths and weaknesses review

The strengths and weaknesses approach is much like the approach a supervisor might take with a professional employee who is generally considered to be performing well but can (as can everyone) continue to improve. This approach sees the establishment of agency and individual goals as a joint project between the board and the executive director and stresses the involvement of the director in establishing a plan for the year.

On page 86 is a form that can be adapted to help structure this kind of evaluation.

No one of these evaluation approaches is likely to be best for an agency all the time. With a proven executive director and a strong board, the report on performance to plan can provide strong accountability and position the agency for growth or dramatic change. The board survey assessment is useful for boards that have not recently evaluated their executive directors or that want a simple, convenient tool; a year or two later the board may wish to move to a more customized approach. And many boards feel most comfortable with the kind of qualitative feedback that can be given in a strengths and weaknesses approach.

Whatever the method, executive directors need feedback all year-round. Like any employee, executive directors need praise and acknowledgment for work well done, and immediate feedback when problems arise. In the best situations, the board president and officers have established good working relationships with the executive director where constant feedback goes in both directions. The annual formal evaluation is an important component of, not a substitute for, that relationship.

Also Try

Executive Director's Performance Assessment, p. 87

Job Description for an Executive Director, p. 70

Firing the Executive Director, p. 95

Sample Executive Director Performance Evaluation: Strengths and Weaknesses Review

Period covered: July 1–June 30

Performance Evaluation Committee members: _____

Strengths and Weaknesses

In this section the board officers and the executive director each make a list "from scratch" and then compare lists and develop an agreed-upon set of areas for improvement.

Strengths	Action plan for building on strengths
• Outstanding community contacts and uses contacts well for the benefit of the organization	• Institutionalize contacts by introducing contacts to several staff members who will also develop relationships with them
• Successful in obtaining government contracts	• Obtain one contract from a new department
• Strong ability to mentor staff to take on new responsibilities	• Consider "mentoring mentors": helping senior management staff become better mentors themselves
Weaknesses	**Action plan for addressing weaknesses**
• Does not take advantage of public speaking opportunities	• Take public-speaking workshop
• "Getting around" to diversifying fund-raising	• Develop written month-by-month plan by February 15; submit at least two foundation proposals for capacity building by March 15
• Working productively with board members with whom there is a disagreement	• Meet individually with two board members with whom there have been recent disagreements and discuss ways of disagreeing more constructively in the future

Additional objectives

• Improve follow-through on board requests for information

• Take skills-building workshop or university extension course in supervision

• Raise issues earlier to the board

How the board can help the executive director achieve these objectives

• Individual members can give feedback on behavior seen as inappropriate at the time it occurs rather than later

• The board chair will have quarterly in-person meetings with the executive director to go over progress on the plan

Executive Director's Performance Assessment
Sample Board Survey

The following assessment is best used as a first draft for your own tool based on the job description for your executive director. You might add items related to audience growth, publishing, or meeting with the press or otherwise adapt this sample to your own organization's work.

The survey should be completed by each board member; don't forget there are several free online survey tools such as Zoomerang and SurveyMonkey. The evaluation committee can tabulate the results for discussion with the full board and the executive.

Also Try

Evaluating the Executive Director's Performance, p. 82

How Much to Pay the Executive Director, p. 76

Firing the Executive Director, p. 95

Performance Review for the Board, p. 128

Executive Director Annual Assessment Form

In one sense, the executive director's performance can be measured by the performance of the organization. Non–chief executive officer jobs are often evaluated based on completion of *activities*. But the executive's job in a nonprofit is more about results than about activities. This assessment form combines results, activities, and attributes: Every board will want to focus it on the areas that have been the most important to the organization.

Please rate your assessment of each category of performance as
Exceptional, Satisfactory, Unsatisfactory, or Don't Know.

Organization-wide: Program Development and Delivery *(Circle one)*

Ensures that the organization has a long-range strategy that achieves its mission and toward which it makes consistent and timely progress.

        Unsatisfactory   Satisfactory   Exceptional   Don't Know

Provides effective leadership in developing program and organizational plans with the board of directors and staff. Acts quickly in response to rapidly changing conditions.

        Unsatisfactory   Satisfactory   Exceptional   Don't Know

Sees to it that the organization meets or exceeds program goals in quantity and quality.

        Unsatisfactory   Satisfactory   Exceptional   Don't Know

Demonstrates quality of analysis and judgment in program planning, implementation, and evaluation.

        Unsatisfactory   Satisfactory   Exceptional   Don't Know

Shows creativity and initiative and responsiveness to constituencies in creating new programs and changing or closing existing programs.

        Unsatisfactory   Satisfactory   Exceptional   Don't Know

Maintains and utilizes a working knowledge of significant developments and trends in the field (such as AIDS, developmental disabilities, community theatre, sustainable agriculture) and in the relevant community (such as neighborhood, city, Latino engineers, healthy seniors).

        Unsatisfactory   Satisfactory   Exceptional   Don't Know

Comments:

Executive Director Annual Assessment Form (continued)

Please rate your assessment of each category of performance as Exceptional, Satisfactory, Unsatisfactory, or Don't Know.

Administration and Human Resource Management *(Circle one)*

Organizes and assigns work effectively, delegating appropriate levels of freedom and authority.

    Unsatisfactory   Satisfactory   Exceptional   Don't Know

Establishes and makes use of an effective management team.

    Unsatisfactory   Satisfactory   Exceptional   Don't Know

Maintains appropriate balance between administration and programs.

    Unsatisfactory   Satisfactory   Exceptional   Don't Know

Ensures that job descriptions are developed and that regular performance evaluations are held and documented.

    Unsatisfactory   Satisfactory   Exceptional   Don't Know

Ensures compliance with personnel policies and federal, state, and local regulations on workplaces and employment.

    Unsatisfactory   Satisfactory   Exceptional   Don't Know

Ensures that employees are licensed and credentialed as required and that appropriate background checks are conducted.

    Unsatisfactory   Satisfactory   Exceptional   Don't Know

Ensures that dimensions of diversity (race, gender, age, sexual orientation, economic background) are identified as important to the organization's mission and business goals and recruits and retains a diverse staff.

    Unsatisfactory   Satisfactory   Exceptional   Don't Know

Ensures that policies and procedures are in place to maximize volunteer involvement.

    Unsatisfactory   Satisfactory   Exceptional   Don't Know

Encourages staff development and education and assists program staff in relating their specialized work to the total program of the organization. Leadership development is embedded in organizational practices as appropriate.

    Unsatisfactory   Satisfactory   Exceptional   Don't Know

Maintains a climate that attracts, keeps, and motivates a diverse staff of top-quality people.

    Unsatisfactory   Satisfactory   Exceptional   Don't Know

Comments:

Executive Director Annual Assessment Form (continued)

Please rate your assessment of each category of performance as Exceptional, Satisfactory, Unsatisfactory, or Don't Know.

Community Relations *(Circle one)*

Serves as an effective spokesperson for the organization; represents the programs and points of view of the organization to other nonprofits, government, foundations, corporations, and the general public.

Unsatisfactory   Satisfactory   Exceptional   Don't Know

Establishes sound working relationships and cooperative arrangements with community groups and organizations.

Unsatisfactory   Satisfactory   Exceptional   Don't Know

Comments:

Financial Management and Legal Compliance *(Circle one)*

Ensures adequate control and accounting of all funds, including developing and maintaining sound financial practices.

Unsatisfactory   Satisfactory   Exceptional   Don't Know

Works with the staff, finance committee, and the board in preparing a budget; sees that the organization operates within budget guidelines.

Unsatisfactory   Satisfactory   Exceptional   Don't Know

Maintains official records and documents and ensures compliance with federal, state, and local regulations and reporting requirements (such as annual information returns; payroll withholding and reporting).

Unsatisfactory   Satisfactory   Exceptional   Don't Know

Executes legal documents appropriately.

Unsatisfactory   Satisfactory   Exceptional   Don't Know

Ensures that funds are disbursed in accordance with contract requirements and donor designations.

Unsatisfactory   Satisfactory   Exceptional   Don't Know

Comments:

Executive Director Annual Assessment Form (continued)

Please rate your assessment of each category of performance as Exceptional, Satisfactory, Unsatisfactory, or Don't Know.

Fundraising and Income (Circle one)

Develops realistic, ambitious fundraising and earned-income plans that combine to form a business plan for financial sustainability.

    Unsatisfactory   Satisfactory   Exceptional   Don't Know

Sees to it that the organization meets or exceeds revenue goals, ensuring that adequate funds are available to permit the organization to carry out its work.

    Unsatisfactory   Satisfactory   Exceptional   Don't Know

Successfully involves others in fundraising and revenue generation.

    Unsatisfactory   Satisfactory   Exceptional   Don't Know

Establishes productive relationships with government, foundation, and corporate funders.

    Unsatisfactory   Satisfactory   Exceptional   Don't Know

Establishes positive, productive relationships with individual donors.

    Unsatisfactory   Satisfactory   Exceptional   Don't Know

Comments:

Executive Director Annual Assessment Form (continued)

Please rate your assessment of each category of performance as Exceptional, Satisfactory, Unsatisfactory, or Don't Know.

Board of Directors (Circle one)

Works well with board officers.

       Unsatisfactory   Satisfactory   Exceptional   Don't Know

Provides appropriate, adequate, and timely information to the board.

       Unsatisfactory   Satisfactory   Exceptional   Don't Know

Provides support to board committees.

       Unsatisfactory   Satisfactory   Exceptional   Don't Know

Sees that the board is kept informed on the condition of the organization and all important factors influencing it.

       Unsatisfactory   Satisfactory   Exceptional   Don't Know

Appropriately balances supporting the board and providing leadership to the board.

       Unsatisfactory   Satisfactory   Exceptional   Don't Know

Comments:

Are there specific performance objectives, either for the executive director or for the organization as a whole, that you would suggest we add for the coming year?

Are there any other comments you would like to make?

Should the Executive Director Have a Vote on the Board?

by Betsy J. Rosenblatt

Traditionally, all members of the nonprofit board of directors are unpaid, and the top executive (executive director or chief executive officer—CEO) is not a member of the board. In contrast, in most for-profit boards of directors, the chief executive is also the head of the board, although recent corporate board scandals have led many bodies (such as the National Association of Corporate Directors) to recommend that voting board membership be taken away from corporate CEOs.

More nonprofit boards seem to be giving board membership and a vote to the executive director: A recent Board-Source/Stanford study shows that 17 percent of boards include the CEO as a voting member (up from 9 percent in 1997). But is this a good idea?

Proponents say that both board membership and a vote give CEOs credibility and respect, in particular with for-profit corporations where such arrangements are the standard. They argue that board membership gives CEOs a way to take stands on board matters and that without a vote CEOs are cast as second-class board members.

Opponents claim that having a vote may give the CEO too much power and that it disrupts the accountability of the CEO to the board. In fact, most nonprofit CEOs are not even members of the board.

The tension that comes from the balance of power between the chief executive and the board is often necessary to keep a nonprofit on the right track. Properly defining the roles and responsibilities of each—and promoting accountability between the two—may be challenging, but it's necessary for a healthy nonprofit.

The board hires, fires, and evaluates the chief executive; in effect, the board as a group is the chief executive's supervisor. The board delegates its authority to the chief executive. For that individual to be voting on the board and influencing decisions about his or her role creates a conflict of interest. If the chief executive were able to sway board decisions by voting, the board's independent role in keeping the chief executive on his or her toes is at risk. The board also sets the chief executive's salary, so it clearly doesn't make sense for the CEO to vote on that decision. Yes, the chief executive could excuse himself or herself from that discussion, but for how many other decisions would excusing be appropriate?

As the top staff person, the chief executive already wields a great deal of power. He or she likely knows better than anyone what goes on in the organization. The chief executive controls much of the flow of information to the board and, for the most part, controls the hiring and firing of staff. A CEO's fear that without a vote the board holds all the influence and control is unfounded. In a healthy board-CEO relationship, the CEO gives reports and makes recommendations. The CEO should exercise his or her influence through the discussion, not by voting.

But what about the argument that board membership and a vote are needed for the CEO to be respected both on the board and with outside constituents? If a vote is necessary for a board to demonstrate

its respect for its CEO, then something else is wrong with the board-staff relationship. And although nonprofit corporations must be as efficient and organized as for-profit corporations, nonprofits have stakeholders, goals, and missions that differ from those of for-profit businesses. Nonprofits have other ways to demonstrate their efficiency and effectiveness rather than by imitating for-profit board practices.

In the organization on whose board I serve, the chief executive relies on the thoughtfulness and perspective of the board to guide the organization. In turn, she carries the confidence and ability to make day-to-day decisions and carry out the mission of the organization. She does her job, and we on the board do ours. It works out.

Betsy J. Rosenblatt is the communications specialist at the Eugene and Agnes E. Meyer Foundation in Washington, DC. She wrote this article while serving as senior editor at BoardSource and a member of the Board Café *Editorial Committee.*

Also Try

Should the Board Hold Executive Sessions? p. 205

How Much to Pay the Executive Director, p. 76

Firing the Executive Director

Boards of directors often fall into one extreme or another when it comes to dissatisfaction with the executive director. In some cases, such dissatisfaction can simmer for years without resolution. But in other cases, boards can be too hasty and fire an executive at the drop of a hat or, more often, abruptly conclude a long period of silent dissatisfaction with a sudden termination. How the executive director is terminated should be considered carefully for its impact on the staff, members, and others. And sometimes just knowing more about how boards fire their directors can help you relax into just working more proactively with your director.

Sometimes it's necessary for a board to fire the executive director. Occasionally the decision is clear to everyone, such as in instances of embezzlement or unethical behavior. But more often, board members get indications over time that the director is either not doing the job or causing problems for the organization.

The prospect of open conflict with the executive director is so dismaying that many board members who are dissatisfied with the director's performance often choose to resign or drop off rather than take on the issue. Others try to look the other way for as long as possible. Dissatisfaction with the executive director often appears first as rumblings, such as a staff member complaining to a board member about morale or committee members confiding their concerns to one another.

When such rumblings appear, the board should hold an executive session and establish an investigative committee to clarify the content and extent of the dissatisfaction and to determine what general approach is appropriate. If, for example, there are rumors of sexual harassment, the committee (or a consultant) can interview staff and volunteers and determine whether the rumors are frivolous or whether they require a more formal investigation. In another example, the committee may find that the executive director simply doesn't understand the administrative approach the board wants to see taken; in such an instance the board may choose to set up a series of meetings with the executive director to clarify directions and improve communication.

One way to put the issue on the table is to call for a "vote of confidence or no confidence" in the executive director. For example, board members may be asked to vote for one of the following resolutions: (a) "I am confident that the executive director is doing a satisfactory job"; or

(b) "I have lost confidence that the executive director is doing, or will be doing in the near future, a satisfactory job." By doing so, board members can express their concerns without having to vote immediately on a "fire" resolution.

If the board has strong reservations about whether the executive director's performance is satisfactory, it should establish a committee to work more closely with the director in a supervisory capacity. Beginning with letting the executive director know the extent of dissatisfaction on the board, the committee can document the problems and take steps to improve the director's performance. If performance doesn't improve over time, and the director is fired by the board, the ongoing documentation can help deter a lawsuit against the agency by the former executive director. No level of documentation can guarantee that a lawsuit won't be brought, but an agency holds a stronger position in court and in the community if personnel policies have been followed, if steps have been taken to improve performance, and if those steps are documented as having failed.

If, after appropriate investigation and deliberation, a board feels that the executive director should leave the organization, it may choose first to have the board officers approach the director and suggest that a resignation would be welcomed. Many executive directors under pressure prefer resignation to being fired, and some board members feel that a resignation leaves the organization in a better light than termination does.

Boards should strongly consider consulting with legal counsel—someone familiar with nonprofits and with employment law—before terminating the executive director. An employment law expert will be familiar, for example, with issues related to protected classes of employees, and nonprofit knowledge is important in understanding the board-executive relationship. Talking with an attorney is a fairly simple step that can reduce the risk of serious problems with termination.

Whichever is chosen, board action to terminate or to accept a resignation should be put into the minutes. The board should document whether there is any severance pay or any remaining tasks to be completed by the departing executive director and close any other financial relationship. The board should develop a straightforward explanation for the resignation that can be communicated to staff, volunteers, funders, and others in the community.

Also Try

Job Description for an Executive Director, p. 70

Evaluating the Executive Director's Performance, p. 82

When the Executive Director Leaves, p. 98

From *Best of the Board Café* (a column in the online magazine *Blue Avocado*), Copyright © 2003 and 2009, CompassPoint Nonprofit Services, published by Fieldstone Alliance, www.FieldstoneAlliance.org. Subscribe free to *Blue Avocado* at www.blueavocado.org.

Sample Letter Accepting Executive Director's Resignation

November 17, _____

Dear _____:

On behalf of the Board of Directors of _____,
I am writing this letter to tell you that the board received your letter of November 15 and has accepted your resignation from the position of Executive Director as of November 30, _____.

By November 30, you will submit a final expense reimbursement request for the period of your employment and return to the office the fax machine that you have been keeping at your home.

Your final paycheck, along with a check for accrued vacation, will be issued on November 30, and represents final payment from the _____ organization for your services.

Sincerely,

_____
Chair, Board of Directors

When the Executive Director Leaves
The Job of the Board's Executive Transition Committee

by Timothy Wolfred, Psy.D.

One board member recently commented, "The executive director of the organization where I'm the president is thinking about retiring. I know this will sound bad, but my main thought is: Don't retire until my term as president is over!" This president's sentiment is understandable but unrealistic; statistics show that most board members will face executive departure if they serve six years or more.*

The departure of an agency executive demands intensive leadership and activity by the board of directors. The obvious primary task is the search for a new chief executive. But regardless of the circumstances under which the executive director is departing, a healthy transition usually entails many other tasks as well:

- Arranging a proper send-off for the departing executive and establishing a consistent message about the departure and transition.

- Determining what work the organization needs to do to prepare for the hire (perhaps almost nothing, perhaps time to work through a sense of loss, perhaps midlevel planning, perhaps major board and structural changes).

- The selection, if needed, of an interim executive, who can act in roles ranging from "caretaker" to "change agent."

- Deciding how to conduct the search and screening process and with what outside help.

- An "organizational audit" to determine the key challenges for the next executive director.

- Planning a structured entry for the newly hired executive that contributes to future success: welcoming rituals, community introductions, performance goals, and an evaluation protocol.

To coordinate all these facets of an executive turnover, some boards find it helpful to create an *ad hoc* executive transition committee. This committee may include only one or two key board officers, or the officers as a group may choose to serve as the transition committee. It's often a good idea to have one or two (nonvoting) staff act as a communications channel between the committee and the staff. An important member and resource to the committee is an identified staff administrator who will be a crucial communications link for the entire staff group and provide logistical support (and who is not a candidate for the job).

A visible and energized transition committee reassures key stakeholders. The departure of a good (or even bad) leader typically can destabilize staff and estrange some donors. A board swiftly and decisively swinging into action as a solid bridge between executive directors gives confidence to all agency constituents about the future.

Money is also an incentive to early convening of an executive transition committee. Foundations that already have made significant programmatic investments in an agency know the value of a well-managed executive director transition to an agency's vitality, and they may be willing to provide some transition funds. As part of its grant application, the committee will be asked to develop a work plan and timeline and to identify any consultants it may want to use for transition guidance.

As a member of the board of directors, you'll want to be sure that you find the right executive for the job and that the organization is ready for that individual's leadership. A conscientious transition committee can make the difference. Good luck in your transitions!

---

* Jeanne Peters et al., *Daring to Lead: Nonprofit Executive Directors and Their Work Experience* (San Francisco: CompassPoint Nonprofit Services, 2001), 20. This study is available to download for free or in hard copy by paid order at www.compasspoint.org.

Dr. Timothy Wolfred founded and manages the Executive Transitions program for CompassPoint Nonprofit Services, a five-year-old program to help nonprofit boards lead successful transition processes. To date, the program has worked with more than sixty boards on their transition needs, including assistance with searches, provision of interim executive directors, consulting on strategic hiring and compensation, and other topics. More information on this program and executive transition in general can be found at www. compasspoint.org/els.

Also Try

Job Description for an Executive Director, p. 70

Searching for a New Executive Director, p. 73

Do you fear that your board is about to make a really bad decision?

What's the right thing to do when you strenuously object to something the rest of the board wants to do? Or when you may think a difficult choice is the right one, but you want to go on record with your concerns? One option is to write your objections in a letter to the board, read it aloud at the meeting where the vote takes place, and have it placed into the minutes. Your letter will be read by those board members who are absent, and it will become part of the organization's permanent record. (For more ideas on coping with this tough situation, see "What to Do When You Really, Really Disagree with a Board Decision," page 110.

CHAPTER FOUR

Big Decisions

Strategic Plans, a 360-Degree View, Mergers, and Closing Down

Some organizational decisions speak so directly to the organization's continuing existence, or to its fundamental purpose, that it's clear they can only be made by the board of directors. These decisions also speak directly to the board's governance role: decisions that call for the board to act as a steward of the public and the organization's constituencies.

These decisions are often most difficult to make when the board and the staff are in conflict. Over time, a strong executive director and a weak board can result in the staff thinking that they are the ones who "own" the organization's future. When, for example, a board starts to discuss bankruptcy or closing down, the staff may mount an outraged attack on the board, blaming board members for not fundraising or even demanding that the board resign. On the other hand, in the face of conflict with the staff, some board members throw up their hands and resign, saying in effect to staff: "Okay, we give up. Do whatever you want to with the organization."

This chapter focuses on these big decisions, decisions that only the board can make. It includes the following articles:

Strategic Plans

by Mike Allison and Jude Kaye*

Good strategic plans have two dimensions: one you can touch, and the other you can only feel. The first is, of course, the written document. The second is organizational consensus and commitment to the priorities outlined in the document.

A strategic planning *process* is one by which the organization learns about itself, its constituencies, and its environment, reviews its values and goals, identifies important choices, and organizes itself to make and implement those choices. Strategic planning involves choosing specific *priorities*—making decisions about goals and how to get there, in both the long term and the short term.

When should an organization consider strategic planning?

- When board members and staff feel a need for greater organizational focus and organization-wide clarity on priorities.

- When core values, goals, and programs have not been examined in a long time.

- When an earlier plan's time frame is over or when it has become obsolete.

Even if one or more of the above is true, strategic planning should be undertaken only when the organization's leaders are truly committed to the effort and can devote the necessary attention.

When would not be a good time to undertake a strategic planning process?

- When the organization is in crisis, such as a financial crisis or a crisis of confidence in the organization's leadership. In such instances, the organization's attention needs to be focused on resolving or mitigating the urgent issues.

- When the organization is choosing a new executive director. Sometimes boards get caught between whether to "plan first" or "hire first." It's appropriate to think through elements of a new vision and the qualities needed in a new executive, but the new leader will need to lend his or her own thinking and vision to the strategic plan.

- When the environment is so turbulent that it makes better sense to wait until key outside factors develop further (if, for example, a major election, funding decision, or community crisis is looming, the outcome of which would dramatically affect the organization's priorities or resources).

- When the issues are not truly strategy issues. In many organizations, discontent or conflict can get characterized as "we need a strategic plan." Instead, the issue may really be one of capable executive leadership, poor working conditions, racial or gender conflict, poor supervision, staff resentment against management, or board-management conflict. Such issues are important, but should be addressed for what they are and with methods appropriate to the situations.

Is it necessary to use an outside consultant?

It depends on the organization and the nature of the planning being considered. In some organizations, an experienced, outside, neutral facilitator is appropriate to lead the process. In others, the board and executive leadership may be experienced with planning and can best direct the process. In some cases a consultant is brought in for part of the process who has special expertise, for example, in epidemiology, real estate, technology development, or some other area. In other cases, a consultant may be used to gather information from constituents (such as clients or donors or city leaders) who might be reluctant to speak candidly to staff or board members.

What does a typical strategic planning process look like?

A useful strategic plan can be sketched out in a few hours, done over a one- or two-day retreat, or take more than a year and involve all board and staff members.

The time (and cost) will depend on several factors, including how much agreement already exists, the amount of new information that needs to be gathered, the degree to which external key stakeholders should be involved, whether an outside consultant is hired, the level of trust among the staff and board, and the size of the organization.

A typical strategic planning process can be outlined briefly as follows:

1. Identify reasons for planning, agree on readiness, and write a "plan for planning" (the process that will be used). It is often useful to identify five to seven questions that the process will answer.

2. Revisit or write your mission and vision statements. Without getting stuck in terminology, a vision is often "a mental model of a future state...built upon plausible speculations...and reasonable assumptions about the future...influenced by our own judgments about what is possible and worthwhile." ** A mission statement often describes an organization in these terms:

   • Purpose: why the organization exists and what it seeks to accomplish ("to foster stability in the city's African American community").

   • Business: the main methods and activities of the organization ("by developing and operating affordable housing and by facilitating home ownership").

- Values: principles or beliefs that guide the organization ("guided by our commitment to social and environmental justice").

3. Obtain up-to-date information on the external and internal environments. External information may be gathered by interviewing clients, patrons, and key stakeholders, conducting an analysis of the field, consulting with experts, and so forth. Internal information may be gathered through surveys, having a consultant interview staff and review operational procedures, and other activities.

4. Examine the business model(s) of the organization and agree on priorities. If, for example, an organization depends on government funding that may be eliminated, the organization will need to decide if funding the program through other means is possible and a priority or whether the program should be closed down. If a program that used to pay for itself in fees is now having to use unrestricted funds, an important discussion would be whether to continue subsidizing the program.

This process may be short, or it may take considerable time, as the organization thinks through how to achieve its goals. For example, a Red Cross chapter may rethink the appropriate roles for volunteers in the organization. A locally successful sports program may need to decide whether it will expand to other counties or go deeper within its home county.

5. Write the plan. Often a small team drafts a plan, which is circulated and which may go through a few revisions. The written plan makes it easy for the organization to refer back to decisions and guidelines and can also be shared with volunteers, donors, clients, funders, and others.

6. Use and evaluate the strategic plan. The plan can be a useful platform for building annual plans, the next year's budget, and ongoing program planning. An important role for the board is monitoring annual plans to be sure they are aligned with the strategic plan and to see that progress is being made toward goals. The board (or a board committee) should revisit the plan periodically to see whether components should be reexamined.

Caution: Strategic planning requires both rational calculations and creative synthesis. Typically new ideas, adjustment to operations, or insights about what the organization is really about emerge during the process. Because of this, most strategic planning processes go through a "messy" period when it's unclear what is going on. This confusion is just part of the creative process and will pass. One of the benefits of strategic planning is the chance to "hold the organization's mind open" for longer than might seem necessary at first. At the beginning of the process, the board and management team may identify questions that later on turn out to be much larger or more complex than originally thought.

What is the board's role in strategic planning?

Strategic planning is at the intersection of governance and management. The mission, vision, and core strategies of an organization are governance matters that demand input and authorization from the board. On the other hand, strategic plans often speak to issues of operations and implementation of the plans where significant latitude may be given to management staff. Thus, the board can neither delegate strategic planning to management staff nor consider strategic planning without having management staff fully involved. The board can authorize a board committee to carry out most of the planning activity with staff, or it can participate in planning as a committee of the whole.

Once the strategic plan has been completed, make it work hard for you. Copies should be distributed to all staff, longtime volunteers, key funders and partner organizations, and so forth. The organization should use the strategic plan as a basis for the annual plan and for setting departmental goals as well as organization-wide goals. Consider posting some of the key language in your lobby, printing it on your letterhead, or giving plaques with the mission statement to board members, staff, and volunteers.

---

* Excerpted from *Strategic Planning for Nonprofit Organizations: A Practical Guide and Workbook*, 2nd Edition, by Michael Allison and Jude Kaye, published by John Wiley and Sons, 2003. Available at www.amazon.com. Mike Allison is the director of, and Jude Kaye a management consultant in, CompassPoint's Consulting and Research Group. Frequently Asked Questions (FAQs) on strategic planning are also available at www.genie.org.

** Burt Nanus, *Visionary Leadership* (San Francisco: Jossey-Bass, 1995), 25.

Also Try

Why Do Nonprofits Have Boards? p. 18

Sample Agenda for a Board–Staff Retreat on Annual Planning, p. 141

A 360-Degree Look, p. 112

Nonprofit Dashboards
An Essential Tool for Boards

by Jeanne Bell and Jan Masaoka

The dashboard in a car gives an instant update on many important factors: speed, gas left in the tank, engine temperature, whether the air conditioner is on. At the same time, it may not give you the most important information: whether you are taking the right road to Chicago—or even whether you should be going to Chicago at all!

A nonprofit dashboard is similar. It gives important information to decision-makers such as executives and boards in a quick-read way. But it may not be helpful on bigger matters: Are we doing the right work? Should we be considering merging or a new initiative? CompassPoint consultants increasingly work with client organizations to develop dashboard indicators. Here are some examples of dashboards that rely on information you are probably already collecting.

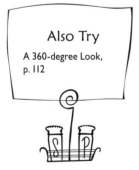

Also Try

A 360-degree Look,
p. 112

■ **Act** ■ **Watch** ■ **Celebrate**

1. Finance

	Target	6 months ago	Now
Days of unrestricted cash on hand	45 days	65 days	18 days
Net surplus or deficit YTD compared with YTD budget	Within 25K or better	$42,500 worse than budget	$28,000 worse than budget-to-date
Government funding year-to-date (52% of budget)	Within 3%	$39,000 worse than budget	$3,200 worse than budgeted
Days from end of month to financial statements	24 days	87 days	48 days

2. Program and Impact

	Target	6 months ago	Now
Number of first-time clients enrolled	360 this year	160	205
GED certificates obtained	90%	70%	82%
E-petition signatures	5,000	Not started yet	6,400
Paid seats per theatre performance	90% of performance space	85% last 3 performances	55% last 3 performances
Presentations to churches, companies, neighborhood groups	15 for year	7 YTD	7 YTD

3. Human Resources

	Target	6 months ago	Now
Performance evaluations completed on time	90%	Had not started counting	82%
Truck accidents per year	0	3	1
% of people of color in exempt positions	55%	20%	32%
Open workers compensation claims	No more than 8	15	6

■ **Act**   ■ **Watch**   ■ **Celebrate** (continued)

4. Board of Directors

	Target	6 months ago	Now
Attendance at board meetings	75%	75%	85%
Executive director performance evaluation completed on time	By February 15	Not applicable	Done by February 13!
New board members	4 new board members by September 30	2 new board members by June 30	August 15 still the same 2

5. Fundraising

	Target	6 months ago	Now
New foundations or corporations	10 this year	6	8
New individual donors	100	11	82

6. Compliance and Risk Management

	Target	As of January 30	As of November 1
Form 990 filed on time	By November 15	Not applicable	Applied for extension October 25
Annual safety drill conducted	By March 31	Not applicable yet	Not applicable

Imagine getting a dashboard like this at every meeting. With a glance, board members could see how the organization is doing and start asking the important questions. The board would also be able to discuss what indicators should be added to the dashboard and which might not be necessary. Board committees could look at expanded sets of indicators within their own areas; for example, the Fund Development Committee might have additional indicators around major donors or attendance at events.

If this dashboard is distributed at each board meeting, the board can zero in on key issues, rather than try to discover issues on their own. Don't forget that a dashboard shows a lot but not everything.

What to Do When You Really, Really Disagree with a Board Decision

Have you ever been in a situation where the board has made a decision that you think is very wrong and will have severe negative consequences for the organization? Or where you think an important decision has been railroaded through?

As a board member myself and something of a contrarian, I've found myself in these situations from time to time over the years. For example, on the board of an organization with a sizable financial deficit, I found myself and one other board member losing a seventeen-to-two vote to take funds from the organization's endowment for current operating expenses. In CompassPoint's consulting work to nonprofits, we see more serious cases, too, such as ones where board members suspect illegal activity or a takeover of the organization by a few very aggressive (and often new) board members.

It's important to remember that reasonable people can disagree on important issues. The following situations may give you some food for thought if an occasion that goes beyond reasonable disagreement were to arise for you.

Question: The board I'm on is about to make a bad decision. Although the last two years have been very tight financially, they refuse to make any cuts to the expenses. But they don't want to do anything different in fundraising either! If we have another bad year, I'm afraid we won't be able to pay our bills.

Answer: Call the board chair and express your concerns. But if you really expect that the decision will go another way, write a letter to the board that explains your reasons for voting against the budget that has been proposed. Bring this letter to the meeting at which the vote will be taken and ask to read your letter aloud and have it entered into the official minutes. You may be outvoted, but your reasoning is in the permanent record, and those who did not attend the board meeting will be able to understand your point of view. Many years from now, someone reading the minutes may also find your comments important and informative.

Question: The board has just voted to repair our playground structures rather than replace them, but I believe strongly that repairs won't do and some child may be hurt. What can I do?

Answer: Consider asking the board for an independent, expert evaluation of the situation, perhaps by a play equipment specialist. Such an evaluation will bring professional, objective information to the decision. If board members won't do that, or if they choose to ignore a report that indicates the structures are dangerous, at least make sure that your no vote is recorded in the minutes. Later, if a child is unfortunately hurt and a lawsuit is brought against the organization, you will not be liable if your vote by name has been recorded. After the vote, simply say, "Please put my name into the minutes as having voted NO on this motion." When the minutes are issued, check to be sure your vote has been recorded properly.

Question: I've just been voted off the board of a nonprofit because I've been asking too many questions about the finances. I think the board president and the executive director are embezzling money. What can I do?

Answer: The first step might be to write a letter explaining your concerns and send it separately to each board member and to the executive director. Ask them to respond to you by a certain date. You can also contact the auditor (if the organiza-tion has a CPA audit) to ask for clari-fication or feedback on your concerns. If these steps still leave you feeling that criminal activities are taking place, you can write a letter to a few of the organiza-tion's key funders and supporters, but be aware that such a step is likely to create a large uproar that could end up backfiring on you. Your final recourse is to bring the charges to the attorney general in your state. That office is responsible for over-seeing nonprofit organizations incorpo-rated within the state; your local state leg-islator may also be helpful in making sure there is an investigation.

Question: I'm still angry and disap-pointed over a decision the board has made. What can I do?

Answer: Once a decision has been made, don't keep bringing it up again or try to take your case to others. For example, if the board has just adopted a budget that you think is unrealistically optimis-tic, don't continue the argument by try-ing to convince staff or others that the decision should be overturned. If you feel that other board members understand your point of view but still disagree, and you feel that you could not openheart-edly work within that decision, consider resigning from the board and state your reasons clearly in a letter to the board. If, however, you can reluctantly live with the decision, make your disagreements clear, but also make clear that you will work with the decision.

Also Try

Removing a Difficult Board Member, p. 138

Conflict of Interest, p. 131

Ten Quick Ways to Invigorate Board Meet-ings, p. 193

Dominating Personalities on the Board, p. 166

The Right Way to Resign from the Board, p. 168

A 360-Degree Look
Seeing Ourselves as Others See Us

Who should judge if a meal is good? The cook? The nutritionist? The restaurant critic? Aristotle had a good answer long ago: "The guest is a better judge of the feast than the cook."

There are 360 degrees in a circle, and the 360-Degree Look places the organization at the center of the circle and looks at it from the viewpoint of its many constituencies. In particular, the 360-Degree Look helps compensate for the board's limited view of how well the organization is functioning. There are several reasons for this limited view. First, board members often have only a little time each month to spend on their volunteer board commitments. Second, board members are often unfamiliar with the program area of the organization, whether that is pesticide research, early childhood development, or nursing home standards. Hopefully, board members do know about the needs and desire of the organization's constituents, but that may not be the case. Finally, board members often receive most or all of their information from the organization's executive—not entirely a bias-free source.

In a 360-Degree Look, the board and the staff management team seek feedback from those who stand around the outside of the circle as well as inside it: clients, the community, volunteers, donors, funders, and staff. While such a project might be seen as threatening or overly time-consuming by staff, it's an infrequent project, done perhaps every five years, or when a fresh perspective is wanted. Having it led by a board-staff task force can alleviate staff fears and create a precedent for such board-staff teams. Like any project, a 360-Degree Look can get bigger and bigger; keep it modest and doable.

The following steps can be considered as examples of ways to obtain input from a variety of constituents and sources:

1. *Clients or patrons (the diners):* Program evaluation techniques are designed to determine the impacts of particular program interventions. A 360-Degree Look is more exploratory, more holistic, looking for how patrons and clients feel about what we do, and seeks unexpected insights. Consider holding one or two focus groups with clients or patrons, facilitated by an experienced focus group leader, where they can give feedback on current services and unmet needs. A more extensive client or patron survey can involve a written questionnaire, a telephone survey, or in-person interviews. Even as few as

five or ten open-ended interviews can provide new, valuable insights. Some example questions:

- How did you first hear about the Spruce Organization*?
- What was your first contact with Spruce like?
- What makes it difficult for you to use Spruce's services or attend Spruce's performances? What bothers you about Spruce?
- What do you wish that Spruce did that it doesn't do now?
- Spruce is thinking about asking patients for donations by mail or changing the matinee ticket price. What would your reaction be to something like this?

2. *Staff (the kitchen and waitstaff):* Consider asking staff to anonymously complete a short questionnaire to learn more about how they see the organization's strengths and weaknesses. Make it clear that this survey is one of the ways, not the only way, that the board is conducting the assessment. While a full report probably shouldn't be given to all staff, the staff will appreciate hearing some of the highlights from what you find. Here are some sample survey statements:

- How much do you agree or disagree with the following statements?

- The Spruce Organization consistently does quality work.
- I am proud to be an employee of this organization.
- I am embarrassed to be an employee of this organization.
- The duties of my job are clear to me.
- I have confidence in the staff leadership of this organization.
- Most of the time, I have enough time to complete my work assignments.
- I worry that our financial situation is unstable.
- I am respected by my supervisor.
- I am respected by people who report to me.
- Our organization does too much/ too little/the right mix. Please comment.

3. *Donors and volunteers (the friends):* Staff and board members can conduct telephone interviews with major donors and key volunteers, asking for feedback on how well the organization involves and informs them and seeking perceptions about the organization's effectiveness. Here are some sample questions:

- How did it come about that you are a donor to Spruce [or a volunteer with Spruce]?
- You have many choices in where to make donations [or volunteer].

What made you choose Spruce as one of those places?

- Have we thanked you appropriately? Too much? Too little? On time? Did you appreciate the framed poster we sent, or did you think it was an unnecessary expense?

- Has our staff been appropriately responsive to you, in giving you information about Spruce's procedures, organization, or clients? What, if anything, do you have questions about?

- If there were one thing you would like to see Spruce change, what would it be?

4. *Foundation, corporate, and government funders (the financiers):* Board members can conduct a series of telephone interviews with foundation and government program officers, in which a board member asks, for example, for comments on the quality of written proposals submitted, quality of communication and interaction with the agency, the organization's reputation in the community, and suggested areas for improvement or change. Here is an excerpt from a sample interview script:

As you know from the letter you received last week, the Spruce Organization is conducting a 360-Degree Look at our organization. I'm a board member of Spruce,

and I want to ask you a few questions:

- How well acquainted are you with Spruce's programs and operations?
- What do you think Spruce does very well?
- Are there some activities you think we do poorly, that should be discontinued, or that need improvement?
- How would you characterize the quality and promptness of our proposals and reports?
- From your direct interactions with Spruce, what is your general impression?
- If there were one thing you would like to see Spruce change, what would it be?

5. *Independent program and management evaluators (the nutritionists and the restaurant critics):* In addition to an annual audit by a certified public accountant, the board can contract with consultants to assess an aspect of the organization's programming or management. Such consultations can involve different components, such as an examination of personnel procedures or an analysis of organizational compliance with relevant regulations. Professional program evaluators assess human service and other types of programs both to find ways that the programs can be improved and to determine the outcomes of the agency's

From *Best of the Board Café* (a column in the online magazine *Blue Avocado*), Copyright © 2003 and 2009, CompassPoint Nonprofit Services, published by Fieldstone Alliance, www.FieldstoneAlliance.org. Subscribe free to *Blue Avocado* at www.blueavocado.org.

services and the impact on clients and the community. Arts consultants look at the artistic quality of an organization and compare its strengths and weaknesses to others. Remember that restaurant critics aren't always right, but if they have a complaint it may be something that's easy to fix.

6. *What's on the web about our organization?* Do a Google or a Yahoo search on the name of your organization. Look at your Form 990 to see what you've told the IRS and the public. See whether and how you have been rated by one of the online charity rating agencies. Create a Yahoo Alert or Google Alert and get e-mails every time your organization is mentioned on the web.

Using the information

The committee or task force that has led the 360-Degree Look has the important responsibility of making sense of all the material. For example, interviews with funders may reveal that grant reports are well written but often late; the executive director should have this feedback. There may be patterns of satisfaction and dissatisfaction among staff that can be useful planning information for the management team. An idea for change can

unexpectedly show up from several different kinds of people—such as a desire for an organizational name change—and should be taken seriously by the board as a suggestion. The interviews may show that the organization is gaining or losing luster in the community; such a finding may bear further investigation.

The committee can make its report to a board meeting, perhaps with the staff management team present. Present it in sections and after each section, ask for reactions and ideas: Is there something we should look into more closely? How can we celebrate good news?

Proceed with caution

The information gathered in a 360-Degree Look needs to be used with care. The staff needs to hear critical as well as positive comments from clients, but they may not need to hear the exact wording of an overly harsh statement by an obvious crank. In addition, a 360-Degree Look is not the same as an evaluation of the executive director. The information gathered may be best used in organizational planning and only used in a secondary way in the executive director's annual assessment.

Also Try

Evaluating the Executive Director's Performance, p. 82

Six Things Every Board Member Should Know about Form 990, p. 237

Abolish Board Committees? p. 180

---

* This is a fictitious name for an organization and, like other such fictitious groups in this book, is named after a tree.

From *Best of the Board Café* (a column in the online magazine *Blue Avocado*), Copyright © 2003 and 2009, CompassPoint Nonprofit Services, published by Fieldstone Alliance, www.FieldstoneAlliance.org. Subscribe free to *Blue Avocado* at www.blueavocado.org.

The 360-Degree Look doesn't replace systems for getting ongoing feedback. But the information you gather may help you decide to offer more fish dishes or pay more attention to the coffee being hot enough. You might change the way the dinner shift turns over. You might think to point out on your menu that you don't use any trans fats, and to frame a restaurant review for your front window. And remember that you can't please everyone. Aristotle also said, "A great city is not to be confounded with a big one."

The board as a safety net

It's not uncommon to see a nonprofit go through some very trying times. In one example, the longtime executive director had recently departed, and the board was struggling with serious financial difficulties—the organization was two weeks late on its last payroll, and there was no immediate "fix" in sight for some long-standing, deep problems. One positive factor was the way that board members stepped up to the plate. The board members didn't expect these kinds of challenges when they joined the board, but they "declared a state of emergency" and courageously and aggressively addressed the situation. This real story calls attention to an unexpected, yet important, role of boards: acting as a safety net for organizations. For many years of this organization's existence, the board had wondered, "Why are we here when staff are so competent?" Any organization can get into trouble over time; if the board had not been there in this case, surely the organization would have folded. Instead, there was immediate attention for the issues for clients and staff, and long-term cause for hope.

Should Your Nonprofit Be Considering a Merger?

by David La Piana

Should your nonprofit be considering a merger, long-term collaborative management, or other arrangement that goes beyond "cooperating"? Mergers, joint ventures, back-office consolidations, fiscal sponsorship arrangements, and virtual nonprofits are all examples of "strategic restructuring" options that nonprofits are viewing with increasing interest. Strategic restructuring goes beyond collaboration to bring the organizations into more formal, long-lasting, and profound forms of alliance.

You and your board might be interested in these intense partnerships:

- If your organization is, alas, weak—that is, unable to find or keep an executive director; unable to maintain an active board; too small to compete effectively in a particular market—you might seek affiliation with a larger organization that has what you lack or with other smaller organizations with whom you can develop the necessary strengths.

- If you are ready to grow—that is, want to augment a continuum of services; want to create a program from scratch; need to increase market share; hope to reduce competition—you are probably a strong nonprofit and see mergers or other partnerships as ways to further grow the organization.

- If you think a merger might enhance your mission and services—that is, reduce consumer confusion; lower overhead and put more dollars into direct service; increase political clout by speaking with one stronger voice— you might partner with others with whom you have a significant mission, program, or identity overlap.

For both the voluntary and paid leadership of nonprofits, strategic restructuring choices often come after years of building organizations, so such partnerships may threaten the organization's autonomy and identity. If our true goals are to serve our communities (rather than our own agencies), however, shouldn't we be as willing to serve by partnering as we are willing to serve by building our own organizations?

David La Piana is principal of La Piana Associates, Inc., a consulting firm providing services to nonprofits and philanthropy on "strategic restructuring" and other strategic issues. He can be reached at 510-655-3455 or at lapiana@lapiana.org. For a longer report by the same author, see "Beyond Collaboration: Strategic Restructuring for Nonprofit Organizations," available at http://www.lapiana.org/research/beyond.html.

Note: Available free online is A Board Member's Guide to Nonprofit Mergers by Alfredo Vergara-Lobo, Jan Masaoka, and Sabrina Smith, at www.blueavocado.org.

Also Try

Thinking about Closing Down, p. 118

The Right Way to Go Out of Business, p. 120

Strategic Plans, p. 102

Thinking about Closing Down

It's very hard to break the ice on a board and open a discussion about closing down. The nonprofit board of directors is responsible for the organization's future—whether to grow, change, downsize, merge, evolve, or close. And although nonprofit board members don't have personal financial stakes in the organization, they have invested their time, their energy, their financial contributions, and their hearts. At the same time, few nonprofits are destined to thrive for centuries . . . there may be a time for closing and for turning to new ventures.

For many nonprofit boards, this is the unthinkable: closing down or going out of business. There may be a crisis, or serious warning signs, or simply a lack of energy in the organization. In other cases, conditions may have changed and the organization is no longer viable, at least in its current form. Whatever the long-term causes may be, a board may find itself wondering whether to go out of business, what the implications will be, whether the organization can still be saved, whether the organization should choose bankruptcy or dissolution, and how to go about closing down.

In most cases the board finds itself facing an obvious crossroads. Perhaps the organization has lost all its funding or a substantial funding source; perhaps key staff have departed; or perhaps the organization has lost a valuable facility or donated service. Other indicators may be a sudden awareness of significant debt or unpaid payroll, a scandal or seriously damaged reputation, or a serious legal challenge.

By the time the board arrives at this crossroads, there's usually a history of less-than-successful efforts to turn things around. For example, in the previous year the organization may have laid off staff, cut costs, or undertaken a new fundraising drive. As a result, board members often enter the discussion tired or resentful. It's not easy for such a board to find the strength to consider all the strategic options objectively, to pursue possible mergers, or to manage a bankruptcy process well.

One important step is for the board to describe, or "declare," the situation a crisis or emergency, or at least an "urgent and unusual situation." Such a declaration helps board and staff members to feel that it is appropriate to hold extra or unusual meetings, to take unusual measures to cut costs, and to ask for financial or political help. Declaring a crisis also gives the board a chance to see if there are supporters who step forward to help. Perhaps most important, declaring a special situation gives people permission to talk more openly about problems facing the organization and to think more creatively about what options exist.

Some organizations create a special options task force of a few board members or a board-staff team that is charged with developing strategic options. The task force can talk with key creditors, key funders, allied organizations, and staff. The task force may consider these strategies among others:

1. *Buy time to consider options at a more deliberate pace.* Examples: A job training program may be able to obtain a delay on loan payments or ask a government funder to renegotiate contracts to allow the organization to keep funds although services have not been delivered. In a few cases a donor may be willing to make an "emergency grant" to keep operations going while the board investigates its choices.

2. *Restructure services and operations in a way that will permit long-term viability.* Examples: An under-enrolled child care center may be able to combine classes, reduce staff, and eliminate part-time care options in order to operate on a break-even basis. A membership organization may dramatically reduce member services and refocus attention on advocacy, anticipating lower membership income but lower costs as well. A homeless shelter may spin off a money-losing job training program to an employment organization that can run it more cost-effectively. A nonprofit art gallery may close the gallery but set up

arrangements with two coffeehouses that will provide free exhibit space.

3. *Find a merger or acquisition partner who will take over services, staff, location, and other matters.* Example: An after-school tutoring organization might become a program or department of a nearby community center or church.

4. *Close down.* Example: A neighborhood newspaper may find it is simply running out of steam. The board decides to cease publication and gives the copyrights and name rights to a neighborhood association.

Whatever choices are made, the board will need to find ways to involve the staff, funders, clients, patrons, and others appropriately in the decision making. Clear communication is also crucial to ensuring that the decisions—whatever they are—can be implemented successfully.

A good resource on cutback strategies is *Coping with Cutbacks: The Nonprofit Guide to Success When Times Are Tight*, by Emil Angelica and Vincent Hyman. Available at http://www.fieldstonealliance.org/. A free list of cutback strategies can be found online at www.FieldstoneAlliance.org

Also Try

The Right Way to Go Out of Business, p. 120

Why Do Nonprofits Have Boards? p. 18

The Right Way to Go Out of Business

The article "Thinking about Closing Down" talks about how a nonprofit board facing a crisis can think through its options—whether to restructure services, seek a merger partner, close down, and so forth. This article looks at just one of those options: going out of business and the dissolution (dissolving) of the nonprofit.

When a nonprofit board has to shut down, or "dissolve," the organization, it often finds itself swimming in a sea of unpaid bills, demanding creditors, frustrated and anxious staff, and desperate clients. Going broke, like other things in life, can be done poorly or well. Managing insolvency well can mean that client or patron services are not disrupted, that staff are given assistance in their job transitions, or that creditors can receive some satisfaction. Here are some steps for boards considering dissolution.

Going broke, like other things in life, can be done poorly or well.

1. *Identify your legal and contractual obligations.* Consult a lawyer to help you plan and implement the dissolution; there may be a lawyer willing to help on a free, or pro bono, basis. Are there government contracts that must be fulfilled? Are building or equipment leases in place? Do you have any restricted money or assets that must be returned to the funder rather than liquidated to pay creditors? Are there any pending lawsuits? In particular, are there any unpaid taxes, such as payroll or sales taxes, which may pose personal liability for board members or staff? Notify and negotiate any outstanding contract, payment, or restricted fund obligations. You may not leave everyone happy, but at least you will leave with a reputation for doing the best you can to meet obligations.

2. *Be frank and direct with the staff about the organization's future.* Enlist their help in the closure. If you have planned ahead, you should be able to pay staff through the closedown.

3. *Identify clients who will be hurt by the closure and explore ways to minimize the disruption to them.* For example, there may be nearby child care centers that can take a few additional children, or a local disabilities agency may be able to take over administration of the support groups operated by your program. There may also be a community foundation or other donor who could donate funds to ensure that client transitions, if necessary, are as smooth as possible.

Also Try

Should Your Nonprofit Be Considering a Merger? p. 117

Strategic Plans, p. 102

Thinking about Closing Down, p. 118

4. *Review the organization's own rules for dissolution as stated in the bylaws and articles of incorporation.* For example, some bylaws may require a two-thirds vote of the board, or a vote of the membership, for dissolution. Take care to hold the appropriate meetings and votes and to record the actions taken. Choose one person who will store the documents for a few years in case there are questions. Certain nonprofits, such as those in the health or counseling fields, may have a legal obligation to maintain client records; if you are in this situation, determine another organization to take on this responsibility for you.

5. *Check your state laws. State laws vary on the steps required for nonprofit dissolutions.* In some cases a petition must be filed with a court, which then appoints a trustee to oversee the distribution of any remaining assets. Ask an attorney for help or contact your state attorney general for information. If the nonprofit has significant assets, such as real estate, it may be necessary to go through a formal bankruptcy process.

6. *If you are able to pay off all debts, make a list of any remaining assets and decide on other nonprofits to receive them.* Government regulations require that nonprofit assets be given to other nonprofits, not be distributed among board or staff. In addition to cash or receivables, assets may include copy-rights, historical photos, and the organization's name and Internet domain name. As examples, a nonprofit may donate its equipment to a nonprofit halfway house, give its publications inventory to a nonprofit bookstore, and give its domain name to an allied organization.

7. *Be proactive about publicity. If an established charity has failed, journalists may be looking for a scandal story.* Write up some key points about the organization's successes, its reasons for closing, and the steps taken on behalf of clients. Choose one or two people who will speak for the organization to the press.

8. *If you can, find a way to celebrate the organization's successes and legacy.* Staff and board might invite former staff, board, and volunteers to a closing dinner at someone's home. An open letter to the public might be sent to a local newspaper. A community has been created around the nonprofit, and it is appropriate and fitting for that community to draw together to mark its transition.

Thanks very much to attorney and Board Café *reader Michael Schley of Santa Barbara, California, for his pro bono assistance on this article.*

From a reader

Facing the demise of a nonprofit is a difficult prospect. Based on my own experience, I would add that because of the psychic investment in one's organization, there is an emotional component. People go through a grieving process, starting with denial, moving through anger and blame, and reaching acceptance and closure. It is particularly important to be aware of the hazards of the blaming stage, because relationships can be needlessly damaged and blame can keep people from being creative in response to the crisis.

—J.K., Menlo Park, California

CHAPTER FIVE

The Board Manages Its Own Affairs

In addition to providing the appropriate mix of governance and support to its organization, a board of directors must be capable of managing its own affairs. The board must understand the technical issues underpinning its authority and responsibilities and learn to manage the rhythm of its work as a board. "Board affairs" covers a wide range of issues, and not all of them are discussed here. This chapter includes the following articles on board management:

The Board's Sense of Self
Bodybuilding for Boards

Perhaps the single most important attribute of an effective board is also its most intangible: an independent sense of itself. This sense of self is the board's identity as a body rather than, for instance, as a loose collection of individuals who each finds ways to support the organization.

As individuals, board members act as supporters of the organization and often see themselves as supporters of the executive director as well. They speak to the community on the organization's behalf: asking for donations, volunteer time, and support. In contrast, when acting as a *body*, the board speaks to the organization on behalf of its constituency. And while individual board members are cheerleaders, the board as a whole is the sharp-eyed team owner looking at both the season record and the bottom line and evaluating the head coach.

Here are five easy ways to strengthen the board's sense of self:

1. *Hold regular executive sessions.* Some boards automatically put executive sessions on, for instance, four meeting agendas per year. Discussions without any staff present allow board members to float ideas and tentative concerns. Making the sessions a standard quarterly event keeps executive directors informed about activities and developments.

2. *Have an annual social event for board members only—no staff, no executive director.* A take-out dinner at a board member's home, drinks after a board meeting, or other nonrequired social events go a long way toward helping board members see themselves as an entity outside the boardroom.

3. *Schedule Board Member Briefings: 7 x 7.* Individual board members are seldom given a chance to shine except as helpers. No wonder it's hard to recognize how Joe's and Carla's professional knowledge and personal backgrounds can inform strategy and drive accountability to the community, when we know only about Joe's fundraising work or Carla's committee work. Try having a board member briefing at every meeting:

The board chair (or the Governance Committee if you have one) can schedule a seven-minute briefing at each meeting by a board member followed by seven minutes of questions

From *Best of the Board Café* (a column in the online magazine *Blue Avocado*), Copyright © 2003 and 2009, CompassPoint Nonprofit Services, published by Fieldstone Alliance, www.FieldstoneAlliance.org. Subscribe free to *Blue Avocado* at www.blueavocado.org.

and answers (total time not to exceed fifteen minutes). Be strict about time! Examples:

- A person in marketing for a bank can present on two marketing concepts board members should understand.

- A former or current client can relate her personal experience as a client.

- A pharmaceuticals vice president can explain to her AIDS board what are the drivers in AIDS drugs development.

- A social worker can talk about the different schools of thought in child development to her board of a learning center.

4. *Annually conduct an evaluation of the executive director.* One venture capitalist we know says about the for-profit boards she sits on: "The main question in my mind at every meeting is simply: Should we fire the CEO or not?" In contrast, a frequent complaint of nonprofit executives is that *they* have to prod the board into completing an evaluation. Whatever the method, just be sure you do it.

5. *As executive director, step back at board meetings and do not dominate discussions.* If you are the board chair, work with your executive to put reports in writing and to take staff reports off the agenda unless there is a decision to be made at the meeting related to the report. If you are a board member, send this article to your executive and board chair and have a brief chat before or after the next meeting. If you are the executive: Be quiet more often! Restrain your instinctive reaction to explain everything every time and instead try seeing your job as "leading the board to lead."

In short: Don't just be a bunch of really great board members. Be a board that sees itself as more than just 1 + 1 + ... When a board has a sense of itself as a body, it will take the time to be sure that it has the information and relationships to act as a body and be more prepared for holding the organization accountable to its constituencies.

Special thanks to Board Café *Editorial Committee member Mike Allison for his thinking on this subject.*

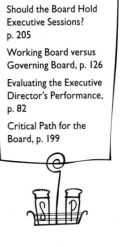

Also Try

Should the Board Hold Executive Sessions? p. 205

Working Board versus Governing Board, p. 126

Evaluating the Executive Director's Performance, p. 82

Critical Path for the Board, p. 199

Working Board versus Governing Board?

Have you ever heard a comment like one of the following?

Said with pride: "We're a working board!"

Said slightly abashed: "We're just a working board...not a board board."

Said with a tinge of regret: "We've been a working board, but we have to become a fundraising board."

Is the opposite of a *working board* a *nonworking board*? And is it true that governing boards don't "work"? Actually, these comments reflect a confusion between what the board does and what board members do.

What's usually meant by a *working board* is one where board members actively do the organization's work—whether it's taking homebound seniors on outings, staffing a fundraising booth at a fair, or keeping the organization's books. In other words, board members participate in program work, fundraising work, and administrative work.

When a board starts to talk about becoming less of a working board and more of a governing board, what it probably means is that the organization needs the board to change its focus of work

- From doing administrative work to oversight of finance and administration
- From doing program work to overseeing program work
- From doing fundraising to...doing fundraising and overseeing fundraising

But there's a difference between what the board does when acting as a body and what board members do when acting as individuals. For example, the board as a whole—not just the board chair—hires the executive director. On the other hand, individual board members can offer mentoring to the executive director, but they do so as individuals, not as a body. And although we say things such as, "Our board raises money," what we really mean is that "board members raise money."

For organizations with staff, the board will partner with the executive director in different ways: as a governing body and as a group of individual volunteers. And over time, the work of the board and of board members will change to reflect what the organization needs at that time.

Instead of thinking that board members will do less, discuss how staff and volunteers (including board members) will work together to do program work. Instead of thinking that the board is turning over decisionmaking to the executive director, discuss how the executive and the board chair will work together to decide what decisions can be made by staff and which need to come to the board. Hopefully, the board will combine the strategy and oversight work of the board (as a body) with the talents of board members (as individuals). Examples:

- The board reviews program plans (developed by staff) and achievements (of the programs), while individual board members volunteer as legal advocates, meal deliverers, and tree planters.

- The board makes sure the budget for income is realistic and individual board members raise money through raffles or by talking to county officials.

- The board makes sure that there is adequate insurance for the organization, while an individual board member (who knows about insurance) helps the staff choose a broker.

In short, the work that the board does as a body is different from the work that board members do as individuals. Both need to be done. So how about this phrase instead: "We're a working board. And part of that work is governance."

Also Try

The CompassPoint Board Model for Governance and Support, p. 20

Governance and Board Development Committees, p. 181

A Board-Staff Contract for Financial Accountability, p. 220

From *Best of the Board Café* (a column in the online magazine *Blue Avocado*), Copyright © 2003 and 2009, CompassPoint Nonprofit Services, published by Fieldstone Alliance, www.FieldstoneAlliance.org. Subscribe free to *Blue Avocado* at www.blueavocado.org.

Performance Review for the Board

We evaluate—or try to evaluate—how well individuals, groups, and organizations perform. So it only makes sense to evaluate how well the board of directors has performed. Yet few boards undertake such evaluations on a regular basis, and among those that do, the process typically focuses on the wrong things.

Why are regular board evaluations relatively rare? Well, they often just don't feel necessary. Board members often feel that "we're doing a good job but not a great job" and suspect that they won't find out much different from an evaluation. And they're often right. It takes leadership and drive to get a board to conduct an evaluation. And some boards just aren't sure how to go about it.

Typical board self-assessment tools use a survey of board members and ask questions such as "How satisfied are you that the board has adopted adequate human resource policies?" and "How would you rate the board's financial oversight?" A significant advantage of such tools is that they are easy: boilerplates can be found on the web and they take only a few minutes to complete. But they suffer from being internal self-assessments only and often result in driving attention to process

and documentation rather than organizational impact. One can easily imagine the board of Lehman Brothers or a high-profile nonprofit sincerely giving itself high marks right before its downfall.

But the deeper reason for neglect of board evaluation is probably lack of clarity about what the board is supposed to do. We typically have opinions about what board *members* as individuals should be doing. They should be coming to more meetings, raising more money, or following through on things they said they would do. But we're less clear about what the *board as a body* should do.

We propose a different approach to board evaluation—one that combines the strengths of the board survey with a stronger focus on the performance of the organization and that brings in comments from the executive as well. Once the board and the executive have completed their forms, a conversation comparing and discussing them should happen first in a small group (such as the board president, the chair of the Governance Committee, and the executive director) and then a discussion by the full board should follow.

Also Try

A 360-Degree Look, p. 112

The Board's Composition and Profile, p. 144

Governance and Board Development Committees, p. 181

Nonprofit Dashboard: An Essential Tool for Boards, p. 106

From *Best of the Board Café* (a column in the online magazine *Blue Avocado*), Copyright © 2003 and 2009, CompassPoint Nonprofit Services, published by Fieldstone Alliance, www.FieldstoneAlliance.org. Subscribe free to *Blue Avocado* at www.blueavocado.org.

Board Survey

Section 1: On a scale of 1–5, with 1 being "Very unhappy" and 5 being "Very happy," how do you assess

1. The organization's overall performance over the last year?	1	2	3	4	5
2. The organization's impact on its targeted community and on behalf of its targeted community?	1	2	3	4	5
3. The organization's management performance over the last year?	1	2	3	4	5
4. The organization's financial performance over the last year?	1	2	3	4	5
5. The organization's CEO's or executive director's performance over the last year?	1	2	3	4	5
6. The board and its members' impact on organizational overall performance?	1	2	3	4	5
7. The board and its members' impact on quality and reach of programming?	1	2	3	4	5
8. The board and its members' impact on management effectiveness?	1	2	3	4	5
9. The board and its members' impact on the organization's meeting revenue goals for earned income such as fees and contracts?	1	2	3	4	5
10. The board and its members' impact on meeting organizational revenue goals for donations, grants, and other types of contributed income?	1	2	3	4	5

Section 2: Critical path for the organization and the board (these are open-ended questions)

11. What were the two most important things for the organization to have accomplished this last year? Were they accomplished? To what degree did the board contribute to success or failure?

12. If there were two things you would change about the board, what would they be?

13. If there were two things—anything at all—that you would change about the organization, what would they be?

14. What makes you the most proud of this board?

Board Survey (continued)

Section 3: Priority areas for improvement

There are always dozens of things that can be improved. What's harder is choosing which areas are priorities.

15. Which of the following areas do you think the board should improve this coming year?

- ❑ Attention to financial oversight
- ❑ Attention to changes in the environment or community and what organizational responses will be necessary or appropriate
- ❑ Board meetings
- ❑ Board–executive director relationship
- ❑ Board member recruitment
- ❑ Holding individual board members responsible for follow-through
- ❑ Committee performance, be specific:
- ❑ Which committees we have or don't have, be specific:
- ❑ The board chair's leadership

Section 4: A questionnaire to be completed by the executive
On a scale of 1–5, with 5 being the best, how do you assess

16. The organization's overall performance over the last year?	1 2 3 4 5
17. The organization's impact on its targeted community and on behalf of its targeted community?	1 2 3 4 5
18. The organization's management performance over the last year?	1 2 3 4 5
19. The organization's financial performance over the last year?	1 2 3 4 5
20. The board and its members' impact on quality and reach of programming?	1 2 3 4 5
21. The board and its members' impact on management effectiveness?	1 2 3 4 5
22. The board and its members' impact on the organization's meeting revenue goals for earned income such as fees and contracts?	1 2 3 4 5
23. The board and its members' impact on the organization's meeting its revenue goals for donations, grants, and other types of contributed income?	1 2 3 4 5

24. What were the two most important things for the organization to have accomplished this last year? Were they accomplished? To what degree did the board contribute to success or failure?

25. If there were two things you would change about the board, what would they be?

26. If there were two things—anything at all—that you would change about the organization, what would they be?

Conflict of Interest

At some point, most boards become concerned about a conflict of interest between the interests of the organization and the interests of an individual board member. For example, if your organization is hiring a new bookkeeper and the board president suggests hiring his sister, questions may arise as to whether this is appropriate. On one hand, the board president's sister is an experienced bookkeeper who, because of her personal connection to the organization, will be particularly committed to the work. On the other hand, the executive director may be reluctant to supervise the board president's sister. Still another worry may be that collusion between the board president and his sister might result in embezzlement.

Cyril Houle, in *Governing Boards*,* defines three types of conflict of interest: potential conflict of interest, actual conflict of interest, and self-dealing. The example above is a *potential conflict of interest*. The relationship between the board president and the bookkeeper creates a situation where a conflict *might arise* between the interests of the organization and the personal interests of the board president.

A second type is *actual conflict of interest*. If the bookkeeper is hired, and at a later time the executive director wants to eliminate the position of bookkeeper, an actual conflict of interest exists if the board president must take a stand as to whether or not the position should be retained.

A third type is *self-dealing*, or self-interested decisions, when a board member advocates a decision that results in *personal* advantage to himself or herself or to a family member.

To these three, a fourth might be added: *competitive conflict of interest*. In this instance, there is concern that a board member may use knowledge not for personal advantage but for the advantage of a competing company or nonprofit. For example, suppose an individual is on the boards of two nonprofits, one a scouting organization and the other a boys and girls club. The boys and girls club has just discovered a little-known government grant opportunity and is preparing a proposal to bring to that government agency. If the scouting organization were to hear about this opportunity, it likely would want to apply as well. At the next meeting of the scouting organization, when the question comes up of seeking new government funding, should this board member say something, or keep quiet?

Relationships that board members have are a part of the contributions they bring to the table. That is what makes all these types of conflict of interest so difficult. If the organization is buying a computer, for example, and a board member owns a computer store, the organization may well benefit from discounts and extra service by buying the computer at that store. It would be a mistake to rule out working with board members as vendors. Similarly, having board members of a preschool who also are parents in the school can be tremendously helpful in ensuring that a parent perspective is brought into decision making. But, at the same time, board members who are parents may find themselves in a difficult position if the preschool is considering eliminating a service that is used by very few parents other than themselves.

In the area of competitive conflict of interest, having board members on multiple boards can be an important way to forge connections between organizations. But while organizations may share similar goals, they still do compete for funding, talent, and connections. Such a situation can lead organizations to feel as if they are competing for the loyalty of a board member they have in common.

Three straightforward safeguards can go a long way toward preventing conflicts of interest. First, the organization can establish a policy related to conflict of interest that is signed by all board members at the time they join the board. The statement can be a simple declaration of expected behavior, or it can require detailed information about the board members' financial interests. (A simple version follows this article.)

Second, establish disclosure as a normal habit or practice. Board members should find it customary for someone to say, for example, "This next agenda item relates to joining a collaboration with other mental health agencies that receive county funds. Because I am on the staff of one of the agencies involved, I have a potential conflict of interest, and I am going to excuse myself from the room for this discussion." In another situation a board member might say, "I have started to date the clinic director and as a result feel that I must resign from the board. I would like to continue as a member of the Fundraising Committee, but not as a board member." Disclosures and excusal from voting should be recorded in the meeting's minutes.

Third, if major purchases are involved, competitive written bids should be obtained to ensure that prices and product are comparable if there will be a financial benefit to a board member.

Perhaps even more than written policies, board and staff leadership must establish by example and attitude an atmosphere of personal integrity. Some situations may need only a brief, informal comment to maintain that climate. In other situations a decision may be delayed because of the need to ensure that the decision has been made truly in the best interests of the organization. Each of us, by our words and actions every day, contributes toward a culture of integrity and responsibility.

---

* Cyril O. Houle, *Governing Boards: Their Nature and Nurture* (New York: John Wiley and Sons, 1997), 5.

Also Try

A Board Member Contract, p. 26

Performance Review for the Board, p. 128

Sarbanes-Oxley and Nonprofits, p. 31

Sample Conflict of Interest Policy

The standard of behavior at the Willow Organization* is that all staff, volunteers, and board members *scrupulously* avoid any conflict of interest between the interests of the Willow Organization on one hand, and personal, professional, and business interests on the other. This includes avoiding actual conflicts of interest as well as perceptions of conflicts of interest.

I understand that the purposes of this policy are to protect the integrity of the Willow Organization's decision-making process, to enable our constituencies to have confidence in our integrity, and to protect the integrity and reputation of volunteers, staff, and board members.

Upon or before election, hiring, or appointment, I will make a full written disclosure of interests, relationships, and holdings that could potentially result in a conflict of interest. This written disclosure will be kept on file and I will update it as appropriate.

In the course of meetings or activities, I will disclose any interests in a transaction or decision where I (including my business or other nonprofit affiliation), my family or my significant other, employer, or close associates will receive a benefit or gain. After disclosure, I understand that I will be asked to leave the room for the discussion and will not be permitted to vote on the question.

I understand that this policy is meant to be a supplement to good judgment, and I will respect its spirit as well as its wording.

Signed_____   Date_____

---

*This is a fictitious name for an organization and, like other fictitious groups in this book, is named after a tree.

Orientation and Integration of New Board Members

In the movies, it looks pretty easy for the hero to jump onto a moving train. Joining a nonprofit board as a new member feels a good deal harder.

When new on a board, it's easy not to say much, but instead to listen and observe. Later on, it can be easy to *stay* quiet, because by then it's embarrassing not to know more about what everyone's talking about. In contrast, some board members err in the opposite direction; they don't take a moment to listen or observe, and instead jump in giving forceful advice when they really don't have the basis for such opinions.

Joining a board and *fully joining* as an active, contributing member of the team are quite different.

Imagine being on a basketball or baseball team and having a new member join the team. What are ways to educate and integrate that individual?

One way is a formal orientation: a sit-down discussion that goes over the official matters. Many boards hold special sessions with new board members, where they are introduced to the history of the organization, given a tour of facilities, briefed on current board issues and discussions, made acquainted with how the board works, and introduced to key staff and board members. This is a good time to go over the responsibilities of board members and the board member contract (and give them this book and a subscription to the *Blue Avocado*!).

A good addition to such orientations is a discussion that confirms or solidifies the contributions individual members will make over the next year in their supporting role to the organization. For example, one board member might agree to develop a marketing plan with one of the staff, while another might agree to help on the silent auction in anticipation of chairing it the following year. A board member might make a short list of individuals to introduce to the executive director or development director, or analyze web sites of ten similar organizations and make recommendations on how to improve the organization's site. Creating this kind of work plan for each board member will clarify for all sides what is expected and also help to bring new members immediately into activities.

In addition to a formal orientation, many new board members appreciate having a "buddy," a longer-time board member who is one of those "in the know." The buddy can explain otherwise mystifying events, such as why Board Member A's volunteering to approach a major donor was ignored (he often overstates his connection to prominent people), why no one said anything about the fact that the audit is six months late (the board officers are quietly investigating whether there is serious mismanagement at the top of the organization), or why Board Member B got so much praise for doing something that seemed very small (she's been criticized in the past for not following through and this was a big improvement). The new member can test suggestions on the buddy without having to take the bolder step of making the suggestion to the whole board.

The buddy can also discover what the new member would like to experience or do while on the board. One new board member might want to learn more about child development, while a second might want to get to know the executive director, and a third might want to connect more with the Salvadoran community. The new board member may have specific concerns. For example, a younger woman may be ignored by older men on the board, or a sole Asian on the board may be expected to speak for all Asian communities. The buddy can suggest ways for the board experience to encompass these objectives and can raise concerns to other board members in effective ways.

Although it's a good idea to involve staff (such as the executive director and staff responsible for fundraising and other major programs) in board orientation, it's valuable to have board members lead the orientation.

Whatever formal and informal orientation is given to new board members, the objective is to involve them quickly and effectively. If board members have been on for several months but don't seem to be integrating into the board, there are probably reasons that should be addressed. Having had an orientation will make these situations less common and can also provide a good basis for following up with inactive board members at a later time.

Also Try

A Board Member Contract, p. 26

Why Do Nonprofits Have Boards? p. 18

Alligators in the Boardroom, p. 11

The CompassPoint Board Model for Governance and Support, p. 20

Table of Contents for a Board Binder, p. 36

What to Do with Board Members Who Don't Do Anything

"He never comes to meetings or does anything. Why does he even stay on the board?"
"She always says she'll take care of it and then she doesn't follow through. Aaagh!"

Whose responsibility is it to "do something" about a board member who is AWOL, deadwood, undependable, a procrastinator, or worse? Answer: Yours. Every board member shares in the responsibility to involve each board member in contributing to the well-being of the board and the organization. If you're the board president or an officer, your responsibilities include monitoring nonparticipation and intervening with board members when necessary. In some cases you may need to talk with the executive director about improving the way he or she works with board members. If you're the executive director, you may need to discuss the situation with board leadership.

You *must* do two things in the case of a board member who is not participating. First, you must do *something*. The problem is likely only to get worse, and nonparticipating board members have a demoralizing impact on even the best of boards. Second, *be confident and hopeful*.

Many board members just need a little reminder to be more conscientious, and others will be grateful that you've given them a graceful way to relinquish tasks or even leave the board. Things will work out.

Short-term strategies

- Check to be sure that expectations were made clear to the board member before he or she joined the board. "I know you joined the board recently and I'm not sure that you realize that we ask all board members to attend the annual dinner and, hopefully, to help sell tickets. Let me explain to you what most board members do, so you can see whether you'll be able to work on this with us."

- Hold a board discussion at which expectations are reconsidered and reaffirmed. Agree on a list of expectations for *every* board member.

- Be sensitive to possible health issues or personal reasons why a good board member isn't participating as much as he or she has in the past.

- Transfer responsibilities to someone else. "I'm concerned about finishing the revision of the personnel policies. Since you're so busy, maybe it would work out for the best if John took your notes on the policies and developed a first draft."

- Together with the board member, explore whether he or she really has the time right now to be an active board member. "I'm calling to check in with you since you haven't been able to make a meeting in the last several months. Are you just temporarily a lot busier than usual? We really want to have your participation, but if it isn't realistic, perhaps we should see if there's a less time-consuming way than board membership for you to be involved."

Longer-term strategies

- Make it possible for individuals to take a leave of absence from the board if they have health, work, or other reasons why they cannot participate fully for a while. An individual can, for example, take a six-month maternity leave or a disability leave.

- Have a board discussion or conduct a written board survey on what makes it difficult for people to participate fully. "Are there things we can change about the frequency, day, time, or length of board meetings that would make it easier for you to attend?" "Are there things about the way that board meetings are conducted that would make it easier for you to attend or that would give you more reason to want to attend?"

- Consider whether board participation is meaningful to board members. Have lunch with semi-active members or the executive director: "I'm sensing that board participation just isn't as substantive or significant as some board members want it to be. What do you think are the reasons, and what do you think we can do to make board membership more meaningful?"

- Revise what is expected of board members. Perhaps responsibilities have been given to a board member that are unrealistic for any but the super-board-member. Reduce the number of committees and utilize short-term task forces instead. Redesign jobs and responsibilities to fit the ability of a busy achiever to accomplish them.

> **Make it possible for board members to take a leave of absence from the board if they have health, work, or other reasons why they cannot participate fully for a while.**

Also Try

Removing a Difficult Board Member, p. 138

The Board's Composition and Profile, p. 144

Performance Review for the Board, p. 128

A Board Member Contract, p. 26

Removing a Difficult Board Member

Perhaps the most common reason for wanting to remove a board member is nonattendance or inactivity. But occasionally, a board member needs to be removed because he or she is preventing the board from doing its work. In some cases, an ongoing conflict of interest or unethical behavior may be grounds to remove an individual from the board. In other cases, the behavior of a board member may become so obstructive that the board is prevented from functioning effectively. More frequently, a problem board member discourages others from participating, and the board may find that members attend less frequently or find reasons to resign.

Strongly felt disagreements and passionate arguments are often elements of the most effective boards (and genuine debate). Arguing for an unpopular viewpoint is *not* grounds for board dismissal. But if a board member *consistently* disrupts meetings, is unwilling to let the majority prevail, or prevents the organization from working well, it may be appropriate to consider removing the individual from the board.

Although board member removal is rare, organizations should provide for such removal in their bylaws. The following three strategies can be used to remove troublesome board members:

1. *Term Limits*: Many boards establish not only board terms but also term limits, such as two-year terms with a limit of three consecutive terms. In such a situation, a board member cannot serve more than six consecutive years without a "break" from the board. After a year off the board, an individual can once again be elected to the board. Proponents of term limits feel that such limits provide a nonconfrontational way to ease ineffective board members off the board, and point out that terrific board members can be invited back onto the board after one year. Proponents also feel that having a constant infusion of fresh thinking acts as a preventive measure for problem board members. Opponents of term limits believe that, with proper board leadership, errant board members can be guided toward either improving their behavior or quietly resigning from the board.

2. *Personal Intervention:* One-to-one intervention by the board president or other board leadership is a less formal solution to managing difficult board members. If a board member has failed to fulfill his or her responsibilities, many

Also Try

What to Do with Board Members Who Don't Do Anything, p. 136

What to Do When You Really, Really Disagree with a Board Decision, p. 110

Key Documents, p. 28

From *Best of the Board Café* (a column in the online magazine *Blue Avocado*), Copyright © 2003 and 2009, CompassPoint Nonprofit Services, published by Fieldstone Alliance, www.FieldstoneAlliance.org. Subscribe free to *Blue Avocado* at www.blueavocado.org.

board presidents take the opportunity to meet informally with the board member in question. In person or on the telephone, the board president can discuss the matter with the person and suggest that resignation may be appropriate (sometimes problem board members are relieved to have this as an option).

3. *Impeachment:* Organizational bylaws should describe a process by which a board member can be removed by vote, if necessary. For example, in some organizations a board member can be removed by a two-thirds vote of the board at a regularly scheduled board meeting.

What do you wish someone had told you?

When board members are asked how they learned to be effective board members, they usually scratch their heads and say something like "I went to board meetings and watched how people did things." Here's a better idea from a California environmental justice organization. First, the organization asked each board member to answer the question, "What do you wish you had known when you first became a board member—things that you were never told, but would have made a difference in your understanding of this board's work?" The organization then compiled the answers into a *Welcome to Our Board* sheet for new board members.

Ban on board e-mail

Has your board experienced lots of harsh words being passed around to board and staff members by e-mail? One all-volunteer organization erupted into conflict as board members accused one another of inappropriate practices. The board president acted decisively: he declared a three-week ban on e-mail. He told all board members not to send e-mail, or to read any they received. By preventing hastily written, angry messages, and by forcing board members to talk on the phone instead, this action calmed the situation and, at the next meeting, people were ready to try working together again. It's just too easy for impulsive, negative e-mail messages to get passed along and passed along.

Should We Have a Board Retreat?

A retreat is a special meeting of the board that allows time to step back from the day-to-day operations of the organization and to examine questions in a more open-ended way than is usually possible at a regular board meeting.

Some boards schedule an all-Saturday retreat each year, during which they review the accomplishments of the previous year and establish plans and priorities for the coming year. Sometimes a board will schedule a half-day retreat to discuss one topic in detail. For example, a board might have a special session that begins with a presentation on managed healthcare, and then discusses strategic questions around the organization's possible transition to a managed care system. In another example, a board may have one evening meeting during which it doesn't conduct regular business, but clarifies its own role and responsibilities in the organization.

Because board members and staff members often have little contact with one another, some organizations also choose to have retreats that bring both together for social as well as work time. Working directly with the board on a special topic or in planning work helps staff to understand the board's priorities and concerns. Board members often find that contact with the staff makes them more aware of the day-to-day challenges and more connected with the organization's real-life activities and impact on the community.

Following is one example of what a retreat agenda might look like for a board-staff retreat focused on annual planning.

Also Try
Strategic Plans, p. 102

Sample Agenda for a Board-Staff Retreat on Annual Planning

This organization has determined that a retreat is needed to look at planning for the upcoming year, and that both staff and board should participate in the discussion. As a result, the organization planned for both staff and board members to meet in the morning and have lunch together, and for the board to meet by itself at the conclusion of the day.

Saturday
9:00 a.m.– 4:30 p.m.

Part I: Program and Administrative Priorities

Participants: entire board, executive director, and program managers

	Time Frame
Introductions, review objectives for the meeting, review agenda	9:00–9:20 a.m.
"State of the Nonprofit Technology Field and Our Organization" report by executive director and "State of the Board" report by board chair	9:20–9:40
Setting program and organizational priorities	
• Identify programmatic and organizational strengths and weaknesses; identify opportunities and threats: political, economic, social, technological, demographic, and legal trends impacting the organization	9:40–10:15
• Review of previous program and administrative strategies and priorities	10:15–10:30
Break	10:30–10:45
• Identify key issues; either discuss one or two issues or develop a plan as to how and when to address them	10:45–Noon
Lunch	Noon–1:15 p.m.
• Propose future program and administrative strategies and, if possible, agree on them	1:15–2:30
Break	2:30–2:45

Part II: Board Priorities

Participants: board members only

	Time Frame
Review of board and committee accomplishments: strengths and weaknesses in achieving objectives, how the board has worked together, and the board–executive director working relationship	2:45–4:00
Board and committee priorities and commitments for the upcoming year. Review of next steps, by when, and who responsible	4:00–4:15
Evaluation of retreat (what worked; recommended changes for next year)	4:15–4:30

CHAPTER SIX

Composition and Recruiting

Who Is on the Board and How Did They Get There?

Despite the common responsibilities of boards, there are also broad choices of structure that each board must decide for itself. It must decide what mix of people is needed, what officers and committees to have, how often to meet, and how to divide responsibilities and tasks. The following articles can help with these decisions:

The Board's Composition and Profile

Like baseball, nonprofit boards are a team sport. Just as a baseball team will evaluate its strengths and weaknesses, and then go out and recruit a good catcher or an outfielder or both, boards of directors must first assess their composition to determine which new players they should bring onto the team.

There are some characteristics that each and every board member should possess, and other characteristics that only one or two members need possess if the organization is to have a well-rounded team. For example, *every* baseball player must be able to run the bases and get to practice on time, while only one or two players must be able to pitch. The point is to select team characteristics best suited to the job, rather than attempting to reach some generic ideal. Let's look at the mix of characteristics.

Every board member must have

- A commitment to the work of the organization and to the people served, with the understanding that this is a commitment of energy to the mundane as well as to the glorious.

- A willingness to represent the organization to the public and to speak in support of the organization.

- An ability and a commitment to participate in meetings, events, and other board-related activities.

- Common sense and the ability to exercise good judgment.

The following characteristics must be present on the board as a team, but each characteristic may be possessed by only one or two people.

Representation of specific constituencies and points of view: Board members may be recruited to ensure that specific constituencies and their viewpoints are represented on the governing body of the organization. For example, an organization serving two cities may decide it's important to have some people from each city on the board. Another organization begun in a Methodist church may find it important to include board members from both the neighborhood Catholic church and the local mosque.

Skills for the priority work of the board in the near future: Rather than assume that "of course we need a CPA," for example, look at what the board will be doing in the next couple of years. If the organization will be building a new shelter on its current parking lot, board members with real estate and construction skills will be important.

Standing and reputation in the relevant communities: Based, for example, on the revenue strategy, it may be important to have professors or researchers who are respected by foundations, business leaders who are respected by prospective corporate sponsors, and so forth.

Race and ethnic background: Many organizations choose to have boards that reflect the racial and ethnic backgrounds of their client populations. As a result, an organization serving a Latino neighborhood may have a board with all or nearly all Latino members. An organization serving a racially mixed population may choose to have at least one or two board members from each of the populations served. (Some government agencies may require that your board try to reflect the racial and ethnic populations you serve.)

Gender, religion, sexual orientation, age, disability, and other social-demographic characteristics: As communities are increasingly diverse in a broad range of demographic variables, many organizations find it important to be intentional—rather than accidental—about having a mix of backgrounds on the board. For some organizations, diversity has a mission-based reason, such as an Asian-serving organization that includes as board members people from Chinese, Filipino, Asian Indian, Vietnamese, and other Asian backgrounds. In other instances, diversity of gender and age, for example, are

important ways of bringing multiple, valued perceptions and connections. And in still other cases, organizations will choose to keep their boards relatively homogenous in line with their mission, such as a women's organization that has a board of all women.

Program-related diversity: Board members may be chosen to bring a range of perspectives related to the organization's programs. For example, in an organization of adult adoptees, birth parents, and adoptive parents, there is a commitment to having at least two board members from each "corner of the adoption triangle." One AIDS organization had a board that was composed entirely of people with AIDS or HIV-positive status. After much consideration the organization decided to add three members who were HIV-negative. A senior home requires that 50 percent of its board members be sixty years old or older, but also that 25 percent be forty-five years old or younger.

Disability: With nearly 20 percent of Americans having one or more physical disabilities, boards are making the organization—including its board—accessible to people with various disabilities. One way to keep this awareness present is to value the participation on the board of people with disabilities and those who speak out against discrimination against people with disabilities.

Also Try

Eleven Cool Ideas for Finding Hot New Board Members, p. 148

Questions to Ask Candidates for the Board, p. 159

The Diversity Issue, p. 151

Critical Path for the Board, p. 199

Young Voices in the Boardroom, p. 155

Diversity for Organizations Based in Minority Communities, p. 157

Uniquely special board members: Finally, sometimes an organization has the opportunity to have a very unusual individual join the board. Such an individual can bring enormous credibility or donations, but may not be able to participate as other board members do. If, for example, Tiger Woods or George Clooney were interested in joining the board but couldn't attend 75 percent of the meetings, would it be wise to turn him down? Instead, consider designating a very limited number of spots (one to three) for these board members with not-the-usual contributions to make.

A board composition matrix is a tool that allows a board first to identify the desired mix of constituencies, skills, and demographics and then to see what gaps exist. As shown in the example on page 147, the names of current board members are filled in on the left. Each characteristic the board member represents is indicated in the appropriate box. As prospective new board members are nominated, their names and characteristics can also be filled in to see what the overall impact on the board would be if they were added.

Sample Board Composition Matrix

Here's an example of how one board mapped out its needs:

Qualities We Seek

Name of current board member or potential board member	Constituency or affiliation					Skills/experience						Demographics and background								Can work on upcoming priority			
	Corporations	Government	Small business	Medical	Churches	Finance and accounting	Medical	Human resources	Legal	Nonprofit management	Marketing and PR	Male	Female	African American	Asian Pacific Islander	European and White	Hispanic and Latino	Native American	Disabled	Special events	Major gifts contacts	Foundation contacts	Planned giving exp.
Kathleen	X				X			X					X	X								X	
Carlos		X				X				X		X					X						
Renée			X	X				X				X					X						
Sylvia		X				X	X				X		X			X				X			
Ben	X								X			X				X				X	X		

Twleve Cool Ideas for Finding Hot New Board Members

A saying with much truth goes like this: For short-term success, hire a good executive director; for long-term success, recruit good board members.

The tasks of recruiting new board members are often those for which no one volunteers. One reason is that although new board members are often told they have been recruited for their "connections," it hasn't been made clear that an important use of these connections is in board member recruitment. A second and more subtle reason is that many people are reluctant to recruit board members from among people whom they perceive as being more important (by whatever standard) than themselves. The techniques below help overcome these barriers and others.

Create a one-meeting nominating committee to accelerate the process of attracting board members with increased clout and influence.

1. Form a "one-meeting nominating committee." Draw up a list of twenty well-connected people of the type you would want on the board, who you suspect wouldn't join, but who might know someone who would be a good board member. Call those twenty people and ask them to come to a one-time meeting over lunch. Tell them that at the lunch they'll be told more about the organization and what it's looking for in board members. At the end of lunch, they'll be asked simply for the name of one person they think would be a good board member. The day after the lunch, call up each of the nominees and begin by explaining who nominated them.

2. Take out a "Help Wanted—Volunteer Board Member" ad in your own newsletter, in the neighborhood newsletter, or in the alumni newsletter of a local college. Example: "HELP Cypress House…We're looking for a few talented and conscientious volunteer board members to help guide our child care, teen, and senior programs into the next century. If you can contribute one evening a month and have skills or contacts in accounting, publicity, or special-event fundraising, call Sister Mary Margaret at 555-1234 to find out more about whether this volunteer opportunity is right for you."

3. Ask the executive director or the volunteer coordinator if there are two or three hands-on volunteers who would make good board members. Hands-on volunteers—such as support group facilitators, practical life support volunteers, meal preparers, weekend

tree-planters, classroom aides, and others—bring both demonstrated commitment and an intimate knowledge of the organization's strengths and weaknesses. Volunteers, donors, and clients should be the first place you look. You don't have to "sell" the organization or its cause—they're on board already!

4. Pick four local organizations where you don't know anyone, but you wish you did (examples: Hispanic Chamber of Commerce, CPA Society, United Cerebral Palsy). (Tip: Your local Yahoo site, www.yahoo.com, is a good place to look for lists of organizations under "Community.") Ask each board officer to call one of the four local organizations and ask to have coffee with the board president or the executive director. Over coffee, suggest that your two organizations recommend to each other board members for limited terms as a way of establishing organizational links and strengthening ties among communities.

5. Read the local paper, especially the profiles of community leaders. When you see someone intriguing, send that person a note (in care of the newspaper if you can't find a business or home address) commenting on the article and asking if he or she would be interested in getting involved as a volunteer board member. Even if the person doesn't respond to the invitation to meet, you will have caught the favorable attention of an influential community member.

6. See if your community has a board recruitment program, perhaps run by the United Way, a volunteer center, or a technical assistance organization.

7. Tell government program officers and foundation grantmakers that you are trying to expand and strengthen your board, and you would greatly appreciate help from them. Ask each person for just one terrific suggestion.

8. Call a community association such as the Chamber of Commerce, the Rotary Club, the Gay/Lesbian Democratic Club, or the Council of Churches. Ask if you can make a presentation at an upcoming meeting about community needs and your organization's services. As part of your presentation, talk about how your organization is seeking dedicated board members with clout and wide community contacts.

9. Contact a friend or colleague who is affiliated with a local university. Ask them to help you identify two or three professors of public health or management, or an administrative dean who might be capable of and interested in serving as board members.

10. Call the head of a local corporate foundation or corporate giving department. Get an appointment and explain your organization's work and the kind of board members you are

Also Try

seeking. It's likely that the executive staff of the corporation are already on boards and would like to see their junior members join boards (for community goodwill and for leadership development). Bring a short "organizational résumé" and ask your contact to circulate it among possible candidates and their superiors.

11. Ask your supervisor at work for suggestions. If nothing else, he or she should be impressed with your community involvement.

12. Offer a modest "finder's fee" (such as a gift certificate to a local restaurant) to board and staff members who recruit individuals who end up being invited onto the board.

From a reader

Q: I'm embarrassed to ask anyone on the board I'm on, but we desperately need new board members, and the organization's in some trouble. Help! What should I do?

A: Use one of the Twelve Cool Ideas for Finding Hot New Board Members, but with this kicker: "I even feel guilty asking someone like you to join a board that's as weak and confused as this one. But this organization has a unique role to play in solving the problem of _____. What's really needed is a total overhaul of the board. Maybe I can't ask you to do that, but maybe I can ask you to be one of the members and help me work toward bigger changes. We meet every month for two hours on Tuesday morning. Could I ask you to consider being on that committee?"

The Diversity Issue

One thing we know about diversity: cookie-cutter solutions don't work, because the situations are so...well, diverse. Consider, as just a few examples, the following situations:

- A summer Shakespeare festival board, currently all white, would like to recruit people of color as one way of helping to expand festival audiences to include minority communities. Although everyone on the board likes the idea of a more demographically diverse board, several board members can't see why a minority community leader would be interested in raising money for this organization (which is the primary activity of the board). What practical steps can and should this organization take in board recruitment?

- A family service agency adds an AIDS program to its extensive list of services. Up to now, this agency's clients have been 80 percent white and 20 percent Native American; statistics haven't been kept on the percent of gay, lesbian, or heterosexual clients. But more than half of the clients in the new AIDS program are either Native American or gay (or both). How might and should the board use this information to inform its board recruitment needs?

- A deaf counseling organization requires that 80 percent of board members be deaf and that all members be fluent in American Sign Language (ASL). Because so few people outside the deaf and deaf-serving community are fluent in ASL, it's been hard to find board members with the political clout the board wants. For example, the mayor wants to join the board, but she is not fluent in ASL.

- A Filipino senior organization finds itself serving more and more people who are not Filipino. Some of the initial non-Filipino clients came because their spouses were Filipino, but now the agency's reputation for quality care is attracting people from a wide range of racial and ethnic backgrounds. In fact, a Spanish-speaking counselor was recently hired to strengthen the work with Latino families. Some board members want to bring on Latino and white board members, while other board members find strength in the organization's Filipino focus and worry that the organization's volunteer base and focus will be diminished if that focus goes away. In addition, this organization has a policy that 50 percent or more of the board must be age sixty or older; some of the younger professionals on the board are concerned that this standard limits the fundraising potential of the board.

The call for diversity in nonprofit organizations grew out of a legitimate concern that many nonprofits serving minority communities had few, if any, staff or board members from those same communities. How, asked community members from communities of color, can you know the needs and perspectives of our communities when you don't have any of us working as providers and managers or serving as board members?

In today's nonprofit sector, diversity has several different dimensions, including

- Diversity among clients, patrons, members
- Diversity among staff, board members, volunteers
- Diversity based on specific demographic characteristics, including race, ethnicity, age, gender, sexual orientation, disability, location
- Diversity based on characteristics specific to the organization's constituencies (examples: adoptive parent, HIV status, immigration status, survivor of domestic violence)

Looking at the nonprofit sector overall, we can also see that there's a role to play for organizations that are for and in a specific community, such as Russian organizations, African American organizations, organizations of mental health patients,

or organizations of nurses advocating a particular cause.

Discussions about diversity are difficult to hold. The topics of race, ethnicity, gender, and sexual orientation evoke deeply felt, complex emotions, and participants in the discussion frequently have quite different points of view. These discussions, though they may be difficult, are an important part of the way a board develops its values and vision, and provide a unique platform where individuals can develop their own thinking.

There is no "right" answer on diversity that is appropriate for all organizations. The discussion about diversity is itself an important process through which a board can consider in what ways diversity may be important in achieving its mission.

Sample policy statements on diversity

Following are some approaches to diversity on nonprofit boards, and sample policies that can act as a starting point for your own board's discussion.

1. A mission reason: Diversity serves the mission. To help ensure that the perspectives of people utilizing services are reflected in planning and operations, organizations should have on their boards members of the communities being served, including clients, customers, and volunteers. (It's hard to imagine an effective board of a disabilities organization with no members who have disabilities, a

Chinese community center with no board members who are Chinese, or a theatre board with no members who attend the theatre.)

Examples

- "We will strive to have two or more members of our board be parents whose children are residents in our treatment program."

- "As one way to ensure our organization is responsive to the diverse community we serve, we are committed to a board that includes individuals from different racial and ethnic communities and individuals of different genders, ages, sexual orientations, and physical disabilities."

2. A business reason: Diversity is a good business practice. An organization's board should include individuals who bring contacts, sensibility, and knowledge related to the communities served.

Examples

- "To help us reach—and reach meaningfully—the Latino population we want to serve, we are committed to a board that is 40 percent or more from the Latino and Hispanic community."

- "Because our organization seeks to serve a racially diverse spectrum of low-income families, we strive for board composition that is racially and ethnically diverse."

3. A responsible corporation reason: Every organization is responsible to its community. Even beyond an organization's client population, today's diverse communities need diverse organizations as community building blocks. As employers and managers of public spaces, organizations have a responsibility to the greater community.

Examples

- "In line with our commitment that our staff and board reflect the larger community we serve, we will strive for a staff and board that have racial and ethnic composition comparable to the civilian labor force in our area."

- "We are committed to making our facilities accessible to visitors and employees, to ensuring that our web site follows designs and practices for accessibility, and to providing sign language interpretation, large-print materials, and other supports to enable us to serve the broadest segment of our community."

4. A definitional reason: Ethnic-specific, gender-specific, and other organizations focused on specific groups should clarify and articulate their policies (whether and how to diversify) as part of their missions or their strategies for working with their communities.

Examples

- "Because our organization is built on the idea of self-help for the immigrant Central American community, a board composition of 100 percent Central American immigrants is an important aspect of how we do our work."

- "We expect that the composition of the board of our Arab American historical society will be predominantly Arab American, but we have no restrictions on race or national origin, and we recognize that others can play valuable roles in advancing our organization's mission."

- "As a group advocating for the advancement of women in science, we see a board composition of 100 percent women as a component of our mission."

Also Try

The Board's Composition and Profile, p. 144

Twelve Cool Ideas for Finding Hot New Board Members, p. 148

Diversity for Organizations Based in Minority Communities, p. 157

Young Voices in the Boardroom, p. 155

From a reader

Regarding the latest feature article "Young Voices in the Boardroom," I don't believe that "young" only refers to those in their teens. I am twenty-five years old and the youngest person on two boards (by at least fifteen years). People in their twenties and even thirties are considered "young" on (most) boards or committees. While young people may be inexperienced in some areas and need some guidance, the involvement of "a new kid" will benefit the organization, and especially the "young voice."

—D. B., Hamilton, Ontario

Young Voices in the Boardroom

by Betsy J. Rosenblatt

One in every four U.S. residents is under eighteen years old. Young people are members of our communities and clients of our organizations as this country's future leadership. That's why more organizations are involving young people in new ways, including as board members. Young people—let's say people approximately sixteen to thirty years old—are willing to work and eager to learn, so why not take them up on it?

Why bring a young person onto your board? There are many reasons, but here is a sampling.

Diversity of viewpoint: Young people offer creative thinking and fresh perspectives that may not be present on your board.

Long-term growth: How better for young people to learn about nonprofits, leadership, and contributing to their community than through board service? How better for your board to ensure it won't wither and die when current members retire from service?

Community outreach: Youth have powerful and effective informal networks. If you want to reach young people in your community, recruiting them to serve on your board may be a great way to do so.

When you bring up this idea with others on your board, some people may object. They might say that teenagers don't know how to be board members or that graduate students will leave the area after graduation. It *will* take commitment from the adults on the board to make the inclusion of young people work. You may need to adjust meeting times, bylaws, or board member requirements. But some of the changes you might enact—such as reducing the use of jargon and acronyms, making financial reports easier to understand, or creating a board member mentor mechanism—are changes that can be good for everyone on the board.

Following are potential obstacles to young people serving on boards and how to overcome them.

Legality and bylaws: Most state laws are silent on the issue of minors serving on boards, but you might want to check with an attorney or local resource center who can outline your state's laws. Many organizations specify age limits for board members, on both ends. It is easy to change bylaws to make your board more inclusive.

Budget: You may need to include money in your budget to make board meetings more accessible to young people. This might include serving food at meetings or giving college students a ride back to campus.

Board member requirements: If your board requires, for example, personal financial contributions of a fixed amount or higher, it may be preferable to change the requirement to "a level that is personally meaningful." In another example, you may need to be willing to accept high school seniors for one-year terms instead of the usual two-year terms.

Want to start now? Here are some steps to get you started.

Assess your willingness and readiness: Are your board and staff willing and able to make changes?

Look to your constituents: Whom are you serving? Find two or three young people who are in your pool of clients, students at local schools, or involved in activities related to your mission.

Call your local volunteer center: See if staff members can help find potential young board members. Many volunteer centers have or know of special programs to train and place young people on boards.

Plan a strong orientation: Young people need the same background on your organization as adults, as well as some basics on the nonprofit sector and how meetings are conducted.

Conduct training: Both young people and adults benefit from ongoing board development programs.

There was a time when all board members were new to nonprofits and philanthropy and had to find their way around. What better time to make that happen than when people are young and open to new ideas and full of creativity and energy?

An organization called Youth on Board has done a great deal of thinking about how and why to bring young people onto the board. It publishes *Fifteen Points for Successfully Involving Youth in Decision Making,* $29.95; www.youthonboard.org.

Betsy J. Rosenblatt is the communications specialist at the Eugene and Agnes E. Meyer Foundation in Washington, DC. Betsy was the senior editor at BoardSource, under thirty, a board member of a neighborhood organization, and a member of the Board Café Editorial Committee.

Also Try

The Diversity Issue, p. 151

The Board's Composition and Profile, p. 144

Twelve Cool Ideas for Finding Hot New Board Members, p. 148

Diversity for Organizations Based in Minority Communities, p. 157

Diversity for Organizations Based in Minority Communities

In this book and elsewhere, the issue of boards and diversity comes up—whether diversity in race and ethnicity, age, gender, areas of expertise, personal income, or other dimensions. Discussions of diversity in the abstract tend to assume that the organization is a "mainstream" organization—mostly white, mostly male, mostly able-bodied, and so forth. While many diversity concerns are equally applicable to organizations based in specific under-represented communities, there are special considerations for women's organizations, Jewish organizations, Latino arts organizations, and others.

For example, many local YWCAs and women's organizations have held discussions about whether to invite men onto the board. Most have ultimately decided they have a mission-related reason for maintaining a board composed of all women: that such composition helps further the mission of empowering women and girls (including as leaders of non-profits!). Many people of color have made personal choices to join boards because they shared race or ethnicity with all the other board members or because they wanted to be the only or first people of color on the board.

The *Board Café* talked with Adrian Tyler, associate director in the Regulatory Department of Pacific Bell in San Francisco. Adrian, who is African American, has served both on boards with a wide diversity of members and on several all–African American boards, including economic development organizations, a Black adoption organization, a Black chamber of commerce, and an African American holistic healing institute. Some of his thought-provoking comments follow:

"I get a little uncomfortable when someone asks me to be on a board [that is mostly white, seeking racial diversity] by saying, 'We need to have an African American on the board.' Because that question tells me they may have expectations about my experience, my skills, my networks, my access to resources, that may not be accurate. If you know ME, and you know what I can and can't do, and you're asking me to be on a board knowing that, then I feel more comfortable with the invitation.

"I understand the power of all–African American boards. I remember one board I joined [of an agency serving the African American community] where I walked into a high-powered corporate board room and, of the eighteen African American board members, one was president of a college, one was a vice president at a hospital, etc.…. it was very empowering to find that level of community, and that was important to me as well as to the organization's mission.

"At the same time, here [in San Francisco] African Americans are a fairly small percentage, 8 to 10 percent of the total population, so it can be jarring to leave a work environment, then go to a board meeting where everyone is African American, and then go out again into the general community.

"Often we can find the people we need within the African American community. But we need to have a plan for dealing with that wider market, that external environment, and one way (not the only way) is to have non–African Americans

on boards that are based in African American communities. Here, too, prospective board members should be considered based on a broad set of needs (not just diversity).

"To me, first and foremost, I want a set of board members that brings together a broad set of skills, networks, and resources. Sometimes boards can be shortsighted by looking only at a person's skills, and not at everything that person is; while at other times, boards look only at what the person 'is' and not the skills and abilities brought to the table. I can categorically say that a racially mixed board doesn't necessarily perform better or worse than one where everyone is African American, or Asian American, etc. We have to remember that people's networks aren't limited to what we might assume they are… life is fuller than that. I want to be sure we don't forego any opportunities to get the best available person who can make the commitment to fill an organization's needs."

Thank you, Adrian, for these candid and helpful comments.

Also Try

The Board's Composition and Profile, p. 144

The Diversity Issue, p. 151

From *Best of the Board Café* (a column in the online magazine *Blue Avocado*), Copyright © 2003 and 2009, CompassPoint Nonprofit Services, published by Fieldstone Alliance, www.FieldstoneAlliance.org. Subscribe free to *Blue Avocado* at www.blueavocado.org.

Questions to Ask Candidates for the Board

Board committees charged with recruiting new members often meet with potential board candidates over lunch to allow both sides to become more acquainted with each other. The following questions can help the board committee and the candidate see whether there's a good match.

Frequently a first meeting with a prospective board member is set up for lunch or coffee with a current board member and the executive director. It's a good idea to state clearly at the beginning that this is a "get-to-know-you" meeting and that no decisions need to be made before the meeting ends. Usually a follow-up call with the candidate confirms whether or not he or she is still interested in joining the board and, if so, the candidate's nomination is brought to the next board meeting for approval.

An alternative process is to have profiles of several candidates brought to the board. Board members choose those they are quite certain they would like to recruit. The board then authorizes the nominating committee or other group to meet with the candidates and allows the nominating committee to add individuals to the list from the board. This shortens the screen-ing process and a new board member can often go to his or her first meeting within weeks of being asked. In either process, it's important not to let months go by between when the candidates are asked and when they can attend their first meeting—in short, months after their interest has been sparked.

Questions to ask prospective board members

- What interests you about our organization? What aspect of our organization interests you most?
- What are some of your previous volunteer experiences or leadership roles?
- What appeals to you about board service as a volunteer activity?
- What are you hoping to get out of your board experience?
- What skills, training, resources, and expertise do you feel you have to offer?
- One of the reasons we're talking to you about possibly joining our board is because we think you can help us connect with other public school parents in the African American community. Are these connections you could help us make?
- Do you have any worries about joining the board?

If fundraising is an important activity for board members, be sure to raise it now:

- We're hoping that if you join our board, you'll be a member of the fundraising committee. In fact, we hope that you will be able to ask five or ten of your friends for contributions of over $1,000 each. Is this something you think you could do?
- What would you need from this organization to make this experience a successful one for you?

Questions you should be prepared to answer, if the candidate asks you

- Why are you interested in me as a board member?
- What role do you see me playing on your board?
- What are your expectations and commitments?
- What is unique about your organization? What do you feel is unique about your board?
- Are there particular discussions this board has difficulty handling?

- What weaknesses are there in the way the board works together and with staff?
- What are the major issues this board is facing?
- How are you addressing them now?
- If I were to join this board, what would you want me to do during my first year?
- If I were to join this board, what could I reasonably expect to get out of the experience?

At the end of the get-acquainted meeting, you might want to suggest that each side think about the candidate's joining the board. Say that you'll get in touch with the candidate within a week once you've had a chance to talk over the "fit" with others on the board. Encourage the candidate to think it over, call you with any questions, and let you know within a week if he or she wants to commit to being on the board.

Also Try

The Board's Composition and Profile, p. 144

Why Do Nonprofits Have Boards? p. 18

The CompassPoint Board Model for Governance and Support, p. 20

Speed up recruitment by "prequalifying" prospective board members

Traditional recruitment processes can take months to bring on new board members...months during which the candidates become less interested. For instance, if a board meets every other month, the board might discuss a list of possible candidates in January, agree in March which ones to approach, hear back from the Governance Committee after interviews and vote in May, and a new recruit's first board meeting is in July. Some boards invite potential recruits to observe a board meeting, which adds even more time.

To accelerate this process, some boards invite candidates to the board meeting at which they will be voted on. The hitch, of course, is that it makes it very difficult for a board *not* to approve someone who is already in attendance (albeit asked to sit in the hall for a few minutes).

Instead, think about "pre-approving" some candidates. Often a few candidate names arise of people who are already known by several other people on the board. In such cases a candidate might be pre-approved, meaning that the Governance Committee will approach the person, discuss how the interview went, and if the Governance Committee agrees, the person can be immediately notified of his or her acceptance and can attend the next board meeting.

From *Best of the Board Café* (a column in the online magazine *Blue Avocado*), Copyright © 2003 and 2009, CompassPoint Nonprofit Services, published by Fieldstone Alliance, www.FieldstoneAlliance.org. Subscribe free to *Blue Avocado* at www.blueavocado.org.

Questions to Ask Yourself before Joining Your Next Board

Okay, you're having a great time serving on a board, but your term limit is coming up, or you're moving to a new community, or you just need a change. If asked why you joined your current board, chances are you'd reply, "Because someone asked me." As you consider another board to join, here are some questions to ask yourself.

Is this the right cause and organization for me?

Approach this decision as if you were planning to make a major donation: you would probably begin by thinking of areas where you have strong feelings—perhaps care for the elderly, or civil rights, or the environment. After settling on a subject area, you might then learn about several different organizations working in that field and investigate ones that seem to have high impact and are well managed. Only after you were fully satisfied would you make the donation.

The next time you consider joining a board, first ask yourself whether you truly feel strongly about the type of work that the organization does and the people it serves. Since, as a board member, you'll be investing not only money but also time and energy, ask yourself whether the organization seems to be a good risk as an investment.

Can I work with this organization and this board at this particular stage in its life?

At one time in an organization's life, board service may be fairly smooth with a few bumps, while at another time board service may involve a hair-raising roller-coaster ride (of course, an unexpected event can throw any board for a loop). What type of board seems right for you right now? You may want a board that really lets you roll up your sleeves and get to work with the other board members, or you may want a board that is stable and can let you learn about board work in a gradual way.

What can I, and what *will* I, contribute to this organization?

Often board members find that some of their talents and contacts never seem to get utilized by the boards they're on. Perhaps you gave up a music career for accounting, or have writing skills that are not used at your job. Perhaps your customer network includes dozens of influential community leaders. Consider first what you bring to the table and, then, whether you are willing to give that to the organization. Look, too, for vehicles for your skills: if you can't see a specific vehicle (work on an event, help market a service, work with the treasurer), your desire to contribute may well go unfulfilled. Ask yourself:

- Do I believe in this organization enough to introduce my customers to it?
- Can I make a commitment to attending at least 75 percent of the meetings?
- Am I willing to give up one or more evenings a month?
- Am I willing to make a generous donation?
- Can I volunteer with other board members on occasional Saturdays?
- Would I feel comfortable having my name on its letterhead or on its brochure?

The right time to ask these questions is before, not after, you have joined the board.

What do I want to accomplish, learn, or do before leaving this board?

This final question is one that potential candidates should ask themselves and one that active board members should periodically reexamine during their board service.

An all-too-common experience for board members at the end of their terms is a feeling that they didn't, after all, really get deeply involved and don't, as a result, feel that they either contributed as much or got as much as they had hoped when they first joined. Board members who plan and ask for what they want in the board will contribute more as well as gain more. For example, if you don't have a finance background but wish you knew more about finance, consider asking to be appointed to the finance committee. If there's a community leader on the program committee whom you would love to get to know, ask to be on the program committee and put in the time to be sure you get to know all the members well. If one of your reasons for joining the board was to meet new people, volunteer to help put on the annual luncheon or staff the table at a street fair.

Also Try

A Board Member Contract, p. 26

Reasons to Have—and Not to Have—an Attorney on the Board

by Mark J. Goldstein

"We should have an attorney on the board." It's conventional wisdom we've all heard. We expect that an attorney would bring legal expertise (so we wouldn't have to pay a lawyer) and that she'll have a skill set, personality, and community stature that would benefit our organization. Attorney Mark J. Goldstein of Milwaukee shares some thoughts, which also suggest similar guidelines for working with certified public accountants, human resource specialists, and other professionals.

Not all attorneys are wise, expert, facilitative, financially generous, and well regarded. (You knew that!) With more than one million lawyers and 196 law schools in the United States, it may be hard to find the Abraham Lincolns and Atticus Finches of the profession. As a result, and because a board's success depends upon its gestalt as much as the traits of its individual members, boards should think a bit about the contributions an attorney might make.

Advantages of having an attorney on the board

1. *Professionalism, conscientiousness, attention to detail.* Notwithstanding all the lawyer jokes, attorneys are learned professionals. They are typically detail oriented, conscientious, and risk averse. Many are citizens and activists committed to doing the right thing (admittedly a fluid concept). Such an attorney is an asset to any board.

2. *Legal knowledge and skills.* Attorneys are trained in law school to take in legal and factual information, to analyze that information, and to make recommendations based upon fact, law, financial risk, and other factors. There are many instances where—short of serving as the organization's attorney—this point of view can be very helpful.

Disadvantages of having an attorney on the board

1. *The wrong specialty.* The constantly increasing rules and regulations mean that the law is far more specialized than ever before. How helpful will an intellectual property attorney be with respect to nonprofit lobbying rules?

What might a real estate attorney contribute to a discussion on responding to allegations of harassment? The attorney herself may not know what she doesn't know.

2. *The "smartest guy in the room" phenomenon.* The good traits of attorneys (such as the ability to form a convincing argument) may compel other board members to give unreasonable weight to the attorney's point of view, and other board members may even feel that to disagree is to risk legal exposure. The attorney himself may feel a need to be the expert or to imply that his way is the only legal way.

A good attorney board member will acknowledge the boundaries of her expertise and defer to outside counsel on issues beyond her own areas of knowledge.

3. *Serving two masters and over-legalizing issues.* More common than some might think, an attorney might encourage the organization to hire his firm or push for a position that benefits his firm, such as taking a stance that leads to costly litigation as opposed to working creatively to avoid litigation. In other cases an attorney may insist on (paid) legal review of documents for which such review is unnecessary. Such actions can be done with the best of intentions, but the attorney may have prompted the organization to take a position that is justifiable in a strictly legal sense but not in the organization's financial or other best interest.

Following are three tips on how best to work with attorneys on your board:

1. Do reference checks with boards on which the attorney has served before. Does the attorney bring the best of the profession to the boardroom?

2. When recruiting attorneys as board members, consider which types of issues your organization regularly confronts and seek an attorney with expertise in those areas.

3. Give the attorney (and the board chair) a copy of this article.

Concluding thought: No doubt, a good lawyer on the board is an invaluable resource. But one who doesn't know her limitations, or takes a combative, overly legalistic approach to the deliberative process, can be demoralizing to other board members and can lead a board to poor decisions. Make sure you get a good lawyer.

Mark J. Goldstein is an attorney practicing in Milwaukee, Wisconsin. In addition to helping his clients (and their boards) resolve business and employment issues, he serves as vice president of his local school board.

Dominating Personalities on the Board

by Mike Schley

Nonprofits exist to serve the public good. In this attorney's twenty-plus years of advising nonprofits and volunteering on boards, it has been apparent that the public purpose can become subverted when a strong personality—whether on the board or in executive management—ends up dominating meetings and organizational processes.

Some examples of this problem:

The dominating board member: Some board discussions are dominated by the personality of a powerful board member—usually an extremely dedicated and capable individual who has recruited many of the other board members. Out of respect, other board members may be unwilling to contradict the dominating board member, thereby limiting the organization's potential.

The executive who dominates the board: Many nonprofits are started or built by a hardworking executive director, and both the executive and the board members come to feel that the organization "belongs" in some way to the executive director.

The insistent legal advisor: Nonprofits often look to an attorney on the board for free legal advice. But sometimes it's hard to distinguish the attorney's legal advice from his or her opinions. Couple this with a strong personality, and you have a board member with disproportionate influence.

How does an organization deal with these problems? The starting point is that every board member needs to take to heart his or her personal responsibility to the good of the organization. This includes expressing your opinion politely ("Excuse me, Sally, but I have a different view that I would like to share…"). Remember that your duty is to express your opinion, not to win the argument. You may need to start a dialogue with others you can approach in confidence. You may be surprised and relieved to learn that others share your concern but felt they were alone and were afraid to raise the issue.

Longer-term solutions that should be part of every nonprofit's structure

Term limits: There are benefits to tenure and history, but most experts agree that a board should be regularly refreshed. Consider structuring your board so that one-third of the members are up for reelection each year and so that no member can serve more than two consecutive terms.

Board recruitment and retirement: Every board should have a strong nominating or board development committee that takes seriously its duty to review individual board member performance. Board members who do too much should be treated in the same manner as board members who do too little—that is, they should be gracefully asked to complete their terms and make room for new board members.

Evaluation of the executive director: The board's most important function is to monitor the performance of management. Its ability to do so is hindered if an executive sits on the board or participates in the board nomination process.

Use of independent advisors: A certified public accountant cannot serve on the board of an organization that he or she audits. The same principle of independence should be respected in the case of lawyers, consultants to the board, and other advisors.

Mike Schley is an attorney in Santa Barbara, California, and a member of the Board Café *Editorial Committee. He can be reached at mike@schleylook.com.*

Also Try

Removing a Difficult Board Member, p. 138

A Board Member Contract, p. 26

Performance Review for the Board, p. 128

What to Do with Board Members Who Don't Do Anything, p. 136

Evaluating the Executive Director's Performance, p. 82

The Right Way to Resign from the Board

Most of us have resigned from a nonprofit board before our terms are up. We might have been angry, disappointed, or just too busy. Don't botch your resignation: do it right.

Very often board members not only complete one term but get to their term limits and leave the board feeling good about what they've contributed. But there are also times when we resign before we get to our term limits. Maybe we just haven't had the time to attend meetings or maybe we're moving to another city. Maybe we really don't feel right about the direction the organization is taking or maybe we feel that board members are treated like "mushrooms": kept in the dark and fed manure! Regardless of your reason, your resignation can be a moment where the board's effectiveness is demonstrated and increased, or it can be an empty gesture. Following are some ways to make significance out of your resignation:

If you have concerns about the organization or the executive director but haven't voiced them, consider raising them to the board president before finalizing your decision to resign. We know one organization where seven former board members were interviewed—and every one of them had resigned because they weren't happy with the executive director, yet they never told anyone. At a minimum, raise your concern to the board chair or an officer you know: "The reason I'm really resigning is because I don't feel confident that Jim is doing a good job as executive director. I can't work constructively with him, but at the same time, I don't want to prevent the rest of you from working with him. I wanted to be honest with you about why I'm resigning, and later on it may be important for you to know why."

If you've been AWOL due to other commitments, be honest about your situation. "I haven't been the board member I wanted to be. And I realize it's demoralizing to everyone when someone is as absent as I have been. I don't think things will change for me, so I've decided to resign." If this is your situation, commit to doing one more specific task after leaving, such as getting two items for the upcoming silent auction or attending the city council hearing on zoning the following month.

If you are resigning because you strongly disagree with a major organizational decision, consider staying on as the "loyal opposition." Hopefully the decision was discussed and debated before being made, and you should be aware that leaving may look like "sour grapes." But if you're out-of-step with everyone else, and you aren't comfortable staying, leave gracefully but with principle. Consider writing a letter to the board explaining your position and read it aloud at your last board meeting. Ask to have it entered into the minutes. The board members who were absent at the meeting will hear your comments, and years later the record of the debate may help the board of the future.

If you simply feel ineffective or useless as a board member, think about why that's so. Is it because the board has an executive committee that decides everything of importance, leaving little for the whole board to do? Is it because neither the executive director nor the board chair really knows what to do with the board and with board members? Is it because the executive acts on his or her own and the board is an afterthought? Can these questions be raised with the board's leaders who can address them with you?

Whatever the reason, resign right. Tell the board chair first, then the executive director, then the whole board. If you will be attending one more meeting, bring cookies or another gesture of goodwill. They will be listening carefully to your "last words," so make the most of the moment to contribute to the organization and its cause—just as you did when you first joined the board.

Also Try

What to Do When You Really, Really Disagree with a Board Decision, p. 110

Questions to Ask Yourself before Joining Your Next Board, p. 162

From *Best of the Board Café* (a column in the online magazine *Blue Avocado*), Copyright © 2003 and 2009, CompassPoint Nonprofit Services, published by Fieldstone Alliance, www.FieldstoneAlliance.org. Subscribe free to *Blue Avocado* at www.blueavocado.org.

CHAPTER SEVEN

Officers and Committees

The legal requirements for the size, officers, and committees of boards vary from state to state, but are generally minimal. While there are few legal requirements, there are some accepted principles that help guide organizations.

This chapter first addresses some basic, frequently asked questions about board structures. The articles then go on to discuss some specific topics:

Frequently Asked Questions

Should boards be big or small?

Most community-based organizations have boards of directors with five to twenty members because this range provides a manageable number of people for meetings. If there are too *few* people on the board, there simply may not be enough hands to do the work. If there are too *many* people, individuals may feel less effective, a quorum may be difficult to achieve, and more staff time is required to ensure that all board members are able to contribute to the organization.

A final, often overlooked consideration is space: The size of an available meeting room may limit the size of the board.

Is an advisory board a good place to put people who want to be involved?

Some organizations have fairly small boards of directors and larger advisory committees. Members of the board not only must be committed to the organization, but also must be willing to attend to the detailed and often mundane work of the organization. Advisory committees and councils can draw on larger numbers of people with expertise and perspectives important to the agency's programmatic work, but who may not want to be involved with the governance of the organization. Caution: Don't make the common mistake of starting an advisory board as a way to get donors involved without having them on the "real" board. If fundraising is the real goal of a group, make it clear through its title, such as "Honorary Committee," or "Friends of . . ."

How many officers should a board have?

Boards of community-based organizations typically have four officers: president, vice president, secretary, and treasurer. Some organizations choose to have two co-chairs and a treasurer. Others have a chair and a vice chair and choose to have committee chairs as officers. The appropriate number of officers and committee chairs, like the total number of board members, depends on the needs and intentions of the organization.

How often should a board meet?

Most local organizations meet monthly. However, some local and regional organizations find it more valuable to meet every other month or once a quarter. Boards need to find the appropriate balance between keeping in touch with the organization and its issues and not overburdening board members and staff with too many meetings.

Should all boards have committees?

Most boards of more than five people work through committees because smaller groups can work more efficiently and less formally. Most boards also try to limit the number of committees so that individual workloads can be kept manageable. If a person is on two or three committees, his or her time is spread too thin to be effective.

Some boards choose not to have committees at all. In some cases work can be more efficiently performed by individual board members working directly with staff. For example, the treasurer may work directly with the staff to review financial affairs. When a task is proposed at a meeting, an individual board member takes on the responsibility, involving one or two other board members on an ad hoc basis if needed.

The advantage of responsibilities assigned to individuals rather than to committees is that fewer meetings need to be held and that work can often be done more efficiently. In the absence of committees, the board president must make extra efforts to be sure that individuals are held accountable to the board for their responsibilities.

Should the Board Have Committees? If So, Which Ones?

Much of the decision-making work of many nonprofit boards is managed through committees. Committees can also serve as an important mechanism for actively involving all board members in the agency's work and for encouraging board leadership to emerge. One longtime nonprofit executive director commented, "When a board member remarks to me that the board isn't tackling substantive issues, that's a sign to me that his committee chair hasn't involved him enough."

Do all boards need committees?

Most boards have committees because smaller groups can work more efficiently and less formally. (The number of committees should be limited so that individual workloads can be kept manageable—if board members sit on two or three committees, their time is spread too thin for the committees to be effective.) Committees can play a helpful role in building teamwork among larger boards. While they require more administrative management from the staff and board president, they also divvy up tasks and expertise efficiently.

Task forces instead of standing committees

Increasingly, some boards are choosing to have only a few standing—permanent—committees at all. In some cases, work can be more efficiently performed by individual board members working directly with staff, such as the treasurer working directly with staff on financial affairs. In other cases, an ad hoc committee or task force is formed to complete a particular task within a few months. Many board members feel more comfortable signing on to a temporary, ad hoc committee than to a permanent standing committee. In addition, assigning responsibilities to individuals rather than to committees may result in fewer meetings and more efficient work.

How much authority does a board committee have?

Board committees are often on both governing and supporting sides of the CompassPoint Board Model. For example, the governance responsibilities of the board are taken up in part by the finance committee through financial oversight and by working with the outside auditor. But some finance committee meetings may also take up support matters, such as making suggestions to staff about collecting receivables or advising in the selection of accounting software.

In most cases, a board committee has no authority to make decisions on its own; its role is to prepare recommendations for the board. Practically speaking, board committees often sort through decisions to determine which should be made by staff with committee suggestions, which can be decided by the board committee, and which should be taken to the full board for discussion, revisions, and approval. For example, a special event committee may decide that staff can choose the centerpieces for the luncheon, that the committee itself will decide on the menu, but that if the menu would necessitate a change in price, the committee will bring the price decision to the full board.

The role of a board committee can be to prepare recommendations for the board, to decide that a matter doesn't need to be addressed by the full board, to advise staff, or, in some cases, to take on a significant project. For example, a detailed review of the cash-flow situation may take place in the finance committee, which then recommends to the board that a line of credit be established. Although the full board is responsible for the decision, board members rely on the diligence and thoughtfulness of the finance committee in making

the recommendation. In another example, the fundraising committee develops a fundraising strategy, which is brought to the board for approval. Anyone on the board can object, and the board can still reject the plan or ask the committee to revise it. Over time, committees gain the confidence of the board by doing their work well.

Can people other than board members serve on committees?

In some organizations, board committees are comprised only of board members. In other organizations, committees have both board members and nonboard members. For example, a site relocation committee may have board members along with real estate professionals and neighborhood leaders. Having nonboard members on committees invites specialized expertise, from people who may not have time to serve on the board or from individuals who may be inappropriate for full board membership.

Board committees can be great fun and more satisfying than being on the board itself. They can also be insulting wastes of time or worse: board committees that exist mainly in the imaginations of the board president and executive director. In short, be sure to create board committees only when meaningful work is to be done and when the committee can and will do that work.

Also Try

Board Committee Job Descriptions, p. 175

Year-Long Agenda for a Board Committee, p. 185

Board Committee Job Descriptions

It goes without saying that there is no one-size-fits-all committee list for boards or descriptions of what the responsibilities or activities should be for each committee. Some boards have *no* standing committees and either work as a whole or with time-limited task forces.

Following are committee job descriptions that you can use to construct the committees that are appropriate for your own board.

Finance committee

The finance committee (often called the budget and finance committee) focuses on the financial governance of the organization. Tasks include

- To review budgets initially prepared by staff, to help develop appropriate procedures for budget preparations (such as meaningful involvement by program directors), and to ensure a consistency between the budget and the organization's plans.

- To report to the board any financial irregularities, concerns, or opportunities.

- To recommend financial guidelines to the board (such as to establish a reserve fund or to obtain a line of credit for a specified amount).

- To work with staff to design financial reports and ensure that reports are accurate and timely.

- To oversee short- and long-term investments, unless there is a separate investments committee.

- To recommend to the board the selection of the auditor and to work with the auditor, unless there is a separate audit committee. Note: In larger organizations it is important to have separate audit and finance committees.

- To advise the executive director and other staff on financial priorities and information systems, depending on committee member expertise.

Fundraising committee

The fundraising committee's job is not simply to raise money. Instead, acting for the board in its governance role, the fundraising committee oversees the organization's fundraising picture and, in particular, fundraising done by the board. To accomplish this, its governance responsibilities are

- To work with staff to establish a fundraising *plan* that incorporates a series of appropriate vehicles, such as special events, direct mail, and product sales, and to take this plan to the full board for its review and approval.

- To oversee the implementation of the fundraising plan, and especially to ensure that commitments by individual board members are met.

- To monitor fundraising efforts to be sure that ethical practices are in place, that donors are acknowledged appropriately, and that fundraising efforts are cost effective.

In their support role, fundraising committee members are committed

- To raise funds through personal activities, such as hosting donor parties or asking for major donations.
- To work with fundraising staff in their efforts to raise money.
- To take the lead in certain types of outreach efforts, such as chairing a dinner or dance committee or hosting fundraising parties.
- To be responsible for involvement of all board members in fundraising, such as having board members make telephone calls to ask for support or visit key donors.

Governance committee or board development committee

In some ways the most influential of all the committees over the long term, the governance committee does what nominating committees do but goes further to include some or all of the following responsibilities:

- To draft priorities for board composition in line with the board's needs.
- To recruit, screen, and recommend new board members to the board.
- To recruit and present a slate of officers to the board.

- To organize board education for both new and ongoing members, whether through training sessions, discussions, reading, outside speakers, and so forth.
- To suggest new, nonboard individuals for committee membership.
- To ensure that the board is composed of individuals who, taken together, are equipped to govern, to support, and, if it becomes necessary, to hire a new executive director.
- To conduct an annual board assessment, whether a self-assessment or with input from others.

Program committees and task forces

Organizations with program committees often compose them of board members who are most familiar with the approaches and operations of the organization's programs.

Depending on its makeup and the organization's programs, the program committee acts in the board's supporting role as a group of advisors to staff:

- To advise the staff on the development of new programs.
- To initiate and work with staff on assessing the impact of programs.
- To facilitate discussions on the board about program priorities for the agency.
- To coordinate the work of board members doing program work.

From *Best of the Board Café* (a column in the online magazine *Blue Avocado*), Copyright © 2003 and 2009, CompassPoint Nonprofit Services, published by Fieldstone Alliance, www.FieldstoneAlliance.org. Subscribe free to *Blue Avocado* at www.blueavocado.org.

Some nonprofit organizations, however, feel that the organization's program— its "products"— should be overseen by the whole board. Increasingly, a better approach is to have program task forces that are formed for a specific task and for a limited time. For example, a Wellness Center Board–Staff Task Force can review and revise programming for the Wellness Center, or a Student Outcomes Board–Staff Task Force can take an intensive look at students in a particular program.

Executive committee

Sometimes an organization with a large board forms an executive committee, which is a smaller group that meets more frequently than the full board. Some executive committees are comprised of the board officers; others include committee chairs; and some choose other configurations, such as the board officers and the fundraising committee chair. A risk with executive committees is that they may take over decision-making for the full board, and other board members will feel they are only there to rubber-stamp decisions made by the executive committee.

Audit committee

The role of the audit committee encompasses interviewing auditors, reviewing bids, recommending selection of an auditor to the board, receiving the auditor's report, meeting with the auditor, and responding to the auditor's recommenda-

tions. For many organizations, the annual audit is the only time the organization's financial systems are reviewed by an independent outsider, and as a result the auditor's report is an important way the board obtains independent information about the organization's activities. On smaller boards, the functions of the audit committee are managed by the finance committee. (California now requires a separate audit committee from the finance committee for nonprofits with non-government income of $2 million a year or more; other states are considering enacting similar laws, so check with the attorney general of your state.)

Public policy committee

Organizations whose mission includes public policy or education may create a public policy committee that stays informed on relevant matters and brings proposals to the table for a board position or an organizational activity. For example, a public policy committee might draft a written position paper related to changes in the Americans with Disabilities Act or propose that the board join a coalition of nonprofits protesting the closure of a library branch or discrimination in the fire department.

Risk management committee or task force

This committee works with staff to identify risks, obtain and review insurance, and institute standards and procedures that reduce risk for the organization. For example, a child care center may decide to have general liability insurance with a $2 million policy and to ensure that fingerprinting of employees and applicants is done regularly, in line with state and county regulations.

Management oversight committee for geographically distant boards

Boards where the members are geographically distant from one another have a difficult time keeping in touch with the work of the staff. The board may meet only twice a year or quarterly, and much of the contact among board members may be through e-mail or only through the staff. To ensure financial and legal oversight in between board meetings, some boards establish a management oversight committee, which meets every six weeks and where two of the three members live near the office (the out-of-state member participates by phone). This committee has finance, audit, legal, and personnel responsibilities that might be done by separate committees if the organization were larger and working in only one city. The management oversight committee provides a report on the organization's operations to each board meeting.

Human resources committee

Whether or not to have a board human resources or personnel committee is often a controversial decision. Many organizations see all personnel matters as man-

agement items delegated to the executive director. There are, however, both governing and supporting roles for a board human resources committee to play. Governance responsibilities include

- Reviewing job descriptions for management staff.
- Establishing a salary structure, and annually reviewing staff salaries to be sure they are in line with the structure.
- Reviewing the benefits package.
- Developing a philosophy and strategy on volunteer involvement.

In its support role, responsibilities can include

- Drafting or revising personnel policies for board approval.
- Acting as a grievance board for employee complaints. Because difficulties can arise if many less serious complaints are brought directly to the board rather than to the staff person's supervisor, it is preferable for the personnel committee to act only on formal written grievances against the executive director or when an employee formally appeals a decision by the executive director to the board.
- Providing expert advice to staff on employment law, procedures, and related matters.

Task forces and temporary committees

Some committees are convened on a temporary basis to address a specific, single event or issue. Often called ad hoc committees, they meet for a few months and then disband once their task is completed. Many nonprofits include staff members on these task forces. Commonly used temporary committees and their designated tasks include the following:

Site Committee

To work with staff to evaluate the existing location and consider a move to a different location, to review a new lease, or to weigh the feasibility of purchasing a building.

Special Event Committee

To coordinate the board's assignments on a particular event, such as an annual dinner, or to be responsible for all aspects of the event.

Executive Director Transition or Search Committee

To seek a new executive director, including recommending guidelines and a search process to the board, and to take steps to help the new executive succeed. Some search committees hire the new executive director, while other search committees present a small group of candidates to be evaluated by the whole board.

Merger Exploration Committee

To pursue a possible merger with another organization, and to bring information and recommendations back to the full board.

Planning Committee

To lead a strategic planning endeavor.

Special Issue Committee

To investigate an unusual problem or opportunity, such as negative publicity in the newspaper, deep staff resentment against the executive director, an unusual grant opportunity, or a possible joint project with another organization. Setting up a special issue committee to research the situation and report back to the board ensures that decisions are based on adequate information.

Bylaws Committee

The bylaws committee reviews bylaws of similar organizations, consults an attorney, interviews knowledgeable individuals within and outside the organization, and drafts amendments to the bylaws or a new set for the board to consider and approve. Periodically all boards should review their existing bylaws. Too often bylaws are only consulted once some serious conflict on the board has emerged and both sides are consulting dusty bylaws for how to outmaneuver the other.

Also Try

Governance and Board Development Committees, p. 181

Key Documents, p. 28

The Board's Role in Human Resource Administration, p. 43

Year-Long Agenda for a Board Committee, p. 185

Annual Report from a Board Committee, p. 187

A Board-Staff Contract for Financial Accountability, p. 220

When the Executive Director Leaves, p. 98

Abolish board committees?

Here's a fresh and radical idea: consider eliminating all (or most) of your board committees. Too many boards are bogged down by inactive or even semi-fictitious committees. And each board member can feel compelled to be on three or four committees.

The reality is that very few committees need to exist in perpetuity. Instead of a permanent Personnel Committee, for example, create a time-limited Human Resources Task Force to oversee policy revision and then disband when the work is done. In place of a standing Program Committee, form a time-limited Library Committee that tackles reviewing library usage—and then dissolve the group. The same folks might volunteer for the subsequent Newsletter Overhaul Committee to reinvent the newsletter and then move on after four months.

Increasingly, organizations have just two or three permanent (standing) committees. One you'll probably need is the Finance Committee, which must oversee financial performance on a continuous basis. Some organizations might also want to keep a Fundraising Committee, while others might replace this body with two task forces: one to coordinate the fall luncheon and one to plan and manage the county fair booth. Others combine fundraising and publicity into an External Affairs Committee.

Task forces, ad hoc committees, and temporary committees all have specific tasks to accomplish in a specific time frame. Signing up to work on a project with a clear goal and a termination point always trumps the prospect of indefinite service on a committee weighed down by a vague purpose.

An added bonus that results from shifting to temporary committees is the changing mix of team participants. Interaction among a variety of members on the board will result in having the right people "on the bus" more often and in board members getting to know more people on the board. And isn't getting to work with more people in new settings one of the reasons we join boards in the first place?

Governance and Board Development Committees

A more descriptive name for govenance committees is probably board development committee or board affairs committee. A governance or board affairs committee is something like the human resources department of the board of directors. Its responsibilities are to

- Recruit, screen, and recommend candidates for new board members.
- Identify and recruit people for board officer positions and manage officer elections, which may involve bringing a slate of officers to the board.
- Pay attention to the integration of new board members.
- Conduct an assessment of the board's performance, either a self-evaluation or involving input from others.
- Organize board education.
- Propose and implement board policies, such as a board conflict of interest policy.

Two to four people are enough for a strong governance committee. Ideally they are in sync with the current board leadership and the executive director, but they are also forward looking. A common mistake is to think first (or only) of veteran board members for the governance committee (or nominating committee). It *is* important to have known and trusted board members on this committee, but often new members better reflect the future directions of the organization and its constituencies. They may also bring fresh energy that helps to improve board functions.

Alternatively, the board president and the executive director make sure that these tasks are performed, often as task forces. Instead of a permanent (standing) committee, the board can create a task force (a temporary committee) to conduct a board evaluation, for example.

A quick look at each of the committee's responsibilities

1. *Recruits, screens, and recommends candidates for new board members.* The governing committee can ask the full board what kinds of board members are needed and for specific suggestions. Some boards bring on new members on a rolling basis, while others recruit a group at a time, sometimes at the end of the fiscal year or to jump-start a fresh board outlook. The full board approves or rejects nominations from the governance committee.

2. *Identifies and recruits people for board officer positions and manages officer elections, which may involve bringing a slate of officers to the board.* A good trend is the movement away from long queues where a person moves more or less automatically up a ladder toward the board chairpersonship. Such a system prevents talented people from taking early leadership, and a person selected, for example, six years ago to be vice president for membership may not be the board president the organization needs right now.

3. *Pays attention to the integration of new board members.* Some boards—especially large boards or those that bring in a "class" of several board members at a time—hold formal orientations that might include a tour of the facility and presentations by senior staff (and perhaps the founding board chair or other community leaders). Others orient board members more informally, perhaps with a lunch held with two new board members, two veteran board members, and the executive. Perhaps more important than the "board orientation" itself is informal, just-in-time coaching and inclusion by others. Governance committee members might be attentive to saying, "Anita, our next meeting is going to focus on the clinic's budget. As a doctor, you have input that we'd appreciate...could you attend the next

finance committee meeting?" or "Victor, now that you've been to a couple of board meetings, would you like to get together for coffee, and I can explain to you why everyone is so hypersensitive about the word *lawsuit*?"

4. *Conducts regular assessments of the board's performance, perhaps as a self-evaluation, perhaps with input from others.* Many boards do a fast survey of themselves to see how satisfied they are with their performance. Survey questions might include the following:

- How satisfied are you with how well the board understands the organization's financial situation?

- How satisfied are you with how well board members follow through on tasks for which they volunteer?

- What improvements would you like to see in how the board and the executive director work together?

- How do you assess the work of our board chair?

In some situations a board will want to look more closely at some aspect of its work. It might conduct an anonymous survey of staff members to see how they perceive board members and what the board does. It might want to hold some small-group meetings with the executive and talk about how he sees the board's work as a whole or how she sees the value of various individual board members.

Don't over-worry about *how* you do the assessment; however you do so, it will spark a board discussion that reflects on what the board is supposed to do and how well it is doing at its job.

5. *Organizes board education.* With a likely parallel in nonprofits, a national study of for-profit boards by McKinsey showed board members felt well informed about their *companies* (such as an airline) but strongly wanted more information about the *industry*. Board members need and want to know about their industries (day care for people with Alzheimer's, ethnic theatre) as well as about the programs, finances, and community positions of their own organizations. In addition to brief staff presentations, have board members make presentations on their areas of expertise. *Board Café* and *Blue Avocado* columns are useful for governance committees because they can be easily copied and handed out (such as previous columns on "Ten Ways to Invigorate Board Meetings," "A Board Member's Guide to Nonprofit Insurance," or "How to Take a Public Policy Stand."

6. *Proposes and implements board policies, such as a board conflict of interest policy.* Rather than clutter the bylaws with policies, it's better to have a set of board-related policies. Following are some worth considering:

- Conflict of interest
- Requirements for board members
- Whistleblower protection
- Policy on taking public policy stands
- Code of ethics
- Gift acceptance policy

One possible pitfall with governance committees is that they can get carried away and start taking over from the executive committee (if there is one) or the whole board. They can forget that they are there to support the full board, the executive, and the board leaders, rather than supplant them or overpower them in areas such as whether to have a board retreat, whether board members should be required to "give or get," and who should be on which board committee.

If these key tasks are already getting done on your board without a board affairs committee, there's no need to create one. But such a committee is often a straightforward way to help define the work of the board, the work of board members individually, and to strengthen that work.

Also Try

Should the Board Have Committees? If So, Which Ones? p. 173

Job Descriptions for Board Officers, p. 189

Performance Review for the Board, p. 128

Twelve Cool Ideas for Finding Hot New Board Members, p. 148

Abolish Board Committees? p. 180

Pass the torch award

Are there members of your board (or other volunteers) who hang on to a project or committee long after they should have passed the responsibility along to someone with new ideas and energy? Sometimes a board member will start to "own" a particular committee or event and will begin to resent ideas for changing the activities. Consider an annual "pass the torch award" to the board member or committee chair who has done the best job that year in recruiting a new leader and handing over the job. Such an award not only sends a message about the importance of succession planning in volunteer responsibilities, but also provides a mechanism for suggesting that the overly responsible volunteer works toward becoming a torch passer.

Year-Long Agenda for a Board Committee

Committees often have a hard time remembering long-term goals when it's easier to respond to urgent issues or, in the absence of urgent issues, not to meet. One easy way to manage a committee is to set up a year-long agenda.

A year-long agenda is also a way that the full board can see the plans that a committee has set for itself, suggest changes, and find ways to support the committee. Here's an example of how a year-long agenda can work.

The Budget and Finance Committee of the Cypress Theatre* consists of two board members and one person who is not a board member but who has experience in finance at another performing arts organization. Anticipating a difficult year financially, the committee expects to work more closely on the budget than in prior years, so members will have monthly meetings this year.

Based on these responsibilities, the budget and finance committee developed the year-long agenda on page 186 for itself.

Such an agenda will help the Cypress Theatre's Budget and Finance Committee get to the big tasks as well as the regular tasks of reviewing financial information. It also gives the board confidence that a matter will be taken up sometime during the year. The accounting staff are better able to support the committee by knowing ahead what documents and questions they should prepare.

---

* This is a fictitious name for an organization and, like other such fictitious groups in this book, is named after a tree.

Also Try

Should the Board Have Committees? If So, Which Ones? p. 173

Board Committee Job Descriptions, p. 175

Annual Report from a Board Committee, p. 187

A Board-Staff Contract for Financial Accountability, p. 220

The Board and the Budget, p. 225

Sample Year-Long Agenda

Standard matters: ....Each meeting
- Review of most recent financial statements
- Cash-flow projections as necessary
- Any significant changes from budget
- Monitoring of accounting department workload

1. Work with staff on the development and approval of the budget

   a) Discuss financial objectives for the coming year, including
   break-even points for performances ....February meeting

   b) Review first draft of budget by staff ....March meeting

   c) Discuss second draft of budget along with cash-flow projections
   for year. If possible, agree on budget to take to the board..................April meeting

   d) If necessary, review third draft of budget.............................late April (conference call)

   e) Bring budget to board for approval ....May board meeting

2. Consider engaging a new audit firm

   a) Discuss question...December meeting

   b) Draft letter to send to prospective audit firms asking for bids,
   and agree on list of firms to which the letter will be sent ....February meeting

   c) Review bids ....April meeting

   d) Invite two best prospects to make presentations at meeting...............June meeting

   e) Call references on prospective audit firms ....Report at July meeting

   f) Decide on recommendation to board................................July meeting

   g) Conduct full board discussion; anticipate approval
   of recommendation ....September meeting

3. Meet with auditors to review prior year audit ....March meeting

4. Review internal controls such as signature requirements on
   checks of various sizes ....November meeting

Annual Report from a Board Committee

by Jude Kaye

Although most committee reports are made verbally at board meetings, some boards ask committee chairs to write an annual report describing their activities and decisions. These reports can be included with the board minutes in the organization's formal, permanent records.

Page 188 is a simple format that committees can use for their end-of-year report or that they can adapt for a monthly report.

Jude Kaye is a senior staff consultant at CompassPoint Nonprofit Services and a frequent consultant to nonprofit boards of directors. She coauthored with Mike Allison the book Strategic Planning for Nonprofit Organizations, *published by John Wiley and Sons and available through Amazon.com or www.compasspoint.org.*

Also Try

Year-Long Agenda for a Board Committee, p. 185

Should the Board Have Committees? If So, Which Ones? p. 173

Abolish Board Committees? p. 180

Ten Quick Ways to Invigorate Board Meetings, p. 193

Critical Path for the Board, p. 199

Sample Committee Report

Committee: _____ Period of time this report covers:_____

Committee chair: _____

Committee members: _____

_____

The main objectives for the committee: _____

Summary of recent accomplishments and current activities: _____

_____

List of activities in progress and upcoming events/discussions: _____

_____

Recommendations for action at this time

1. Recommendation to: (check all that apply)

    Board   Executive Director   Other: _____

    Recommendation: _____

    _____

    Comment (background, time frame, possible alternatives and their consequences,
    or other relevant information): _____

    _____

2. Recommendation to: (check all that apply)

    Board   Executive Director   Other: _____

    Recommendation: _____

    _____

    Comment (background, time frame, possible alternatives and their consequences,
    or other relevant information): _____

    _____

Job Descriptions for Board Officers

Titles and job descriptions vary widely from one organization to another. In all-volunteer organizations, the board officers are often the chief "doers"—the people who get the work of the organization done. In some large institutions, board officers are the chief fundraisers, while in others the board officers are the most visible spokespersons for the organization's cause.

Here are sample job descriptions for president, vice president, secretary, and treasurer—the most typical board officer positions.

President (also called chair or chief voluntary officer, CVO)

General: Ensures the effective action of the board in governing and supporting the organization and oversees board affairs. Acts as the representative of the board as a whole, rather than as an individual supervisor to staff.

Community: Speaks to the media and the community on behalf of the organization (as does the executive director); represents the agency in the community.

Meetings: Develops agendas for meetings in concert with the executive director. Presides at board meetings.

Committees: Recommends to the board which committees are to be established. Seeks volunteers for committees and coordinates individual board member assignments. Makes sure each committee has a chairperson and stays in touch with chairpersons to be sure that their work is carried out; identifies committee recommendations that should be presented to the full board. Determines whether executive committee meetings are necessary and convenes the committee accordingly.

Executive Director: Establishes search and selection committee (usually acts as chair) for hiring an executive director. Convenes board discussions on evaluating the executive director and negotiating compensation and benefits package; conveys information to the executive director.

Board Affairs: Ensures that board matters are handled properly, including preparation of pre-meeting materials, committee functioning, and recruitment and orientation of new board members.

Vice President
(also called vice chair)

General: Acts for the president in his or her absence; assists with president's duties as requested by the president.

Special Responsibilities: Often assigned to a special area of responsibility, such as membership, media, annual dinner, facility, or personnel. Some organizations choose to make the vice president, explicitly or implicitly, the president-elect.

Secretary

General: Prepares the draft minutes from board meetings (sometimes with assistance from staff). May be responsible for preparing and sending out board meeting packets.

Special Responsibilities: Often assigned to a special area of responsibility, such as membership, publicity, or other area suited to the individual's talents.

Treasurer

General: Manages the board's review of, and action related to, the board's financial responsibilities. May work directly with the bookkeeper or other staff in developing and implementing financial procedures and systems.

Reports: Ensures that appropriate financial reports are made available to the board. Regularly reports to board on key financial events, trends, concerns, and assessment of fiscal health.

Finance Committee: Chairs the committee and prepares agendas for meetings, including a year-long calendar of issues. In larger organizations, a separate audit committee may be chaired by a different person.

Audit: Recommends to the board whether the organization should have an audit. If so, selects and meets annually with the auditor.

Cash Management and Investments: Ensures, through the finance committee, sound management and maximization of cash and investments.

Also Try

Should the Board Have Committees? If So, Which Ones? p. 173

Board Committee Job Descriptions, p. 175

Ten Tips for the Board Chair on Meetings, p. 196

The CompassPoint Board Model for Governance and Support, p. 20

CHAPTER EIGHT

Meetings

When board members think about the boards they're on, they usually think of the board meetings—which says a lot about the importance of having good meetings. Disorganized or unproductive board meetings are frustrating to everyone and are enough to drive many board members away.

This chapter includes the following articles:

But first, a word on frequency of board meetings.

How Often Should the Board Meet?

National surveys show that boards most commonly meet once a month but that more and more boards are meeting every other month, or quarterly. Some national and international boards may meet in person only once per year, with conference calls at other times.

The argument for *more* meetings: Board members need to know each other to be able to act effectively as a group, and if there are two months between meetings, it's hard to remember people and to get to know them. And when meetings are only six or four times per year, if you miss a meeting, you've missed a lot. With such a long time between meetings, too many decisions end up being made by the executive director and the board chair without input from others.

The argument for *fewer* meetings: Most people don't have time to attend twelve meetings a year, and for most organizations, monthly meetings are not really necessary. Nothing's more irritating than an agenda without anything substantial on it. If urgent matters arise, it's always possible to add another meeting or two.

Regardless of how often the board meets, most meetings can be made more substantial and interesting. Imagine yourself on the way to a board meeting, looking forward to stimulating discussion and knowing that real work will get done.

Ten Quick Ways to Invigorate Board Meetings*

Board members invest a tremendous amount of time and energy at board meetings. A few simple changes can often make that investment pay off in important ways.

Make a resolution to implement at least one of the following ideas this month:

1. Supply name tags for everyone at every meeting. It's embarrassing to have seen people at several meetings and wondered what their names are ... and later it's *really* hard to admit you don't know their names.

2. Make a chart of frequently used external and internal acronyms (such as CDBG for community development block grants or DV for domestic violence) and post it on the wall of every meeting. (If you distribute the list on paper, it is soon lost.) The chart will help people unfamiliar with the acronyms know what others are talking about.

3. Write an anticipated action for each agenda item. Examples:

   - Finance committee report, brief questions and answers: *Anticipated Action* = no action needed.
   - Volunteer recruitment and philosophy: *Anticipated Action* = form

committee of three to four board members.

   - Public policy committee: *Anticipated Action* = approve organizational statement to city council on zoning changes.

4. Make sure that each person says at least one thing at every board meeting. This is the board chair's responsibility, but everyone should help. "Cecilia, you haven't spoken on this issue. I'm wondering what you're thinking about it?" "Matt, at the last meeting you made a good point about finances. Are there financial issues here that we aren't thinking about?"

5. Avoid one-way presentations from staff. If you have a regular executive director's report on the agenda, or if a staff program director is giving you a briefing, be sure that such presentations need a response from the board. If not, put such reports in writing in the board packet and just ask if there are any questions.

6. Don't include committee reports on the agenda just to make the committees feel worthwhile. If a committee has done work but a board discussion isn't necessary, put the committee report in the board packet. In the

meeting be sure to recognize the committee's good work and refer people to the written report. Schedule committee reports according to the topic at hand, rather than at every meeting. For example, if a discussion is planned on attracting and retaining staff, reports from the finance committee and the personnel committee will be more useful and more memorable.

7. On the agenda, have an open-ended discussion on at least one of the most important matters facing the organization. For example, discuss the economic downturn, changes in government funding, possible reasons for declining preschool enrollment, a competitor organization, the possibility of losing donated space—whatever matters are keeping the leadership awake at night.

8. Encourage "dumb" questions, respectful dissent, and authentic disagreements. Find a chance to be encouraging at every meeting: "Sylvia, I'm glad you asked that 'dumb' question. I wanted to know the answer, too." "Duane, I appreciate the fact that you disagreed with me in that last discussion. Even though you didn't

convince me, your comment helped make the discussion much more valuable."

9. Make sure the room is comfortable! Not too hot or cold or crowded. Offer beverages and something light to eat such as cookies or fruit.

10. Adjourn on time, or agree to stay later. Twenty minutes before the scheduled end of the meeting, the chair should ask whether the group wants to stay later: "If we continue this very interesting discussion, we will have to stay fifteen extra minutes to hear the recommendation on the executive director's salary. Can everyone stay that long, or should we end this discussion and move to that one immediately?"

And a suggestion: once every year or two, survey the board about meetings. Pass out a questionnaire for anonymous return to the board vice chair or secretary, asking, "What do you like best about board meetings? Least?" "Are you satisfied with what's usually on the agenda?" "How could the board chair do more to encourage discussion at the meetings?" "Is the location or time of day difficult for you?"

---

* One of the five most reprinted *Board Café* articles.

Also Try

Ten Tips for the Board Chair on Meetings, p. 196

Better Board Meeting Packets, p. 203

Should the Board Hold Executive Sessions? p. 205

Where should the board chair and the executive director sit?

This question generated a huge amount of mail from Board Café *readers. Most felt very strongly on one side or the other of this question; some even sent in diagrams showing where the board chair, the executive director, and the minute-taker should sit.*

How is a board meeting affected by where the board chair and the executive director sit? Where each sits, particularly in relation to each other, sends a message to the board and could influence how the meeting goes. Some board chairs and executives make a point of sitting next to one another at the head of the table: a clear signal about their partnership and their authority. Some board chairs and executive directors choose to sit at opposite ends of the table to encourage participation from other board members. And, finally, some executive directors deliberately choose to sit away from the table altogether to send a message that they are staff to the board. Most executive directors, however, sit somewhere at the table to reflect their important role in the discussion

Should we allow board members to attend meetings by phone?

With freeways getting more crowded and everyone getting busier, more and more board members are wondering if they can participate in board meetings by telephone. The advantage: more people participate. The disadvantage: there's a lot lost for both the board member and the board as a whole when the meetings aren't in person and face-to-face. One board compromises by allowing new board members to participate by phone *only* after they have been to at least three meetings in person. Another board allows members to participate by phone for no more than one-fourth of the meetings. And some boards don't permit participation by phone at all. If you do decide to have some people phoning in to meetings, invest in a dedicated speakerphone so that everyone can hear.

Board meetings or committee meetings by conference call, video conferences, or real-time chat rooms are regulated by states (not the federal government). Note that the law of the nonprofit's home state applies, not the law where a board member lives, and states often have different names for the office in charge. For example, for California, an excerpt reads: "Participation in a meeting through use of conference telephone…constitutes presence in person at that meeting as long as all members participating in the meeting are able to hear one another." The meeting minutes should show, at the start of the meeting, that all persons attending confirmed they could hear everyone else.

Ten Tips for the Board Chair on Meetings

It's worse than boring to sit through a badly chaired board meeting; it's painful. Attention, board chairs! You have the power to keep meetings stimulating and productive, or you can allow them to ramble on to little resolution. For the sake of the organization, and for the sake of your fellow board members, take it as a personal responsibility to have good meetings.

1. With the executive director, prepare an agenda. For each item, identify who will be in charge and whether action is required. See the sample meeting agenda at right.

2. Make sure board members receive board packets one week ahead of the meeting. The packet should have

   • Meeting time and place
   • Proposed agenda
   • Any items that will be acted on during the meeting, such as the résumé of a prospective new board member or minutes from the previous meeting
   • Executive director's report
   • Financial statements
   • If possible, written committee reports
   • Background material for action items

3. Don't be rigid about how meetings are conducted, such as strictly adhering to Robert's Rules of Order. Instead, make sure that discussion on each item allows everyone a chance to speak and that options are fully discussed before an item is closed.

4. In a controversial matter, it may be best to start a discussion at one meeting but not come to a conclusion until a later meeting. Sometimes it's best to have three options on the table and discussed at once, while at other times it's better to see whether agreement can be reached on a particular proposal before exploring other options.

5. Even if there seems to be a consensus, ask for a vote on formal matters. Always ask for the yes votes, the no votes, and the abstentions. (Some boards prefer to record abstentions only if the abstaining board member requests it.) For legal protection, make sure individual names and votes are recorded on important matters.

6. Lead the group by encouraging discussion, not by talking more than others. Make sure everyone has a chance to participate; listen carefully to what each person says; and keep the meeting focused and on track.

7. If someone has expressed a view that most other board members haven't

Sample Meeting Agenda

Item	Person Responsible	Approx. Discussion Time	Action Requested
1. Approval of meeting minutes (draft enclosed in board packet)	Board secretary, Caroline	5 minutes	• Approve minutes
2. Report from program committee on results of survey on client satisfaction	Program committee chair, Emil	30 minutes	• Discuss possible impact on services, indications about competition; actions may be proposed
3. Report from finance committee on advisability of applying for line of credit	Finance committee chair, Jake, and controller, Kimi	15 minutes	• Recommend finance committee prepare and submit application to two banks
4. Report from parade committee on theme and design for Lesbian and Gay Pride Parade float	Parade committee chair, James	20 minutes	• Revise and approve theme for float • Ask for contacts for needed costumes • Review board fundraising responsibilities for event

agreed with, go up to that person after the meeting and comment that you appreciate board members speaking up and expressing their opinions. Find opportunities to encourage open disagreements as well as consensus building.

8. Demonstrate by your words and actions that you take board work seriously and that you appreciate the efforts and talents of both board and staff members.

9. Ask the vice chair or other officer to take a turn chairing a meeting. After the meeting, discuss how it went; the vice chair will welcome the feedback and preparatory training. Other board members may find an occasional change of meeting chair refreshing.

10. Break down the awkwardness that can develop after a board meeting by calling one of the attendees the day after the meeting. For example, call the executive director, someone who raised some important points, or someone who was unusually quiet. This gives you a chance to debrief.

Also Try

Ten Quick Ways to Invigorate Board Meetings, p. 193

Better Board Meeting Packets, p. 203

Ask for the abstentions

When you're doing voice votes ("Everyone in favor?"), don't forget to call for those opposed and for those abstaining. Even if it sounds as if everyone was in favor, it's important to let those who wish to oppose or abstain know they can without having to insist on it. By acknowledging that there may be board members opposed or abstaining, it also sends a message to everyone that differences of opinion are accepted and even valued.

Critical Path for the Board
Determining the Board's Agenda—and Work—for the Year

What is the board supposed to discuss, anyway? Too many of us have seen months go by on a board without a discussion that felt either genuinely important or interesting. One reason may be that traditional board agendas are heavy on committee and staff reports, such as finance committee report, fundraising committee report, or executive director report. There isn't much to do except listen.

Many boards and their executive directors complain about a "lack of engagement" and bring in speakers or even undertake strategic planning as ways to "get the board engaged." But shouldn't the goal be something more than just lively talking followed by volunteering to raise money? Instead of "How can we get the board engaged?" perhaps the question should be "What should the board engage *with*?"

The term *critical path* was adopted in the field of project management to mean the sequence of milestones that a project must follow to finish in the shortest amount of time. The term has come broadly to mean the path or sequence of decisions and actions that will lead to success. Too often organizations and boards develop "plans" that are really to-do lists. A critical path is different because it focuses attention on the most crucial aspects of organizational success.

One way to get to this critical path for the board is to clarify what the critical path is for the *organization*. At least annually, ask this question of the executive director and the board officers:

What does the organization *need* to accomplish this year? What are the most important two or three things that *have* to get done?

The answer might be, "to be named one of the six city-led health centers," "to move to a new office," "to increase our enrollment," "to either fire or see great improvement in the chief executive officer," "to get our finances under control," "to explore and maybe merge," "to find a way to raise salaries," or "to get the board's act together in preparation for hiring a new executive director."

The Big Job for the organization (or two or three jobs) will lead naturally to two other questions.

First, what does the board need to do in order to get this Big Job done? And second, what do board members need to know in order to do that?

Let's look at an example of a Big Job and the board's critical path, and imagine an organization that matches adult mentors with young people. This organization has two big issues in front of it. First, although they have a waiting list, they don't have enough mentors, so their matches have declined by 18 percent over the last year. What is the problem and what can be done about it? Second, they have enjoyed a substantial three-year grant from the county that will be ending in six months. Should the organization expect to get a renewal? Plan to cut back? Find another source of income?

Old agenda:

- Finance committee report: last month's financial statements
- Fundraising committee: ask members to contribute raffle prizes
- Executive director's report: mentor recruiting

New agenda:

- County funding: Form task force to investigate likelihood of renewal; develop strategy for renewal (such as board member meetings with county officials).
- Matches: Report from board-staff task force on the ten interviews they've

conducted with mentors to learn how they were recruited. Review plan from executive director on staff.

- Work to recruit more mentors. Generate and prioritize list of ways that board members can assist with recruiting.
- Finance committee: Prepare contingency budget if county funding is not renewed.

In short, beginning with what the organization has to accomplish and then what the board has to accomplish—and what it thereby has to discuss—is grounded in the pressing and meaningful real work.

The critical path may have been outlined in a recent strategic plan, or there may be a major "event," such as executive director departure, a substantive funding cut, or other matter. A discussion of the critical path will lead naturally to which committees and task forces are needed, to what kinds of board members need to be recruited, to what individual and group tasks there are for the board, and to what key items the board must hold the executive director accountable.

Finally, a word to executives: *What is the most important issue, challenge, or problem facing your organization? And when did the board last discuss it?*

Three interesting ways to hold board meetings

1. Early, very early, in the morning…many Silicon Valley nonprofits match the speed of local industry by having board meetings at 7:30 a.m.

2. Over a leisurely dinner…the board of one San Francisco AIDS fundraising organization meets monthly for dinner at a restaurant. Each board member has his or her credit card automatically billed by the organization for $30 monthly to pay for the dinners.

3. By conference call…the Alliance for Technology Access, a national network advocating for technology for the disabled, has a regular executive committee conference call every Tuesday and a regular board conference call once a month. The alliance has a "meet me line" where board members simply phone in and automatically join the call.

Use a consent agenda

An agenda can make or kill a board meeting. If you routinely have the same items to approve, try using a *consent agenda*. A consent agenda groups routine items under one umbrella that—unless any board member requests that an item be discussed—can be approved without discussion. Typical items for a consent agenda are accepting committee and board minutes or other documents, approving standard contracts, or confirming conventional actions required by bylaws. Don't forget: Consent agendas should be distributed in advance of the board meeting to allow board members sufficient time to review items and ask for topics to be taken off the consent agenda for discussion if they like.

From a reader

"I used the consent agenda idea with good results. One added tip: When someone removed an item from the consent calendar, the initial tendency was to discuss that item right after approval of the rest of the consent items and before the other items. This had the adverse effect of putting a routine matter at the top of the agenda, which is exactly the opposite of what we intended. Therefore, we adopted the policy that any item removed from the consent calendar automatically went to the end of the agenda. This not only helped me to keep control of my agenda, it also reduced the number of items removed, because the person who removed it felt compelled to stay until the end of the meeting to discuss his or her objection. Whatever the objection was usually seemed much less important to everyone, including the one making it, by that time!"

—K. K., online contribution

Better Board Meeting Packets

Most organizations send a packet of materials to board members a week or so before each board meeting. These packets are often time-consuming for staff to prepare, and time-consuming for busy board members to read. Staff can be tempted to send a ton of stuff, the better to inform and impress the board. On the other side, board members can easily run out of time to read the materials, and get annoyed when the materials are either late or questionably useful.

More than fifty *Board Café* readers sent in their comments about what they like—and can't stand—in board meeting packets. Their crystal-clear message: board members feel disrespected when board packets are late or sloppy, and they feel railroaded when background information isn't included for an upcoming decision.

Irrelevant or unexplained materials provoke anger in board members, who feel that poorly prepared packets indicate that the staff don't value the board's ability, authority, and responsibility to make decisions. In contrast, a thoughtful, carefully prepared packet not only provides the board with the information it needs for the meeting, but also increases board confidence in the staff and in the board-staff relationship.

Here are specific suggestions for board meeting packets:

1. Board members want information that will be needed for the next board meeting. If approval of a new program or a new budget is on the agenda, a clear statement of the proposal must be in the packet, along with identification of who is bringing the proposal (staff? a board committee?) and their reasons behind the proposal.

2. Board members want enough time to read the packet. Some organizations send the packet by e-mail as well as by regular mail, so that board members can read the contents from wherever they might be.

3. Critical, but often overlooked: board members want packets that attend to logistics. The packet must include meeting location, directions to the meeting, hotel phone and fax (if board members travel to the meeting), and an annotated agenda (explaining, for example, who will be making a report and what action will be called for). The text must be large enough for board members to read easily (one *Board Café* reader's organization that serves the blind prepares its packets in Braille, too). The packet should provide names and phone numbers of people to call in advance if there's a question about a given item.

4. Board members want brief and usable updates on priority matters, especially financial status. In financial information, board members want to be able to tell—either from the statements or from a cover memo—whether the organization is on budget and financially sound: in short, "Should we be worried?" Other matters—funding updates, program updates, special news about staff or the board—can be covered in an executive director's report or in a series of brief program reports. If other items such as journal articles are included, let board members know what they should be looking for—is this material nonessential but interesting reading, or is this required background for an upcoming organizational decision?

5. Board members don't want to read things that will be repeated at the board meeting, and they also don't like routine committee reports at board meetings. Put committee reports in the board packet, and don't include the reports on the agenda unless action is needed on a proposal from a committee. At the meeting, allow for questions about the mailed written reports, and say a word of appreciation to committees who submitted reports but who are not giving verbal reports at the meeting.

To be sure that packets are helpful, every couple of years ask board members (in writing or at a board meeting discussion) which components of the board packet they like best or like least, and what might be missing.

P.S. Consider putting a *Board Café* article in each packet!

Also Try

Ten Quick Ways to Invigorate Board Meetings, p. 193

Ten Tips for the Board Chair on Meetings, p. 196

Table of Contents for a Board Binder, p. 36

The pause that refreshes

Although seemingly corny, this idea really works. The board of a local hospice with Buddhist roots rings a small bell at the beginning and end of each board meeting to call for a minute of silent reflection. Any board member can ask for the bell during the meeting, too! "It helps us pause, reflect, and occasionally cool down," says a former board treasurer. Even without a bell, a pause in the conversation can help break an unproductive or overly hurried atmosphere. Try it!

Should the Board Hold Executive Sessions?

An executive session is a meeting (or part of a meeting) of the board without the organization's staff present.

Executive directors frequently object to executive sessions—perhaps because they feel their input is essential to any important discussion. But because one of the board's chief responsibilities is to assess the performance of the agency and its executive director, boards often need to discuss sensitive issues without staff present. Some examples include

- Annual meeting with the auditor
- Evaluation of the executive director and deciding on the executive director's salary
- Conflicts between two board members or serious criticism of a board member by another
- Investigation into concerns about the executive director or to hear a report from a management consultant
- Review of salary schedule, compensation policy, and related matters

Some organizations establish a "semi-executive session" during which the executive director is present, but no other staff. Such sessions may include

- Discussions related to lawsuits, complaints, or grievances from staff or former staff
- Discussions related to individual staff situations
- Discussions of the executive director, evaluations with the executive director

For example, one board member might want to raise a concern about the development director to see whether others share the concern or whether his negative experience was the exception. Another board member might want to discuss an issue involving herself and another board member without getting staff involved. Or the board may want to discuss the executive director's strengths and weaknesses with her to clarify each other's expectations.

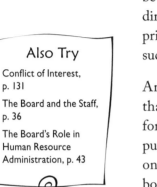

Also Try

Conflict of Interest,
p. 131

The Board and the Staff,
p. 36

The Board's Role in
Human Resource
Administration, p. 43

A certain awkwardness occurs when staff are asked to leave the room, and there may be resistance on the part of the executive director. But some discussions are appropriately held just among board members, such as those listed above.

An effective way to avoid the feeling that "executive sessions mean bad news for staff" is for board chairs to routinely put executive sessions on every agenda or on four agendas per year. That way, the board can meet privately without raising tension simply by doing so. In any case, the board should not feel uncomfortable excusing staff for part of any meeting, and the executive director may even volunteer: "Would you prefer to excuse staff for this next agenda item?"

The minutes of the meeting should indicate that the board met in executive session and report on the topic of the discussion, although the specifics (such as the amount of a lawsuit settlement) may be confidential and appear only in a set of confidential-to-the-board minutes.

From a reader

Executive sessions are rare for the board I'm on. But when we do have them, they often include the executive director. They are mostly used to avoid a written record of confidential issues or to discuss the executive director's salary. I would love to be able to "freewheel" without staff reading this as being "shut out."

—Name withheld

CHAPTER NINE

Boards and Fundraising

A common maxim is that "board members have to give, get, or get out." Many board members and staff as well would assertively state that an intrinsic responsibility of the board is to raise money.

But just what the board's role should be is a source of great debate and greater frustration. Consider the following complaints:

- "Our board members only give lip service to fundraising. No one has raised any real money." (From staff)
- "No one told me the main thing they wanted me to do was to raise money. They told me they wanted me because of my skills." (From a board member)
- "We approved a fundraising position, but the new person hasn't raised a cent!" (From a board member)
- "My new fundraiser can't raise a penny without strategic direction from the board!" (From an executive director)
- "This board can't tell a plan from a paper clip. They're not doing their part; I'm moving on to a better organization." (From the new fundraiser)
- "Fundraising is the board's single greatest responsibility." (From a nonprofit management consultant)

This cycle of finger-pointing has to end. The following articles use the Compass-Point Board Model to help boards and executives be mutually accountable for the governance and support responsibilities around fundraising:

What's the Best Way to Raise Money? Just Tell Me!

It's aggravating to have someone say (at a board meeting, for example), "Look at how they raise money over there! That's better than what we're doing...we should do that!" Or for a funder to tell you what she thinks is the best way to raise money: from major donors, or from government, or from black-tie dinners, or...you get the idea.

Think for a moment about two very successful stores (at least as of 2008): Target and Williams-Sonoma. Both sell cookware. Target sells inexpensive cookware through large stores in outlying areas, and it advertises through newsprint inserts in local newspapers. Williams-Sonoma sells expensive cookware through boutique stores in high-rent districts, and it advertises through glossy, full-color catalogs mailed to high-income zip codes. Each has put together a winning formula.

But what if Target were to try selling its colanders and measuring spoons at the same prices that Williams-Sonoma charges? (Would *you* buy a colander for $60 at Target?) Or if Williams-Sonoma were to try using newsprint flyers instead of its glossy catalogs? Most likely, neither decision would work.

So when we ask "What's the best way to raise money?" we need to start by figuring out who are the best potential supporters of our work and why, what those people are interested in, how to reach them, and how much to ask them for.

Fundraising strategy versus revenue strategy

Fundraising is about income that is contributed rather than earned. Fundraising strategies are ones that bring in money from individual donations, foundation grants, corporate contributions, church giving programs, and the funding programs of other institutions.

Tuitions, ticket sales to performances, magazine subscriptions, and almost all government contracts are examples of earned revenue. If you don't do the work, you don't get the money.

A revenue strategy, therefore, looks broadly at the range of possibilities for financial support and combines both earned income and contributed income. A revenue strategy is a crucial part of any plan for long-term financial sustainability.

The decisions you make about your revenue strategy—that is, who should be supporting your work and how to go about soliciting that support—should be based not only on who is most likely to give you money or pay for your services but what makes the most sense in terms of who you are, what kind of change you're trying to make in your community, and how your funding sources can help you get there.

Most nonprofits these days combine earned income (such as contracts, fees, sales) with contributed income. Like Target and Williams-Sonoma, each organization puts together a package based on its core supporters, its connections and positioning, and its cause.

Different strategies for similar programs

Let's look at how two after-school tutoring programs raise money.

Program A: Started in a racially diverse church, this program works with low-income kids who come for tutoring and after-school care in this mostly Latino, starting-to-gentrify neighborhood. Many of the volunteer tutors and board members are from the church, which draws from many neighborhoods across the city. With several upper-middle-class board members and the active support of the church, Program A raises $80,000 each year through fundraising events and several individual donations of $5,000 each.

Program B: With similar activities as Program A, Program B was started in a similar city quarter by a neighborhood center, itself often struggling for funds. Its volunteer tutors and board members are nearby residents, racially diverse,

many in the helping professions themselves, and some well connected to city politics. Coupling the center's importance to the neighborhood with its board's connections, Program B is able to obtain a modest annual grant each year from city government. In addition, it receives donations from the electric utility and a local family foundation. Car washes and a raffle raise more community spirit than they do funds but are still part of the total budget of $80,000.

Both these community-based programs have developed successful fundraising strategies. Of these methods, which is the best? Individual donations? City grant? Foundations? Fundraising event? Corporate grants? The answer (like the answer to most questions) is: it depends.

It depends on the organization's external environment (the opportunities) and its internal strengths (the assets). Externally, in some cities there are many foundations, while in others there are practically none. Organizational assets include who's involved in the organization—including constituents, board members, volunteers, and staff. Other assets include the relationships the organization has built with other groups and its connections to government agencies, local corporations, and community leaders.

The revenue strategy will be guided by the organization's philosophy about who should form the core of their support.

Finally, the cause itself is important: Some causes lend themselves more naturally to certain kinds of revenue. Corporations are less likely to support a prisoner-support organization than churches or government might be. Older constituents may be less likely to support international causes than younger constituents might be. (Note: These are hypothetical examples.)

Getting from here to there

Even if you don't think you have a revenue strategy, you already do have some kind of configuration of ways to obtain money. Start by taking a good look at the ones you are already using. In most cases a good first step is to expand the revenue areas where you are already having success and to link your various vehicles together. For example, Program A's major gifts program, which relies on about ten board members asking their friends for donations, doesn't take much effort but raises $40,000 each year. In contrast, Program A's walkathon raises about $5,000 in addition to raising community spirit and enthusiasm. Program A should focus its attention on expanding its major donor program, and it should maintain—but not

increase—the walkathon level of activity. It can also link these activities by bringing donors to the walkathon and using the walkathon to identify prospects for larger donations.

Just like the Target and Williams-Sonoma example, it may not work to take a page out of someone else's book. Begin by assessing what your organization has going for it internally and externally, and choose a mix that suits what you've got. Then, and perhaps most important, focus on doing well in those areas and recruiting the right board members and others to increase those fundraising areas before spreading out into new ones.

What's the best way to raise money? The one that has the potential to increase funding (or at least keep it level) and the one that you already have the skills and connections to tap.

This article appeared simultaneously in Blue Avocado *and the* Grassroots Fundraising Journal.

True or False? Board Members Should Raise Money

Here's an all-too-common scenario: The executive director is frustrated because she thinks it's the duty of board members to raise money—but they aren't doing so. A few board members agree and they state (or bring in a consultant to state) something like: "Board members *have to raise money*. That's their main job. You have to do it." Board members typically have three simultaneous reactions to this scenario. First, they resent being required to do fundraising when they were not told of this requirement when invited to join the board. Second, they feel guilty anyway about not raising any funds for the organization. Third, they doubt they could succeed at raising money, even if they were to try. It's as if they were invited to a potluck, arrived with one dish, and then scolded for not having brought birthday cake for the whole party.

To untangle this knot, it's helpful to think of the board as having two roles: a governance role where the board acts as a body to ensure accountability and a support role where board members act as individuals to support the organization through volunteering and donating. Ensuring that the organization has a realistic strategy for raising funds is a critical governance responsibility of the board of directors.

But that strategy may or may not include individual fundraising by board members. The strategy for raising funds will probably include a combination of efforts: fees-for-service (such as tuitions, service fees, registration fees, tickets), government contracts, special events, direct-mail fundraising campaigns, and individual major donor gifts.

There are four crucial rules to fundraising on the board:

1. In its governing role, the board as a body is responsible for approving and monitoring performance of a revenue strategy that will sustain the organization's work.

2. In their supporting roles as individuals, all board members must do something to help implement that strategy.

3. No one has to do everything.

4. Expectations must be clearly and fairly communicated to new board members during the recruitment process.

The board's governance responsibility is to ensure that a suitable financial or revenue strategy is in place. This strategy must have three characteristics: (1) it will result in the funds needed by the organization to do its work; (2) it will provide an emergency reserve, cash-flow smoothing, and cash for organizational investments (such as new computers, carpeting, or a publicity campaign); and (3) it is in line with the organization's ethics and values (for example, whether a community center should accept donations from beer companies).

For an asthma awareness center, the board may consider several funding strategies, such as a combination of foundation grants and an annual dinner dance, a combination of walkathon participation and publication sales, mail appeals combined with major individual gifts, and government contracts combined with foundation grants. The board may decide to adopt a strategy of participating in the walkathon, selling publications, and soliciting major individual donations. This decision is based on what is realistic for the current board and staff as well as on the opportunities most open to them.

As a result, board members, in their support responsibilities, agree that each board member will participate in one or more activities within the fundraising strategy. One board member agrees to bring ten volunteers to help at the walkathon. Another will send out e-mail publicity about publications to book editors and bookstores. A third agrees to hold a party at her house and to ask her friends to attend for $1,500 each. Each board member is supporting either the contributions component or the earned-income component of the revenue strategy in a way that's suited to individual ability.

In short, the board's governance responsibility is fulfilled by its choosing and monitoring a revenue plan, while each board member's support responsibility is fulfilled by participating in the plan's implementation. Clarifying this distinction, as well as the expectations of board members, will go a long way toward calmer, less charged, and more productive discussions about fundraising.

What are the keys to fundraising success?

1. *Leadership.* The board chair or another board member needs to provide an example and act as a leader in fundraising. If you don't have such a leader, wait to launch a fundraising drive; instead, work on recruiting a leader.

   The fundraising leader doesn't need to be a major donor or a board officer. The fundraising leader is a board member who is committed to getting other board members involved with fundraising and who, by attitude as well as in words, brings fundraising matters positively and honestly to board meetings.

2. *Expectations.* Almost nothing is more frustrating for a sincere person than to join a board only to hear for the first time six months later that a major donation is expected of board members. Be sure that your board's policy on individual giving is clearly communicated to prospective board members.

If your board doesn't have a policy, be sure that when you discuss having one, individual board members are aware that policies will go into effect within the next year.

3. *Diverse methods and roles.* A successful fundraising strategy has several different channels through which people can get involved. Not all board members need to be involved in every component. If board members can choose one or two fundraising activities at the beginning of the year, they need not be pressured throughout the year to participate in every activity.

4. *Mentoring and training.* Most people feel best about taking on a job when they are confident they can do the job. Board members aren't any different when it comes to fundraising.

Whether it's planning the annual dinner or asking face-to-face for contributions, board members need both training and ongoing mentoring and support. For example, if a board member is going to accompany a staff person on a visit to a foundation, spend some time beforehand deciding who will say what and anticipating (and practicing!) answers to possible questions.

In some organizations, the board focuses its collective and individual attention more on fundraising than on anything else. Board members are recruited for their eagerness and ability to raise money. But for most community-based organizations, the board must first determine what fundraising duties will be required of its members, and then see that these duties are carried out.

Also Try

The CompassPoint Board Model for Governance and Support, p. 20

A Board Member Contract, p. 26

What to Do with Board Members Who Don't Do Anything, p. 136

Five Ways One Board Member Can Raise $100 to $5,000, p. 215

Eight Easy Ways for the Board to Get Started with Fundraising, p. 217

What is *planned giving* anyway?

Planned giving and deferred giving are ways that people can give funds and assets (such as their homes) to nonprofits so that the donors receive the tax benefits now and the nonprofits receive the assets after their deaths. (It's more complicated than this, but that's the idea.) Some nonprofit board members are finding they want to know more—for their own wills as well as their organizations' planned gift campaigns. A publication entitled "Planned Giving: A Board Member's Perspective" is available from BoardSource by calling 800-883-6262 or visiting http://www.boardsource.org/

Sample Board Member's Budget Pledge Form

Each year, as part of the budget adoption process, one board president collects the following simple form from each board member:

For the fiscal year _____ my contribution toward the support of this organization will be:

1. My personal contribution: $ _____
   - ☐ Check enclosed
   - ☐ Send me a quarterly reminder
   - ☐ Charge my credit card quarterly:

2. My company will match: _____

3. I will make a financial contribution of stock, bequest, other:_____

4. I will participate in preparations for one or more of our special events:

   Annual Gala   Theatre Party   Summer Bash

5. I will assist with fundraising outreach to the following foundations, corporations, individuals:

   _____

6. I can provide or identify in-kind resources or services (for example, computer equipment, office supplies, transportation, furniture, professional services) as follows: _____

   _____

Making this form part of the budget process illustrates how contributions are a fundamental part of how the organization will find needed resources for the coming year.

Thanks to David LaGreca, former Board Café Editorial Committee member, for this great idea.

Five Ways One Board Member Can Raise $100 to $5,000

Frequently two or three board members want everyone to raise funds, but they don't know how to begin to get others on board. Sometimes the best way is simply to start raising money and to involve other board members as individual helpers. And sometimes raising money on your own is simply the best thing to do, whether or not others follow your example. Here are some ways to get started.

1. Make a personal contribution. Write a short, handwritten note to the board president to explain why you are making the contribution and give the check and note to him or her at the end of a board meeting.

2. Get together with one other board member and hold a dessert party at your house or apartment. Invite ten friends and relatives each, and tell them they will learn about the organization, be asked but not pressured to make a contribution, and enjoy a great dessert. Hold the party on a weeknight at 7:00 p.m. The day before the party, call *everyone* again and urge them to attend. Invite three or four other board members so they can learn how to hold a dessert party. Make or buy finger desserts, such as cookies or cream puffs. Make some cupcakes but don't serve them. At the party, have one client speak for three minutes about what the organization has meant in his or her life. Then have one staff person speak for another three minutes. Next explain to the group why you're on the board and why you think the organization is important. Ask your friends if they have any questions you can answer. Then ask them, if they feel it's worthwhile, to make a contribution before leaving the party. Tell them that you'll give them two cupcakes to take home if they make a contribution before they leave (that gives them a "reason" to write the check that evening).

3. Write a letter and send it to ten friends and relatives. In the letter, explain why you are volunteering your time at the agency. Ask them to consider making a contribution to the organization and include the organization's name and address. Give the list to the staff and ask them to tell you immediately if they get any contributions.

4. Volunteer to match the contributions from other board members. Tell the board that you will match, dollar for dollar, every contribution from a board member within the next thirty

Also Try

True or False? Board Members Should Raise Money, p. 211

Eight Easy Ways for the Board to Get Started with Fundraising, p. 217

A Board Member Contract, p. 26

days, to a total of $2,000. The catch: You'll only do it if each and every board member makes a contribution. Alternatively, have a staff member tell the board that an anonymous board member has made this offer.

5. Get together with two or three other people on the board and pledge significant gifts. Then write a letter to all the board members that says, "We—Gerald, Pat, Laura, and Edgar—have pledged to give a combined total of $4,200 to our organization this year. We're making this pledge because we believe in the work we're doing, and we want to make sure we do as much as we can. Won't you join us in building the important work of our organization?"

If you are the only person or one of only a few board members who thinks the board should do more in fundraising, it's smart to start with one of the above steps. After a few of these steps are taken and a few months go by, fundraising will be less mysterious and more familiar to board members, and the board may be open to agreeing on standards of board participation.

What to say to a donor you've run into

Okay, you're at a reception or holiday party and you've just met a donor or funder of the organization on whose board you serve. What do you say?

1. **Thank the donor:** "Glad to meet you. I want to thank you for all the support you've given this organization. It means a lot to us."

2. **Introduce yourself:** "I'm a board member. I got involved because I think this cause is so important."

3. **Ask why he or she gives:** "I'd like to ask you a question…What is it about our organization that made you decide to give a contribution or grant to us?"

4. **Ask for advice:** "If there were one thing you wish we'd change about our organization, what would it be?"

Got it? Thanks—Introduce yourself—Ask why—One change. (Print this phrase on cards to give to board members.)

Eight Easy Ways for the Board to Get Started with Fundraising

Your organization may already have a well-developed, board-based fundraising system that is going gangbusters. If so, congratulations! This article is for the rest of us.

Sometimes board members want to raise funds, but they haven't had experience doing so, either as individuals or as a group. As with any new venture, some early positive experiences can go a long way toward continued success. Try combining these group activities with the individual activities described in "Five Ways One Board Member Can Raise $100 to $5,000."

1. Invite board members from a *similar* organization to come to your board meeting and share their experiences raising money (successful and unsuccessful). For example, if you're a soccer league board, ask a nearby Little League board. Schedule a fifteen-minute presentation and leave time for questions. Don't expect to have any immediate action; this is food for thought.

2. Invite board members from a very *different* kind of organization in your community to come to your board meeting and explain how they raise money. For example, if you're on the board of an after-school program, ask a drug abuse treatment center to send a board member to make a presentation.

3. Schedule a discussion on fundraising. Ask each board member to relate a positive and a negative experience with fundraising. Make a list to help you learn how to avoid having similar negative experiences, and so you can remember how the positive experiences unfolded.

4. If you don't have a fundraising committee, form one. Remember, the fundraising committee doesn't have to raise the money by itself; its first job is to develop a plan for how the organization, including the board, will raise money.

5. If no one wants to be on the fundraising committee, recruit new board members with an interest in and a commitment to starting one.

6. Put the following resolution—adapted for your own organization—on the agenda:

   "We believe the Board of Directors has a responsibility to ensure that a realistic plan is developed and implemented for funding this organization through a combination of fundraising and earned income. In addition, we agree that each individual member of the board will, at a minimum, do the following:

a) Make an annual contribution before June 30 each year at a personally meaningful level, and do so with only one reminder;

b) Donate or solicit donations of items worth $200 or more for the annual silent auction;

c) Participate in at least one other fundraising activity each year."

7. Have the board chair ask everyone to make a personal contribution at a level that is meaningful to them and have the board chair follow up with phone calls.

8. Organize three board members into an ad hoc committee that sets a fundraising goal for the board, such as $10,000 from fifteen board members.

The three committee members then set a target request from each board member, with some board members being asked for substantial gifts and others for modest gifts. Each board member then receives an in-person visit from one of the three committee members during which he or she is asked for the target gift.

Board member fundraising—which is essentially seeking funds from individual donors—is more than a way to sustain the organization financially. Perhaps more important, it's a way of keeping the organization from becoming too dependent on a funding source (such as the government or a foundation) that is likely to have obvious or subtle strings attached. In short, board member fundraising helps keep the organization independent—but accountable to the community—in a way that no other funding vehicle can.

Also Try

Nonprofit bingo: What's the law?

Nonprofits conducting bingo, lotteries, pull-tabs, pickle jars (pickle jars?), and other "games" need to know the whole story on what's taxable to the nonprofit, the special forms that need to be filed, the "volunteer labor exception," and tax withholding on winnings. The excellent IRS "Gaming Publication for Tax-exempt Organizations" goes over it all, and even includes sample spreadsheets for record-keeping. Order it from the IRS (Publication 3079) or download it by visiting http://www.irs.gov/pub/irs-pdf/p3079.pdf.

CHAPTER TEN

Boards and Finance

There may be no governance responsibility more important than responsibility for the financial integrity and accountability of a nonprofit organization. In its role as representative of the organization's publics—its clients, donors, volunteers, and society at large—the board must ensure that the organization uses its funds efficiently, as donors have designated, and in pursuit of the organization's goals. Many of the board's central governance responsibilities fall under the broad area of finance.

But at the same time, many board members are uncertain exactly how they can carry out this responsibility.

Financial matters span a broad range of topics as well as accounting and the budget. Payroll matters, benefits administration, contract management, insurance, compliance with regulations, and other subjects are often handled by staff working closely with the finance committee.

Individual board members also perform supporting roles within the organization, such as advising staff on lines of credit, teaching staff to prepare cash-flow schedules, and other tasks. As a result, the governance and support roles of the board can become confused. The articles in this chapter will help you better execute the board's roles in the organization's finances:

A Board-Staff Contract
for Financial Accountability*

Not all board members need to be familiar with financial terms and concepts, but each organization needs to develop a clear and explicit agreement for how financial accountability will be ensured. The following is a starting point for a "contract" that the board and staff can make to ensure a partnership for accountability.

This agreement should be discussed and renewed when there is a new board treasurer or a new staff head of finance.

---

* One of the five most reprinted *Board Café* articles.

Sample Board-Staff Contract for Financial Accountability

The board and staff agree to the following activities to support financial accountability

The staff will	The board will
Related to tax and legal responsibilities,	
• Immediately notify the board with complete information related to any delays in payroll tax payments or any legal matters • Immediately notify the board of any tax problems or penalties • Immediately notify the board of any legal suits	• Work closely with staff to respond to notification of possible tax problems and develop plans for resolving tax and legal problems • Formally approve any tax and legal settlements
Related to accounting,	

a) Complete monthly or quarterly statements within three weeks of the end of the month:
  • Income and expense statement for each major program and for the organization as a whole (should include statements for the previous month and on a year-to-date basis)
  • Balance sheet for the organization as a whole
  • For large organizations with substantial restricted funds or an endowment fund, a balance sheet for the restricted funds
  • Comparison of actual to budget on a year-to-date basis for the organization and, if appropriate, for each program
b) Mail statements to finance committee in advance of meeting
c) If the statements are not available, explain the delay and estimate a date by which the statements will be completed
d) In a timely manner, prepare end-of-year statements, Federal Form 990, and other federal and state forms
	• Form a finance committee of members who understand financial information and standard accounting terms and practices
	• Carefully read financial information
	• Ask questions to be sure the statements are understood
	• Periodically review key accounting policies, such as depreciation and cash or accrual basis statements
	• Be patient and understanding when statements are occasionally late or infrequent accounting problems occur

Sample Board-Staff Contract for Financial Accountability (continued)

The staff will	The board will
In cash-flow projections,	
• If appropriate for the organization, prepare monthly, quarterly, or annual cash-flow projection • If appropriate, prepare a comparison of actual to projected cash flows • If cash-flow shortages are projected, develop a plan for bridging the shortages • If cash-flow surpluses are projected, develop a plan for maximizing investment	• Pay attention to cash-flow reports • Determine whether preparation of cash-flow reports provides important enough information to justify the staff time required
In financial analysis,	

a) Prepare brief written narrative monthly or quarterly including the following:
  • Highlights of recent period
  • Continuing or anticipated problems
  • Anticipated opportunities
  • Analysis of financial health
  • Comments on recent financial performance
b) As part of the annual budget preparation or at another key juncture:
  • Investigate and analyze outside trends affecting the organization's finances
  • Revisit key decisions related to assets and liabilities, such as mortgages, debt, and investments
  • Prepare vertical and, if possible, horizontal analyses
	• Propose items for ad hoc investigation
	• Discuss analyses with staff; work with staff to improve financial performance
	• In the absence of the expertise on staff, one or more individual board members may be able to do some of the analysis

Sample Board-Staff Contract for Financial Accountability (continued)

The staff will	The board will
In relation to the audit and internal controls,	
• If audited, ensure that audited statements and management letter are completed within four months of the end of the fiscal year • Prepare a written response to comments and recommendations in the management letter • Develop a written set of internal controls and follow procedures in spirit as well as to the letter	• Determine whether or not an audit is appropriate • Take the lead in interviewing prospective auditors and review of bids • Select the auditor • Meet at least once per year with auditor when no staff are present • Receive audit letter directly from auditor • Review written internal control procedures
In relation to the budget,	
• Develop a proposed budget by program and for the organization as a whole • Have the authority to make minor changes (such as shifting dollars among line items or making increases in variable costs that are matched by increases in earned revenue) in the budget without board approval • If significant budget variances occur, explain the variances and proposed action such as better attention to budget control or revised end-of-year projections	• Develop parameters for staff to guide preparation of the draft budget, such as maximum allowable deficit for the year, reduction of days payable, or additions to cash reserve • Give careful attention to budget reports • Engage in long-term planning for funding, such as identifying a target mix of contributed and earned monies • Formally accept the budget, thereby authorizing the beginning of operations as planned

Sample Board-Staff Contract for Financial Accountability (continued)

The staff will	The board will
In salaries and personnel,	
• Prepare an annual report showing each staff position (not name) and salary for the finance committee or personnel committee to review	• Establish salary ranges for each category of employee
• Prepare an annual schedule of individuals to whom 1099s were issued and the amounts	• Approve guidelines for performance-based compensation, if appropriate
	• Negotiate and approve the executive director's salary
	• Ensure that other salaries are within approved salary ranges or, if not, to have approved exceptions
	• Approve personnel policies
	• Periodically review employee benefits
In general,	
• Make a good faith effort to communicate all significant information	• Give serious attention to financial information
• Ungrudgingly complete requests for ad hoc reports	• Be understanding when problems occur
• Appreciate that tough questions are appropriate and not hostile	• Make only reasonable requests for ad hoc reports
• Have good answers	• Work as problem solvers as well as governors
	• Be willing to ask tough questions
	• Respect the difficulty of the work, and express appreciation when appropriate
	• Ask good questions

From *Best of the Board Café* (a column in the online magazine *Blue Avocado*), Copyright © 2003 and 2009, CompassPoint Nonprofit Services, published by Fieldstone Alliance, www.FieldstoneAlliance.org. Subscribe free to *Blue Avocado* at www.blueavocado.org.

The Board and the Budget

Beauty and the Beast?

For many nonprofits, the annual "approving of the budget" is the cornerstone of board financial oversight. However, this annual approval is frequently an empty ritual: one where board members peruse a budget that they are unsure is realistic or appropriate to the planned activities.

Consider the following scene:

> The finance discussion is scheduled for the end of the meeting, which means it will be hurried. Given a complex budget that "needs to be approved," board members react first by looking for things that they can understand . . . usually a relatively small expense item: "Why is this travel budget so high?" "Can this phone budget be reduced?"

> As each question or suggestion is raised by board members, staff respond by explaining why each suggestion is unrealistic. "The travel budget has been funded for Program X so we have to do it." "Actually the phone budget is not that big." After a few instances of staff "explaining" line items, board members realize that asking such questions isn't really going anywhere.

In the backs of their minds is the thought, "It's probably okay. It was okay last year and I didn't understand it then either." So they vote to approve the budget.

In short, board members first nitpick, staff react to questions as evidence of the board's ignorance, and then the board rubberstamps the budget.

The truth is that such approval of the budget isn't a meaningful act on the part of the board. The staff do know more about operations, and appropriately staff should develop the budget. So what would be meaningful work for the board on the budget?

The board has some important perspectives to bring to the discussion of the budget. Here are questions that take advantage of the board's diverse community perspective and the finance staff's knowledge and skill:

Are there specific financial objectives that we want for the next year?

For example, an organization may determine that it needs to have $75,000 in working capital to even out its cash flows over the year. The board may ask the staff to include $15,000 as "surplus" in the budget for each of the next several years to begin building that reserve.

Are there new projects or expansions that the organization's leadership would like to consider?

For example, the staff can be asked to prepare cost estimates for some of the following:

- The financial impact of across-the-board 10 percent raises
- The financial impact of adding a 401(k) retirement plan
- The financial impact of increasing the child care program by one more class of children
- Are there capital projects for which we should be saving? For example, should we be setting aside $3,000 per year to prepare for buying a new phone system? Should we expect to spend $5,000 per year on computer replacements and upgrades?

Is our dollar allocation generally in line with our priorities?

For example, if an organization started as a dance troupe with a few dance classes, it might consider whether the organization's attention over time—as reflected in the budget—has come to overemphasize the classes over dance performance.

An alternative budget process can look like this:

First, the finance committee leads a full board discussion on programmatic goals and financial objectives. The board establishes some broad guidelines for staff to follow as they develop the budget. These might include

- A budget that provides for increased volume in homeless services while keeping other services at the same level or allowing a slight decline
- A budget that plans for a surplus of $30,000 to help build a cash reserve
- A budget that includes the establishment of a 3 percent employer contribution to a 401(k) plan
- A budget that includes a 15 percent increase in board-generated donations

Next, staff prepare a draft budget, with comments about the financial implications of the broad guidelines and projections of anticipated revenue, expense, investment, and cash-flow needs. For example, their comments might be

- Increasing homeless services by 5 percent would cost approximately $85,000 in additional staff, food, and garbage costs. There is some possibility of obtaining a foundation grant for this amount.
- Given the risks of state funding levels this year, a $50,000 addition to cash reserves would be more appropriate and

allow for deliberate closedowns of programs if necessary.

- If the 401(k) contribution is made for all employees (whether or not an employee also contributes), the cost would be $35,000. Establishing and administering a 401(k) plan will take significant staff time over the year as well.

- This last year board-generated donations increased by 15 percent over the previous year. A goal of 18 percent would provide a "stretch" goal.

- The attached draft budget allows for a 2 percent salary increase—somewhat offset by the 3 percent 401(k) contribution.

- Combining staff projections with the board guidelines, a deficit of $20,000 is projected for the coming year.

- One possibility is to decrease the addition to cash reserves from $30,000 to $10,000. Another is to direct staff to make another effort to readjust the budget and bring back a revised budget and projection.

At this point the finance committee and the staff jointly review the draft budget and, through a couple of iterations, end up with a revised budget that meets some but not all of the board's guidelines. In this example, the revised budget may contribute only 2 percent to the 401(k) plan and increase profitability in some other areas.

Finally, the finance committee presents the budget to the full board. The board can see the extent to which the guidelines are met and what implications there are for other parts of the budget. The board authorizes the staff to proceed as the budget outlines.

For many organizations, the budget process is, in fact, the process through which board and staff decide on the organization's priorities, interpret its vision in operational terms, negotiate compromises, and agree to go forward together. In different organizations, this process is bound to look different. A key in all processes is finding a way for the board to act in a meaningful way, exercising its governance role in both financial oversight and maximizing resources.

Also Try

A Board-Staff Contract for Financial Accountability, p. 220

Cash and Investment Management, p. 228

Six Things Every Board Member Should Know about Form 990, p. 237

CompassPoint Board Model for Governance and Support, p. 20

Year-Long Agenda for a Board Committee, p. 185

Cash and Investment Management

As part of its governance responsibilities, the board is responsible for safeguarding the organization's assets and ensuring that funds are used to further the organization's goals. In addition, the board must ensure that donor designations are honored and that cash and other investments are managed prudently.

Specifically, the board should review three areas related to investments: cash management, asset management, and endowment fund management.

1. Cash management

Cash management refers to ordinary transfers, usually of small amounts, between the checking account and other liquid accounts such as savings accounts. For example, if an organization anticipates having excess cash for a few months, staff may open an account that earns more interest and temporarily hold cash there.

While staff typically manage these tasks, the board has a responsibility to oversee cash management and periodically review staff work. In most boards, the finance committee meets periodically with finance staff to review cash management guidelines and practices.

2. Asset management

Whether assets are in an organization's general fund, in its endowment fund, or in other funds, these assets should be invested wisely. The following are key decisions the board should make related to financial assets:

a) *Should we hire a portfolio manager or investment advisor, or make our own investment decisions?*

Organizations with substantial assets often hire portfolio managers or investment advisors. Organizations with fewer dollars to invest usually rely on the expertise of a board member or the finance committee.

The portfolio manager, typically employed at a bank, brokerage, or investment advisory firm, is responsible for making investment decisions for the organization. The portfolio manager will meet with the finance or investment committee to learn about the organization's financial objectives and other concerns, and then make investment decisions throughout the year to meet those objectives. The portfolio manager should give the organization a monthly or quarterly written report that shows all the trades made in the period, the investments at the end of the period, and the value of each investment.

Portfolio managers and investment advisors are generally paid on a retainer basis (a flat monthly fee) for their services, although some are paid as a percentage of the portfolio and others by commissions on trades (this last creates an incentive to make frequent transactions). Great care should be taken in selecting a portfolio manager, and the investment or finance committee should routinely review the manager's performance in detail (usually by making comparisons to the returns in the financial markets and the returns on mutual funds that have similar investment objectives as the organization), just as they should when working with other professionals such as auditors and attorneys.

Some organizations that have identified and agreed on an investment strategy choose to invest directly in a mutual fund with similar investment objectives, rather than hire a portfolio manager.

b) *Should we create a board investments committee?*

Organizations with little money or little investment activity often choose to have their finance committees oversee investments. Some organizations with substantial assets choose to create a second committee to oversee investments. One common arrangement is for the investments committee to be chaired by an experienced member of the finance committee and to include both other board members as well as nonboard members, with board members comprising a majority of the investments committee. Having nonboard members on the investments committee allows the organization to use the expertise and perspectives of individuals who may not have the time or other qualifications to be members of the board.

In some cases, the investments committee or the finance committee makes specific investment decisions itself, such as to move funds from treasury bonds into mutual funds, to sell a specific stock, or to modify the mix of equity and income funds. In other cases, the committee selects and meets regularly with the portfolio manager and, if necessary, recommends changing to a new manager.

c) *What guidelines should we establish for the investments committee or for the portfolio manager?*

Whether a committee or a hired manager handles investments, the board must set investment guidelines. The following questions are examples of concerns that boards take up in investment management. Often these questions are discussed primarily in the investments or finance committee, where committee members are more likely to be familiar with financial terms and the implications of financial decisions. Some organizations delegate these questions to the investments or finance committee, while other organizations require proposed guidelines to be brought to the whole board for approval. The answers to these questions will change over time as the organization's needs change; the appropriate committee must be in touch with board concerns as well as with the following questions:

- Is our primary objective short-term earnings or long-term equity growth?

- What level and types of risk are acceptable to our organization?

- Should we establish any *nonfinancial* guidelines for investments, such as a preference for locally owned companies or avoidance of companies whose products conflict directly with our mission?

- How quickly must our investments be convertible to cash?

3. Endowment fund management

An endowment fund, also called permanently restricted net assets, is typically created when a donor stipulates that the principal amount of his or her gift (the amount of the contribution) will not be spent, but will be maintained "in perpetuity," while the income can be used for specified purposes. For example, a donor may give $1 million with the proviso that the $1 million be kept intact, but that interest from the $1 million can be spent on operating costs.

In some cases a donor will create a term endowment fund that specifies a time period or event after which the principal may be spent as well.

The board's key responsibilities with endowment funds are to ensure that the principal is maintained and that the endowment is invested "as a prudent person would." Assets held in the endowment fund (cash, stocks, bonds, land, works of art, and so on) should be managed prudently, according to fund management guidelines that the organization has adopted. When organizations need cash, either because of an ongoing deficit or short-term cash deficits, they may be tempted to borrow from endowment funds. Any such loans from the endowment fund should be approved by a formal vote of the board, and a repayment schedule should be established. Because such loans put the principal of the endowment fund at risk, they should be discouraged.

It is the responsibility of the board to establish guidelines for the management of the endowment fund. These guidelines are typically discussed by the finance or investments committee, which makes recommendations on policy to the board.

Some of the most important guidelines to establish are the following:

a) *Shall the principal be maintained at face value, or should the endowment be managed so that the value of the endowment increases at the rate of inflation?*

Over time, inflation will reduce the purchasing power of an endowment fund; $2 million today will be worth less as years go by. Some organizations choose to reinvest an amount of the earnings equal to inflation in the endowment fund, in essence defining "maintaining the principal" as "the principal adjusted for inflation." This is sometimes achieved by adopting a "spending rule." For example, some organizations assume long-term inflation at 4 percent, and average portfolio return at 9 percent, and thereby adopt a rule to "spend 5 percent of the average market value of the endowment over the last three years."

b) *Shall gains on contributed, noncash assets be treated as additions to principal (and therefore to be held in perpetuity) or as income (and therefore available for current expenditure)?*

For example, imagine an organization receives a contribution of ten shares of stock valued at $1,000 each, for a total of $10,000. A year later, the organization sells the stock, now valued at $1,100 a share, for a total of $11,000. Must the organization now keep $11,000 in perpetuity, or can it keep $10,000 in the principal and take $1,000 into income for current purposes? (In some cases a donor may place restrictions on the contributed assets, such as specifying that a donation of stock cannot be sold.)

c) *How often will we transfer interest income from the portfolio into the checking account of the general operating fund?*

Some organizations choose to take the earnings from the principal out of the investment accounts only once a year. Others pull out the earnings quarterly, or even monthly. Of course, the longer the intervals between withdrawals, the more income will be realized (because the income will be earning interest, too, until it is withdrawn).

When an organization has enough funds to invest, the board has a responsibility to see that those funds are invested wisely *and* used wisely. These broad guidelines and questions are meant to provide a starting point for a series of discussions where the organization's values, mission, and technical knowledge can come together.

Also Try

A Board-Staff Contract for Financial Accountability, p. 220

Board Committee Job Descriptions, p. 175

Year-Long Agenda for a Board Committee, p. 185

Annual Report from a Board Committee, p. 187

Loans from Board Members

In many nonprofits, a time comes when the question arises: Should the organization accept personal loans from board members? This article does not try to answer that question. It does try to outline—very briefly—some of the choices in how such loans can be made. Use this article as a starting point for a discussion with the board or a discussion with your personal financial advisor.

There are many examples where board members have lent crucial funds to their organizations, making it possible to get through a temporary cash shortage or get started on a new venture, and where those board members have been paid back promptly. But there are also examples where loans from board members have led to resentments and accusations, and where loans are not repaid to some or all of the board members who made loans. In short: a loan from a board member is a risky venture.

For any of the types of loans discussed below, be sure to do the following:

- Have legal documents drawn up and reviewed by an attorney for the organization. Each board member who loans money should have the documents reviewed by his or her own lawyer or financial advisor.

- The board should formally vote to accept any loans from board members and approve the terms of such loans, and any board members lending money should be excused from the vote.

- If all or the majority of board members are lending money, the loans and the legal documents should be accepted by roll-call vote of the board and recorded in the minutes.

- Make sure the lending board members understand that in bankruptcy or liquidation, lenders who are board members are considered "insiders" whose loans may be "subordinated"—pushed down to the last in line for payment—for reasons such as perceived board mismanagement of the organization.

Remember that discussions and decision making are likely to be influenced by loans from board members. Board members who have lent more than others may feel their opinion is more important, as they are the most financially at risk. Others who may not have lent money tend to defer to those who have. Disagreements that were once spirited can become bad-tempered and disruptive.

1. Unsecured loans

In a nutshell:
An individual board member (or several board members) lends money to the organization without collateral.

Example:
Each of five board members individually agrees to make unsecured loans of $5,000 each, at no interest, to be paid back within 120 days.

Be sure to:
Execute (draw up and sign) a loan document for each loan that specifies the amount, the interest due on the loan (if any), when the loan will be paid back (in installments or all at once), and what recourse (if any) the lender has if the loan is not paid back on time.

Comments:
- For the organization: unsecured loans are fast and uncomplicated, particularly for small amounts of money.
- For board members: do not lend more than you could easily afford to lose.

Risks:
- Failure to repay the loan will likely be resented by board members who have lent money.
- If the organization closes and goes bankrupt, other creditors (such as the landlord, the copier lease company) will be repaid before unsecured loans.
- In some cases, individuals who have made loans may feel that their opinions are weightier than those who

have not, and board decision-making processes may be disrupted.

2. Secured loans

In a nutshell:
An individual board member (or several board members) lends funds to the organization to be paid from a specific anticipated income, or secured by specific assets of the organization.

Examples:
- Before the annual luncheon fundraiser, a board member lends $3,500 to the organization with the agreement that he will be the first creditor repaid from the gross receipts of the luncheon.
- Two board members each lend the organization $25,000 with the parking lot (which is fully owned) as collateral.

Comments:
- Because secured loans are "backed up," lenders may feel more confident they will be repaid and, as a result, may be willing to make loans, larger loans, or loans at lower interest rates.
- On the other hand, an organization can lose an important asset over a relatively minor loan.

Be sure to:
- Act with a great deal of caution when considering secured loans.
- Do not use a large asset (such as a building) to secure a small loan.

3. Guaranteeing a loan or line of credit

In a nutshell:

The organization approaches a bank for a line of credit or a term loan, which is guaranteed by (cosigned by) a board member.

Example:

A bank gives the organization a line of credit for up to $10,000 and an individual board member agrees to repay the loan if the organization defaults on repayment.

Comments:

- A line of credit allows the organization to borrow funds as it needs them, up to a limit allowed by the bank. This method permits a board member to help without actually laying out cash (assuming the bank loan is eventually repaid).

- It's easy for disputes to arise if an organization has funds in other accounts but refuses to repay the line of credit or has made decisions deemed unwise by the board member making the guarantee.

- In the event of bankruptcy, the guaranteeing board member may have to honor the guarantee at a time when there is no prospect of repayment from the organization.

- A board member's guarantee can be secured by a pledge of collateral, just as in a secured loan.

4. Pooled loan

In a nutshell:

A number of board members place $10,000 into a pooled bank account. Two board members lend $2,500 each (or 25 percent each of the total), and five board members lend $1,000 each (or 10 percent each of the total). The organization can use funds from this account, using any one of the three options listed above. If, at the time agreed upon for repayment, there is not enough money to repay the board members, the amount available is repaid proportionately. In this instance, if there were only $2,000 for repayment, each of the first two board members would get $500 back (25 percent of $2,000), and each of the five other board members would get $200 back (10 percent of $2,000).

Comment:

This arrangement allows all board members to share in the risk, rather than having to decide which board member would get repaid first, second, and so on.

Be sure to:

Have signed loan documents that specify whether the loaned funds will be used directly or to guarantee other loans, the interest rate and interest payment schedule (if any), dates for payment(s), and recourse, if any, that board members have in the event of a loan default.

5. A "floating endowment"

In a nutshell:

Most often used by private schools, board members (or parents whose children are in the school) make unsecured loans to the organization for a specified period of time.

Example:

At the time of a child's enrollment in the school, his or her parents are required (or strongly encouraged) to make a loan to the school of $2,000, at no interest, which is repaid to the parents at the time the child leaves the school. These loaned funds are held in a special account and used to guarantee the line of credit obtained by the school.

Comments:

- In a way that parents or board members may find relatively painless, the organization has the ability to obtain a significant line of credit.

- Craft the arrangement so that, if departing parents can't be fully repaid, all parents (not just those departing that year) share the burden.

- The requirement to help with a floating endowment can be much more difficult to bear for some parents than for others.

6. Issuing a bond

In a nutshell:

A nonprofit can issue bonds to board members and members as a way of borrowing funds from those same people. Typically there is more risk to these bonds than those available on the open market, but members, board members, and others may be willing to accept this higher level of risk in order to raise funds for a large investment such as a new wing. In addition, nonprofits can issue tax-exempt bonds through government entities (a city, for example). In such a case, the organization—let's say a local museum or YMCA—issues a tax-exempt bond and sells the bonds to the public. The bond—usually not worth doing unless the bond is for more than $2 million—is paid back with interest over a number of years (ten or more) with funds earned in the future.

Comments:

- Bonds are complex transactions that many people feel they cannot understand.

- Issuing a bond requires expert legal and banking assistance. You may have a volunteer parent or board member with such expertise, but be sure to get an outside opinion as well.

Also Try

Thinking about Closing Down, p. 118

The Right Way to Go Out of Business, p. 120

Conflict of Interest, p. 131

A Board-Staff Contract for Financial Accountability, p. 220

Remember...

This article describes only some of the ways that loans can be made and accepted. Perhaps a more important question is whether loans from board members or others are appropriate at all. If an organization is in serious financial trouble, it's unlikely that loaned monies will help solve the problems. (And consider how difficult it might be, in a last ditch, to try to raise money to pay back board members.) On the other hand, if an organization is waiting for a guaranteed payment in the future, or if the board members are willing to make personal investments in the organization, loans can help an organization get through a temporary difficulty to where a bright future can be built.

What's on the Internet about your organization?

Take a quick look by going to http://www.yahoo.com/ or http://www.google.com/. Type in the name of the organization on whose board you serve (be sure to put quotation marks around the name, as in "Olive Tree Nonprofit Services") and see what you can find out!

Six Things Every Board Member Should Know about Form 990

by Jeanne Bell

Thanks to investment banker Paul Rosenstiel of E. J. De La Rosa for assistance with this article.

Federal Form 990 from the Internal Revenue Service (IRS) is like a tax return for nonprofits, but because we are tax-exempt, it's called an "information return." Because the 990 delivers key financial and other information to the IRS and to the public (Forms 990 are available to the public at http://www2.guidestar.org), they have crucial compliance and public image aspects and merit close board member attention.

You may have heard by now that the IRS Form 990 has been substantially revised for the fiscal years ending in 2008 and in the future. The issues disclosed on the form that especially interest the media, potential donors, and the general public still include executive compensation and overhead costs, but with this revised form, the IRS has entered the territory of "good governance" as well.

In fact, in a November 2008 speech, IRS commissioner Steve T. Miller said, "We have pushed to require [new] reporting on how organizations are managed. The crown jewel of this effort is the governance section of the revised Form 990, effective for 2008." This broader IRS scrutiny means that board members and executives of community nonprofits should feel even more urgency to review and understand what's being submitted each year.

Here, very briefly, are six things that you should know about the revised nonprofit tax return. You can find all the details about these and other changes at http://www.irs.gov/charities/.

1. Your organization's 990 is due four and one-half months after the close of your fiscal year: If your fiscal year ends June 30, your 990 is due on November 15; if your fiscal year ends December 31, it's due May 15, and so on. It is very common to obtain an extension of time to file by submitting Form 8868, so that you can use your final audit numbers in completing the Form 990. Our recommendation: The board chair should review and sign the 990 and copies should be given to each board member.

2. It used to be that most small tax-exempt organizations—those with annual gross receipts below $25,000—didn't have to file the 990 annually, but now every year they must file the new Form 990-N, "Electronic Notice (e-Postcard) for Tax-Exempt Organizations Not Required to File Form 990 or 990-EZ."

3. Part III of Form 990-N is an expanded *Program Service Accomplishments* section that requires you to describe succinctly your three largest programs, how much you spent on each of them in the prior year, and even whether you discontinued any core programs since your last filing. Our recommendation: Don't just let your auditor complete this section as a routine task. This is a key opportunity to tell the story of your organization's impact to the world. Make full use of it.

4. A new section is Part VI of the revised form, *Governance, Management, and Disclosure* that asks about the organization's board structure, policies, and practices. Examples: Whether your organization has a conflict of interest policy and whether it posts its 990 on its web site. It also asks whether the executive director and other key employees received an annual compensation review that included a review by independent persons, the

use of comparability data, and other factors.

5. The expanded scrutiny of employee, director, and contractor compensation requires that full compensation be disclosed for all current board members, trustees, and key employees. It also asks whether the organization paid a *former* board member or key employee more than $100,000 in the prior year. And, the organization must disclose its five highest-paid employees and independent contractors making more than $100,000.

6. Part IX, the *Statement of Functional Expenses,* is still the place readers will find out how much of every dollar your organization spent last year on your nonprogram activities: fundraising and management. It is important not to overstate these overhead costs due to poor accounting allocation methods. We recommend that board members ensure that finance staff or contractors have appropriately classified both direct and shared costs across the core functions of the organization.

The IRS is allowing for a rolling adoption of the new form depending on current organizational revenue and asset size. Again, be sure to check the directions at www.irs.gov/charities.

Also Try

Key Documents, p. 28

Why Do Nonprofits Have Boards? p. 18

A Board–Staff Contract for Financial Accountability, p. 220

A Board Member's Guide to Nonprofit Insurance

Many board members don't think about the organization's insurance until something adverse happens. And even given how significant insurance expense is, the budget line item is seldom scrutinized. As one *Blue Avocado* reader commented: "Insurance isn't sexy, but it's as essential as a roof over your head." In these tight times, it's tempting to make insurance a low priority, but this strategy can be penny wise and pound foolish. *Blue Avocado* asked Pamela Davis, president and CEO of the Nonprofits Insurance Alliance Group (and a *Blue Avocado* Steering Committee member) to give us the lowdown on liability.

Q: What are the most common insurance claims against nonprofits? How much do they end up costing?

Pamela: Almost all of the claims—90 percent—reported by nonprofit organizations are accidents and injuries related to automobiles or slips, trips, and falls at nonprofit locations and special events. Interestingly, though, these 90 percent of incidents actually result in only 65 percent of dollars paid out in claims because while auto claims and slip and falls tend to be fairly common, they are usually not large claims involving prolonged litigation. The other 10 percent of claims result from allegations of improper employment practices (such as wrongful termination), professional errors and omissions, and sexual abuse. While less frequent, these tend to be more difficult and expensive claims to resolve and account for 35 percent of claims dollars paid.

Q: Given that, what types of insurance do we need?

Pamela: There are just a couple of types that every organization needs and other types that depend on the kind of work you do. All organizations should purchase general liability, typically thought of as "slip and fall" insurance, which comes into play when someone is hurt or their property is damaged in your office, theatre, clinic, or other area. Even organizations that don't have offices are subject to claims for damages such as a slip and fall at a program or damage to an antique rug at a home where a fundraiser was held.

You should also purchase "non-owned/hired" auto insurance, in case an employee or volunteer is involved in an auto accident and their personal insurance is inadequate. Organizations that have any employees, even just one, need to be fully covered with directors and officers liability insurance (see below).

Other types of insurance to consider include

- Property insurance for damage to property (including computer and other records) owned or leased by the nonprofit
- Fidelity insurance for possible embezzlement
- Social services professional coverage for errors and omissions that could arise in the course of carrying out the missions, providing counseling, advice in support groups, and so forth
- Accident insurance in case a volunteer, program participant, or gallery patron is injured on the premises
- Improper sexual conduct insurance, particularly if the organization works with vulnerable clients.

If you want to purchase limits of more than $1 million in coverage, consider an umbrella policy that would provide extra limits over many different coverages at the same time. The above list is not exhaustive of insurances purchased by nonprofits, but it does represent the most common types.

Q: One thing that confuses a lot of us is how much insurance to get. Some people say $1 million, some say $5 million, some say we don't need most of it. How much insurance does a nonprofit really need?

Pamela: I wish there were an easy answer to this question. If an organization could tell me what accidents or injuries will occur in their future, I could say how much insurance that organization should buy. For most nonprofits, the amount of insurance they buy relates to their specific situation, their insurance broker's assessment of their risk, and the risk tolerance of their board of directors.

In practice, the majority of community-based nonprofits purchase $1 million in coverage, and that has been sufficient to cover 99 percent of the claims we have seen in our twenty years.

However, organizations with significant assets should consider purchasing higher limits. For example, an organization with assets of $500,000 may consider purchasing an umbrella policy with $1 million or $2 million in limits to go over their basic $1 million policy. Those with fleets of vehicles or many-passenger vehicles should definitely consider higher limits. Some organizations are required by a government funder to have higher limits as part of contract requirements. But, absent a contract requirement, there is no rule of thumb for the right amount.

Q: What is directors and officers (D&O) insurance, and do we need it?

Pamela: With the predominance of wrongful termination lawsuits, if the organization has even one employee, D&O insurance with employment practices coverage is probably essential.

Typically, lawsuits are filed when someone is hurt by some sort of accident and that person believes that someone, or some organization, is responsible for that accident. For example, a person tripped because the stairs were not properly lit or a person injured in a car accident because someone else ran a red light.

In contrast, a different type of claim is one made not because of the accident itself, but because someone believes that the board took an intentional and improper action. The most common lawsuit of this type would be one alleging that the board of directors allowed an improper termination of an employee. Insurance for these types of claims against nonprofits is typically found in the D&O policy.

In terms of D&O insurance, almost 95 percent of claims against D&O policies are employment related, including harassment, discrimination, and wrongful termination. According to our data at the Nonprofits Insurance Alliance Group,

in any given year approximately one in twenty-five nonprofits will have a D&O claim against them, nearly all of them employment related. The average D&O claim will cost $35,000 to resolve—a combination of legal defense costs and in a few cases, settlement payments. However, one out of ten claims will cost more than $100,000 to resolve.

If an organization has no employees, its risk of claims against board members is low, but so is the premium for such coverage. It makes sense to buy it, if for no other reason than to give board members peace of mind.

D&O insurance typically protects individual board members as well as employees, volunteers, and the organization itself in the instance of a civil suit. But because each policy is different, sometimes with different features even at the same insurance company, it is important to confirm with your broker that both individuals and the organization are covered and that coverage for employment practices is included.

Q: How much does D&O insurance typically cost?

Pamela: Organizations with no employees can purchase $1 million in D&O limits for around $600 per year. Organizations *with* employees can expect to pay anywhere from about $1,200 for those with just a few employees, to around $4,000 to $5,000 for fifty employees. The cost of D&O insurance varies widely depending on the insurer, the breadth of coverage provided, prior claims, and the quality of employment practices at your organization. Remember that D&O insurance covers both the legal costs of defending your nonprofit as well as any settlements that might arise. Remember, too, that D&O cannot cover board members for responsibility for payroll taxes and retirement payments that were withheld from employee paychecks but not submitted to the proper institutions. (If insurance could cover us for not paying taxes, we might all buy insurance and then not pay taxes!)

Q: I don't understand the difference between a broker and the insurance company. Do we need both?

Pamela: Brokers are professional advisors or consultants who are intermediaries between nonprofits and insurance carriers. This is somewhat similar to how a financial advisor might work with you to help you understand what type of savings strategy or retirement program might be best for you and who would then purchase the stocks or bonds on your behalf. In most cases, organizations must go through a broker to obtain insurance from an insurance company.

Brokers work with nonprofits to determine

- Types of coverage needed (Do we need social services professional insurance? Sexual abuse coverage?)
- Coverage limits (Should our vehicle liability be at $1 million? $3 million?)
- Services needed (Do we need assistance with personnel policies? Training for volunteer drivers?)

Based on these guidelines, the broker approaches various insurance companies for price quotes, from the all-purpose firms such as Aetna or Hartford, to insurance companies that specialize in nonprofits such as NIAC and ANI-RRG. The insurance companies determine the premium (cost) at which they will offer a certain policy and, if selected by the nonprofit, will issue the insurance policy and become responsible for adjusting and paying covered claims. In addition to the above criteria, nonprofits will want to know about an insurance company's track record in prompt, hassle-free, and fair payment of claims.

Insurance companies pay commissions to brokers. This can lead to a situation where brokers might be tempted to recommend an insurance company or a type of insurance that gives them a larger commission rather than the company that is best for the nonprofit. For instance, some companies give brokers extra commissions at the end of the year if they establish and then meet a commitment to a level of premiums sold from that insurance company.

Q: What simple steps can the board take on risk management and insurance oversight?

Pamela: Every member of a board of directors needs to realize that there are risks to operating any nonprofit and that through appropriate policies and procedures and staff training, these risks can be reduced. Insurance is there to cover those things that happen when the risk mitigation strategies are not completely successful. Some steps the board can take to avoid insurance oversight are to

1. *Monitor suits, threats of suits, and accidents.* The board (or a risk management committee of the board) should be informed of *any* insurance claims made against the nonprofit *and* when threats of suits arise. In some organizations it's appropriate for the board to set goals and monitor progress on safety and risk reduction, such as reports on the number and type of automobile accidents and whether there were injuries and what might have been done to prevent an accident.

2. *Periodically review risks, risk-reduction practices, and coverages.* Depending on the size of the organization, the board, a board committee, a board-staff task force, or other group should develop a list of the key risks faced by the

nonprofit and have a process to periodically review incidents or claims. Obvious areas of concern are driver selection and training, policies to protect vulnerable clients, and potential for fraud and damage to property. Less obvious risks are potential damage to reputation and staff morale from poor management.

3. *Review and consider changing brokers.* Every few years, the board should review its relationship with its broker, just as it reviews the relationship with the auditor. In this review board representatives should look over what coverages are being purchased, at what rates, from which insurance companies, and whether the nonprofit is getting the services (such as prompt payments) it deserves. We at NIAC and ANI-RRG are proud of the other services we provide free or at low cost to the nonprofits that insure through us: services such as driver training and monitoring (for organizations with vehicles), informational booklets (such as the issue of serving alcohol at special events), and webinars on risk reduction.

Q: Just one more question: What's different, if anything, about insurance for nonprofits compared to for-profits?

Pamela: It pays to work with insurance brokers and insurance carriers who understand how to make sure that the insurance

Also Try

Key Documents, p. 28

The Board's Role in Human Resource Administration, p. 43

policies purchased are sufficient to cover a nonprofit's risk exposure, which can be more complex than a for-profit's risks.

It is not necessarily being nonprofit that makes our sector's insurance needs so different but rather the fact that we work so intensively with clients and provide services to some of the most vulnerable and the most troubled in our communities. A nonprofit day care, for example, may not have risk exposures all that different from a for-profit day care, but a nonprofit residential program for troubled teens certainly is a much different risk than an assisted living center for seniors. Nevertheless, the standard insurance industry rates classify both of these living arrangements simply as residential risks.

Nonprofits—and not-for-profits—need to have insurance for injury caused by and to volunteers. And because nonprofits often serve as the hubs of their communities, they frequently conduct many different programs, while for-profits tend to have more of a single focus. For example,

a nonprofit may run a school, a day care, a senior residential center, and a food bank all under the umbrella of one organization. A for-profit firm would typically operate just one of those.

Key differences also include medical malpractice risk and social service professional risks such as counseling and providing other professional and quasi-professional services to vulnerable populations. And most nonprofits who work with children, the developmentally disabled, and fragile seniors need to have protection for allegations of sexual or other abuse.

Pamela Davis is president and CEO of two nonprofit insurance companies: Nonprofits' Insurance Alliance of California (NIAC) and Alliance for Nonprofit Insurance, Risk Retention Group (ANI-RRG), and a founding member of the Blue Avocado Steering Committee. She is passionate about nonprofit insurance "because I'm passionate about the work that nonprofits do."

Concluding Words

IN EVERY COMMUNITY, on the third Thursday or the second Tuesday or other nights, nonprofit board members gather in offices, homes, houses of worship, and community centers to discuss how their organizations can best serve. Some of these boards are setting up new organizations, others are guiding organizational growth, while others are considering closing down or merging. Across all types of nonprofits, volunteer community members do a remarkable job of making things work.

Why do we have all these nonprofit organizations anyway?

Forty years ago, none of the following existed:

- A Patient's Bill of Rights
- Acceptance of women in executive positions
- An international movement to stop torture
- Affordable housing units built and owned by Latino organizations for low-income Latino families
- Sidewalk curb cuts to allow people with wheelchairs (and people with hand trucks) to cross streets
- The Clean Water Act
- Respite care so that caregivers for relatives with Alzheimer's can have a break
- Farmland protection legislation
- Safety standards for children's toys and clothing
- Support groups for women with breast cancer
- A national movement against drunk driving
- Financial and legal rights for victims of crime

All these, and many more improvements in our daily lives, are the result of people working in groups, through nonprofit organizations to make change. Nonprofit organizations are, and will continue to be, vehicles for democracy, where small groups of dedicated persons can create movements that change laws, change conventional thinking, change communities…change the world.

Each nonprofit organization today, under the governance of its board of directors, and with the support of its board members, has the potential to change the world for the better. As a nonprofit board member, executive director, volunteer, staff member, donor, or other participant, *you* are part of this worldwide movement for democracy and community. Each and every one of us benefits from your work. Thank you.

Resources

Newspapers, Magazines, Books, and Web Sites

About.com
http://nonprofit.about.com/.

This commercial web site has a strong nonprofit section.

All Hands on Board: The Board of Directors in an All-Volunteer Organization (AVO)
Jan Masaoka
New York: National Center for Nonprofit Boards, 1999, 22 pages. Download free at http://www.blueavocado.org.

A short guide written for boards of all-volunteer organizations (AVOs) such as sports leagues, neighborhood associations, and community choirs. Not an extensive exploration of the importance or complexity of AVOs, but a distilled practical approach.

Are You Chairing a Board by the Seat of Your Pants?
Susan Scribner
Long Beach, CA: Scribner and Associates, scribnerearth@earthlink.net, 1997, 68 pages. $15 at 562-426-9444 or at http://www.AllBookstores.com/.

Along with her subsequent book *Boards from Hell*, Susan Scribner's funny and insightful booklet includes excellent annotated model bylaws, rules for "nondeadly" meetings, and tips on managing the board chair or executive director relationship.

The Best Defense: Ten Steps to Surviving a Lawsuit
Melanie H. Herman
Washington, DC: Nonprofit Risk Management Center, 1998, 54 pages, at 202-785-3891.

This book from the Nonprofit Risk Management Center is easy to read and understands the nuances of nonprofit relationships, such as in the following example: "A church involved its members in carpentry and other tasks associated with the renovation of the sanctuary. One of the members fell off a scaffolding and died. The deceased's wife (also a member of the church) filed suit against the church."

Blue Avocado and one of its columns, Board Café

A free e-mail newsletter for people working and volunteering in community nonprofits. Subscriptions and archived issues at www.blueavocado.org. Much of the material in this book was originally published as the *Board Café* column in *Blue Avocado*. To subscribe, send an e-mail to editor@blueavocado.org with "subscribe" in the subject line, or by visiting http://BlueAvocado.org/.

Boards That Make a Difference: A New Design for Leadership in Nonprofit and Public Organizations, 3rd Edition
John Carver
San Francisco: Jossey-Bass, 2006, 448 pages (hardcover); 2006, 256 pages (e-book). $38 for either edition at http://www.josseybass.com/WileyCDA/.

John Carver's critique of conventional wisdom is inspired, but the model he proposes doesn't sustain the brilliance of the critique. Although his "Policy Governance" model is often characterized as "the strong executive, weak board model," Carver deserves a great deal of credit for opening up the debate on nonprofit boards and letting fresh air in.

Chronicle of Philanthropy

1255 23rd Street, NW, Suite 700, Washington, DC 20037, 202-466-1200 or e-mail help@philanthropy.com.

A biweekly newspaper in tabloid format. A trade journal for foundations that also includes nonprofit sector news. Subscribe 1 year for $72 print or $62 online only (24 issues) at http://philanthropy.com. (Subscriptions can also be bought for 6 months, 1, 2, and 3 years as well as per issue—online only)

Daring to Lead 2006: Nonprofit Executive Directors and Their Work Experience

Jeanne Peters, Richard Moyers, Timothy Wolfred

San Francisco: CompassPoint Nonprofit Services, 2006. Free download at http://www.meyerfoundation.org/downloads/4DaringtoLead2006d.pdf or order hard copy for $15 at www.compasspoint.org.

The third in a set of national reports examining tenure, career background, and work experiences of executive directors. Frames recommendations for executive directors, boards of directors, and funders.

Executive Transition Monograph Series

Tom Adams, Tim Wolfred, et al.

http://www.aecf.org/knowledgecenter/publications-Series/ExecutiveTransitionMonographs.aspx.

The series includes: *Building Leaderful Organizations: Succession Planning for Nonprofits, Capturing the Power of Leadership Change: Using Executive Transition Management to Strengthen Organizational Capacity, Founder Transitions,* and others.

From the Top Down: The Executive Role in Volunteer Program Success

Susan J. Ellis

Philadelphia: Energize, Inc., Revised, 1996, 210 pages. $24.95 at http://energizeinc.com/.

Despite a somewhat confusing title, this well-written book proposes a refreshing philosophy and a sturdy set of practices for positive volunteer engagement.

Fundraising for Social Change, 5th Edition

Kim Klein

Oakland, CA: Chardon Press, 2006, 560 pages. $40 at http://www.josseybass.com/WileyCDA/.

There isn't a better book about fundraising for community-based nonprofits.

Governance Is Governance

Kenneth N. Dayton

1200 Eighteenth St, NW, Suite 200, Washington, DC: Independent Sector, 1987, 15 pages. Free download at http://www.outward-bound.org/docs/staff/governance.pdf

This is the classic pamphlet that distinguishes governance from management, and warns boards of the dangers of forays into management's territory.

Governing Boards: Their Nature and Nurture

Cyril O. Houle

San Francisco: Jossey-Bass, 1997, 256 pages. $32 at http://www.josseybass.com/WileyCDA/.

This landmark book articulates what became the traditional model of "programs, administration, policy." Cyril Houle's warmth and erudition make this a classic.

Grassroots Fundraising Journal

An outstanding resource of practical ideas about fundraising, grounded in an understanding of smaller social-change organizations. Subscribe for $39 per year (6 issues) at http://www.grassrootsfundraising.org/ or at 888-458-8588.

Guidestar.org

http://www.guidestar.org/.

A database of approximately 700,000 U.S. nonprofit organizations, which can be searched by organization name. A short description supplied by the organization is included, as is a summary of the organization's Form 990 and, when available, a link to the organization's web site. A great place to find out the budgets, program statistics, and salaries of similar organizations (but don't forget the information is usually two to three years old).

How to Form a Nonprofit Corporation (National Edition), 8th Edition
Anthony Mancuso
Berkeley, CA: Nolo Press, 2007, 416 pages. $27.99 at http://www.nolo.com/.

Step-by-step instructions from this do-it-yourself legal publisher.

Improving the Performance of Governing Boards
Richard Chait, Thomas Holland, and Barbara Taylor
Greenwood Publishing Group, Inc., 1996, 176 pages. Special order at http://www.barnesandnoble.com/.

An exceptionally useful book. In particular, Richard Chait has made a tremendous contribution with the concept of the Dashboard, a set of indicators that helps the board set, monitor, and change the objectives of the organization.

The Second Legal Answer Book for Nonprofit Organizations
Bruce R. Hopkins
New York: Jossey-Bass, 1998, 422 pages. $135 at http://www.josseybass.com/WileyCDA/.

A practical approach to common nonprofit legal concerns, including board liability, lobbying limitations, and planned giving.

The M Word: A Board Member's Guide to Mergers
Alfredo Vergara-Lobo, Jan Masaoka, and Sabrina Smith
San Francisco: CompassPoint Nonprofit Services. Order a hard copy for $12 at http://www.compasspoint.org/.

This booklet begins with discussing the circumstances in which mergers are proposed and includes key criteria and process steps for deciding whether a merger is a good idea and, if so, how to conduct negotiations and the implementation successfully.

Making the News: A Guide for Nonprofits and Activists
Jason Salzman
Boulder, CO: Westview Press, 2003, 304 pages. $12.71 at http://www.amazon.com/.

This practical book gets to the real questions: How to Write a News Release, How to Handle Unsolicited Media Attention, How to Generate News Coverage without Staging a Media Event, How to Publish a Letter to the Editor, and more.

The New Governance Series
Washington, DC: BoardSource, 2009, 610 pages. $88 for members, $124 for nonmembers at http://www.boardsource.org/.

A series of six pamphlets from BoardSource (formerly the National Center for Nonprofit Boards), including "Ten Basic Responsibilities of Nonprofit Boards" and "Legal Responsibilities of Nonprofit Boards." Larger, institutional organizations tend to find this series more useful than do community-based organizations.

Nonprofit Insurance Alliance Group
http://www.insurancefornonprofits.org.

These two nonprofit insurance companies focus solely on nonprofits, and their web site has a wide range of practical information about insurance and legal matters.

Nonprofit Kit for Dummies (with CD-ROM)
Stan Hutton and Frances Phillips
New York: Hungry Mind, Inc, 2001, 356 pages. $19.98 at http://www.amazon.com/.

A comprehensive guide to nonprofits written by the About.com web site manager and a foundation program officer. Friendly; covers a remarkable amount of territory well.

**Nonprofit Mergers Workbook Part I:
The Leader's Guide to Considering, Negotiating,
and Executing a Merger, Updated Edition**
David La Piana
Saint Paul, MN: Fieldstone Alliance, 2000, 240 pages.
$34.95 at http://www.fieldstonealliance.org/.

A guide to the issues that arise in a nonprofit merger.

Nonprofit Quarterly
A print journal on nonprofit practices. Subscribe
by going to http://www.nonprofitquarterly.org/
1 year subscription $49.00 (4 issues).

NonProfit Times
A monthly newspaper in tabloid format. Good news
coverage and some excellent columns on nonprofit
management. Available free by application at http://
www.nptimes.com/.

**Raise More Money: The Best of the
Grassroots Fundraising Journal**
Kim Klein and Stephanie Roth, Editors
San Francisco: Jossey-Bass, 2001, 200 pages. $33 at
http://www.josseybass.com/WileyCDA/.

This compilation of articles from the *Grassroots
Fundraising Journal* has everything, from mail appeals
to raffles to board roles to major gift campaigns, and is
written in such a straightforward style you won't notice
the research and complex thinking behind it.

Robert's Rules of Order
Generally Robert's Rules of Order are more suited to
large legislative bodies such as the U.S. Congress than
to community-based nonprofit organizations. But if you
need to look them up, a good site is: http://www.
jimslaughter.com/robertsrules.htm.

**Self-Help Accounting: A Guide for the
Volunteer Treasurer, 2nd Edition**
John Paul Dalsimer Philadelphia: Energize Press, 2003.
116 pages, $10, at 800-395-9800 or http://energizeinc.
com/.

A simple bookkeeping system and accounting guide for
the heroic volunteer treasurers who take care of their
organizations' books.

**Strategic Planning for Nonprofit Organizations,
2nd Edition**
Michael Allison and Jude Kaye
New York: John Wiley and Sons, 2003, 320 pages.
$26.37 at http://www.amazon.com/.

A practical and classic approach to strategic planning.
The two authors are consultants at CompassPoint
Nonprofit Services, and the book is based on their years
of work with nonprofits of all types.

**Tax Planning and Compliance for Tax-Exempt
Organizations: Forms, Checklists, Procedures,
4th Edition**
Jody Blazek, Editor
New York: John Wiley and Sons, 2008. $75.66 at
http://www.amazon.com/.

Step-by-step guide to forming a nonprofit organization
and ensuring that the organization complies with
relevant laws and regulations.

Volunteermatch.org
http://www.volunteermatch.org/.

This free web site allows nonprofits to post volunteer
opportunities, including board service openings. The
site also allows individuals to search for ways to
volunteer locally.

Why Boards Don't Govern
Jan Masaoka and Mike Allison

First published in *Taking Trusteeship Seriously* by the
University of Indiana Press, this article has been
reprinted in numerous places and is available online at
http://www.compasspoint.org/assets/69_whyboards-
dontgoverngfj200.pdf.

Organizations and Associations

Many organizations have written booklets and guidelines for their own boards and may be willing to share these with others. In addition to local organizations, national organizations that have developed board materials for their local chapters include the YMCA and YWCA, Campfire, the American Red Cross, the NAACP, the Arthritis Foundation, and the American Lung Association.

The following organizations offer consulting, workshops, written resources, and other technical assistance.

Alliance of Nonprofits for Insurance, Risk Retention Group
P.O. Box 8546
Santa Cruz, CA 95061-8546
800-359-6422
http://www.insurancefornonprofits.org/

A nonprofit insurance company dedicated to providing reasonably priced liability insurance. Modeled after the highly successful Nonprofit Insurance Alliance of California (NIAC).

BoardNetUSA
6 E. 39th Street, Suite 602
New York, NY 10016
212-447-1236
http://www.boardnetusa.org/

This free program, based at the Volunteer Consulting Group in New York, allows individuals seeking board opportunities to find nonprofits seeking board members.

BoardSource (formerly the National Center for Nonprofit Boards)
1828 L Street, NW, Suite 900
Washington, DC 20036-5114
202-452-6262
http://www.boardsource.org/

BoardSource works nationally and internationally on matters of nonprofit governance. It offers an extensive publications catalog, conducts research, and provides speakers on nonprofit boards of directors.

CompassPoint Nonprofit Services
731 Market Street, Suite 200
San Francisco, CA 94103
415-541-9000
http://www.compasspoint.org/

CompassPoint is a leading consulting and training firm working with nonprofit organizations. CompassPoint's mission is to increase the effectiveness and impact of people working and volunteering in the nonprofit sector.

CompassPoint Silicon Valley
Sobrato Center for Nonprofits
600 Valley Way, Suite A
San José, CA 95035
408-719-1400
http://www.compasspoint.org/

Junior League
132 W. 31st Street, 11th Floor
New York, NY 10001-3406
212-951-8300
http://www.ajli.org/

This longtime service club for women has chapters in many U.S. cities and a highly developed system for training leaders within its own board and board committees. The Junior League has a distinct style and organizational culture. It not only develops board leadership skills among its own members but also provides valuable community service.

National Association of Corporate Directors (NACD)
1828 L Street, NW, Suite 801
Washington, DC 20036
202-775-0509
http://www.nacdonline.org/

A membership organization of individuals serving on for-profit corporate boards. Several chapters throughout the country offer speakers series and networking events open to the public. The organization's magazine and web site offer an intriguing look at corporate boards—ofte n with relevant ideas for nonprofit boards. If there's a local chapter, it may also be a good place to recruit board members for your nonprofit board.

National Minority AIDS Council (NMAC)
1931 13th Street, NW
Washington, DC 20009-4432
202-483-6622
http://www.nmac.org/

The National Minority AIDS Council publishes practical guides for AIDS organizations in communities of color. The guides are also useful for most nonprofits. Some of the organization's books are available free at its web site, including *The Program Development Puzzle*.

Nonprofit Risk Management Center
1001 Connecticut Avenue, NW, Suite 900
Washington, DC 20036-5504
202-785-3891
http://www.nonprofitrisk.org/

Excellent, inexpensive booklets on various aspects of insurance and risk management, such as insurance matters for special events, volunteer drivers, and other issues. The web site also has good material on many insurance-related topics.

Volunteer Center National Network/Points of Light Foundation
1400 I Street, NW, Suite 800
Washington, DC 20005
202-729-8000
http://www.pointsoflight.org/

Many communities have independently incorporated volunteer centers that are linked through this association of volunteer centers. Some volunteer centers offer varieties of board recruitment and matching services. A search function on the web site lets you find a nearby volunteer center.

Subscription Form for *Blue Avocado* Newsletter

(copy or tear this page out)

❑ **Yes!** Please give me a free subscription to the *Blue Avocado*:

E-mail address: _____

Organization(s) for which you are a board member (optional): _____

_____

Three ways to subscribe:

1. Fax this form to the *Blue Avocado* at 415-723-7155

2. Mail this page to: *Blue Avocado*
      731 Market Street, Suite 200
      San Francisco, CA 94103

3. Subscribe by sending a blank email to: editor@blueavocado.org.

Index

f indicates form   *s* indicates sample

f indicates form   s indicates sample

More Results-Oriented Resources from Fieldstone Alliance

Practical books are just one of the resources Fieldstone Alliance has to offer. We also provide consulting, training, and demonstration projects that help nonprofits, funders, networks, and communities achieve greater impact.

As a nonprofit ourselves, we know the challenges that you face. In all our services, we draw on our extensive experience to provide solutions that work:

EXPERT CONSULTATION

Our staff and network of affiliated consultants are recognized nonprofit leaders, authors, and experts with deep experience in managing organizations, teaching, training, conducting research, and leading community initiatives. We provide assessment, planning, financial strategy, collaboration, and capacity-building services. Contracts range from short-term assessments to the management of multi-year initiatives.

PROVEN TRAINING

Training can be a powerful change strategy when well designed. Our experienced staff, authors, and network of experts from across the United States provide practical, customized training for nonprofits, foundations, and consultants. From one-hour keynote addresses to multi-session programs, we offer expertise in various aspects of capacity building, nonprofit management, leadership, collaboration, and community development. Coupling training with books and follow-up support increases retention and application of what is learned.

DEMONSTRATION PROJECTS

Fieldstone Alliance conducts research and hosts demonstration projects that have promise for improving performance and results in the nonprofit sector. Through this work we mine best practices, package the findings into practical, easy-to-apply tools, and disseminate them throughout the sector.

Free Resources

GET FREE MANAGEMENT TIPS!

Sign-up for *Nonprofit Tools You Can Use,* Fieldstone Alliance's free e-newsletter. In each issue (arriving twice a month), we feature a free management tool or idea to help you and your nonprofit be more effective.

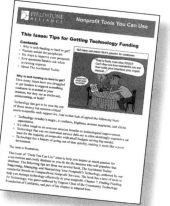

Content comes from our award-winning books, our consultants' direct experience, and from other experts in the field. Each issue focuses on a specific topic and includes practical actions for putting the information to use.

ONLINE RESOURCES

Here are other free resources you'll find on our web site:

Articles
In-depth information on nonprofit management issues.

Assessment Tools
See how your organization or collaboration is doing relative to characteristics of a successful nonprofit.

Research Reports
See research that was done to inform our demonstration projects and consulting practice.

Other Fieldstone Alliance Books

Financial Leadership for Nonprofit Executives
Guiding Your Organization to Long-term Success

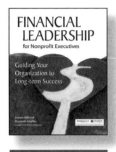

Provides executives with a practical guide to protecting and growing the assets of their organizations while accomplishing as much mission as possible with those resources.

by Jeanne Bell & Elizabeth Schaffer | 144 pp | 2005 | ISBN 978-0-940069-44-2 | order no. 06944X

Coping with Cutbacks
The Nonprofit Guide to Success When Times Are Tight

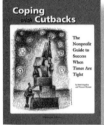

Practical ways to involve business, government, and other nonprofits to solve problems together. Also includes 185 cutback strategies you can put to use right away.

by Emil Angelica & Vincent Hyman | 128 pp | 1997 | ISBN 978-0-940069-09-1 | order no. 069091

Venture Forth!
The Essential Guide to Starting a Moneymaking Business in Your Nonprofit

A time-tested approach to identifying, testing, and launching a nonprofit business venture.

by Rolfe Larson | 272 pp | ISBN 978-0-940069-24-4 | order no. 069245

Seven Turning Points
Leading Through Pivotal Transitions in Organizational Life

To remain strong and effective, organizations must periodically adjust their leadership, management, structure, governance, and operating style to fit their changed circumstances. *Seven Turning Points* identifies key times when nonprofits must reassess the way they operate and make fundamental changes or risk decline.

by Susan Gross | 120 pp | 2009 | ISBN 978-0-940069-73-2 | order no. 069732

The Nonprofit Strategy Revolution
Real-Time Strategic Planning in a Rapid-Response World

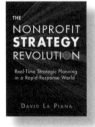

This ground-breaking guide offers a compelling alternative to traditional strategic planning. You'll find new ideas for how to form strategies, and the tools and framework needed to infuse strategic thinking throughout your organization. The result: your nonprofit will be more strategic in thought and action on a daily basis. When the next opportunity (or challenge) comes along, you'll be able to respond swiftly and thoughtfully.

by David La Piana | 208 pp | 2008 | ISBN 978-0-940069-65-7 | order no. 069657

(continued)

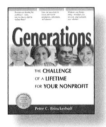

Generations
The Challenge of a Lifetime for Your Nonprofit

What happens when a management team of all Baby Boomers leaves within a five year stretch? Peter Brinckerhoff tells you what generational changes to expect and how to plan for them. You'll find in-depth information for each area of your organization—staff, board, volunteers, clients, marketing, technology, and finances.

by Peter Brinckerhoff | 232 pp | 2007 | ISBN 978-0-940069-55-8 | order no. 069555

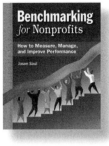

Benchmarking for Nonprofits
How to Measure, Manage, and Improve Results

This book defines a formal, systematic, and reliable way to benchmark (the ongoing process of measuring your organization against leaders), from preparing your organization to measuring performance and implementing best practices.

by Jason Saul | 144 pp | 2004 | ISBN 978-0-940069-43-5 | order no. 069431

The Five Life Stages of Nonprofit Organizations
Where You Are, Where You're Going, & What to Expect When You Get There

Shows you what's "normal" for each development stage which helps you plan for transitions, stay on track, and avoid unnecessary struggles. Includes an assessment.

by Judith Sharken Simon with J. Terence Donovan
128 pp | 2001 | ISBN 978-0-940069-22-0 | order no. 069229

The Manager's Guide to Program Evaluation
Planning, Contracting, and Managing for Useful Results

Explains how to plan and manage an evaluation that will help identify your organization's successes, share information with key audiences, and improve services.

by Paul W. Mattessich, PhD | 112 pp | 2003 | ISBN 978-0-940069-38-1 | order no. 069385

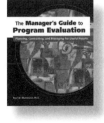

Nonprofit Stewardship
A Better Way to Lead Your Mission-Based Organization

You may lead a nonprofit, but it's not your organization; it belongs to the community it serves. You are the steward—the manager of resources that belong to someone else. The stewardship model of leadership can help you make decisions that are best for the people you serve by keeping your mission foremost.

by Peter C. Brinckerhoff | 272 pp | 2004 | ISBN 978-0-940069-42-8 | order no. 069423

www.FieldstoneAlliance.org

Fieldstone Alliance publishes a number of other books in the fields of nonprofit management, community development, funder effectiveness, and violence prevention. You'll find information about Fieldstone Alliance and more details on our books, such as table of contents, pricing, discounts, endorsements, and more at www. FieldstoneAlliance.org. You can also sign up to receive our e-newsletter, *Tools You Can Use*. It features a free management tool or idea to help you and your nonprofit organization be more effective.

ORDERING INFORMATION

Order by phone, fax, or online

Call toll-free: 800-274-6024
Internationally: 651-556-4509

Fax: 651-556-4517

E-mail: books@FieldstoneAlliance.org
Online: www.FieldstoneAlliance.org

Mail: Fieldstone Alliance
Publishing Center
60 Plato BLVD E, STE 150
St. Paul, MN 55107

Pricing and discounts

For current prices and discounts, please visit our web site at www.FieldstoneAlliance.org or call toll-free at 800-274-6024.

Do you have a book idea?

Fieldstone Alliance seeks manuscripts and proposals for books in the fields of nonprofit management and community development. To get a copy of our author guidelines, please call us at 800-274-6024. You can also download them from our web site at www.FieldstoneAlliance.org.

Our NO-RISK guarantee

If you aren't completely satisfied with any book for any reason, simply send it back within 30 days for a full refund.

Quality assurance

We strive to make sure that all the books we publish are helpful and easy to use. Our major workbooks are tested and critiqued by experts before being published. Their comments help shape the final book and—we trust—make it more useful to you.